Communications in Computer and Information Science 475

T0213894

More information about this series at http://www.springer.com/series/7899

Valentina Presutti · Milan Stankovic
Erik Cambria · Iván Cantador
Angelo Di Iorio · Tommaso Di Noia
Christoph Lange · Diego Reforgiato Recupero
Anna Tordai (Eds.)

Semantic Web Evaluation Challenge

SemWebEval 2014 at ESWC 2014
Anissaras, Crete, Greece, May 25–29, 2014
Revised Selected Papers

 Springer

Editors
Valentina Presutti
Diego Reforgiato Recupero
Semantic Technology Laboratory
ISTC-CNR
Rome
Italy

Milan Stankovic
Université Paris-Sorbonne
Paris
France

Erik Cambria
School of Computer Engineering
Nanyang Technological University
Singapore
Singapore

Iván Cantador
Universidad Autónoma de Madrid
Madrid
Spain

Angelo Di Iorio
University of Bologna
Bologna
Italy

Tommaso Di Noia
Polytechnic University of Bari
Bari
Italy

Christoph Lange
University of Birmingham
Birmingham
UK

Anna Tordai
Elsevier B.V.
Amsterdam
The Netherlands

ISSN 1865-0929　　　　　ISSN 1865-0937　(electronic)
ISBN 978-3-319-12023-2　　ISBN 978-3-319-12024-9　(eBook)
DOI 10.1007/978-3-319-12024-9

Library of Congress Control Number: 2014952190

Springer Cham Heidelberg New York Dordrecht London

Printed on acid-free paper

Springer is part of Springer Science+Business Media (www.springer.com)

Preface

During the last 15 years the Semantic Web evolved from being a pure vision to a set of novel technologies impacting the nature of the Web, which now includes huge amount of structured data represented with a homogeneous model (i.e., RDF) that fosters empirical research toward the development of intelligent applications and devices.

Although the Semantic Web scientific community successfully developed a significant amount of methods and techniques for dealing with Web content semantics, this research field still suffers from a general lack of common benchmarks, established evaluation procedures, tasks, and datasets, etc., making it sometimes hard to assess the current state of the art.

Being a relatively young field this is not surprising, and it is even a positive sign if we consider that innovation and creativity are the most important ingredients for pushing a field and identifying open and interesting problems. In other words, Semantic Web researchers often experience the identification of new tasks during their research work, which cannot be easily compared to existing related works for assessing a proper evaluation. In such cases, researchers are obliged to define new specific settings for empirically evaluating their results.

However, they are expected to provide the scientific community with proper settings and tools for assessing the state of the art on addressing the problem, by enabling replication of results and direct comparison to existing solutions. The Semantic Web community is therefore increasingly sharing raw evaluation data, algorithms, and results.

A solid way to support empirical research and to assess the state of the art with respect to a specific problem is to invite the related community to compete in a challenge in order to directly compare different methods and techniques, and to assess the best performing one at a certain point of time.

Based on this rationale, we have organized the first edition of the "Semantic Web Evaluation Challenge" (SemWebEval) as part of ESWC 2014 conference (held in Crete, Greece in May 2014), one of the most important international scientific events for the Semantic Web research community.

SemWebEval invited the state of the art and groundbreaking submissions on applications dealing with some of the most interesting challenges that the Semantic Web community is currently facing. In particular, the first edition focused on three areas: semantic publishing (sempub), concept-level sentiment analysis (ssa), and linked-data enabled recommender systems (recsys). A total of 23 teams were accepted to compete at different challenges (8 to sempub, 6 to ssa, and 9 to recsys). The event attracted 51 attendees, many of whom came to the conference specifically for attending the challenge, indicating that SemWebEval was much welcomed by the community and brought added value to the conference.

This book includes the descriptions of all methods and tools that competed at SemWebEval 2014, together with a detailed description of the tasks, and evaluation procedures and datasets, offering to the community a snapshot of the advancement in those areas at that moment in time, and material for replications of results.

The editors have divided the book content into three chapters, each dedicated to one area (and challenge). The first chapter refers to "Concept Level Sentiment Analysis," the second chapter to "Semantic Publishing," and the third to "Linked Data-enabled Recommender Systems." Each chapter includes an introductory section by the Challenge Chairs providing a detailed description of the challenge tasks, the evaluation procedure, and associated datasets.

I would like to thank my co-editors, who worked hard during the organization of ESWC and SemWebEval 2014. Thanks to their work, we experienced a successful and inspiring scientific event, and we are now able to deliver this book to the community.

August 2014   Valentina Presutti

Organization

Organizing Committee

General Chair

Valentina Presutti — STLab ISTC-CNR, Italy

Program Chairs

Fabien Gandon — Wimmics, Inria, I3S, CNRS, University of Nice Sophia Antipolis, France

Claudia d'Amato — University of Bari Aldo Moro, Italy

Local Chair

Irini Fundulaki — Institute of Computer Science – FORTH, Greece

Poster and Demo Chairs

Raphaël Troncy — EURECOM, France
Eva Blomqvist — Linköping University, Sweden

Workshop Chair

Harald Sack — Hasso-Plattner-Institute for IT Systems Engineering, University of Potsdam, Germany

Tutorial Chair

Nathalie Aussenac-Gilles — MELODI, IRIT – CNRS, Université de Toulouse, France

PhD Symposium Chairs

Steffen Staab — Institute for Web Science and Technologies - WeST, Universität Koblenz-Landau, Germany

Mathieu d'Aquin — Knowledge Media Institute, The Open University, UK

Semantic Web Evaluation Challenges Coordinator

Milan Stankovic — Universié Paris-Sorbonne, STIH and Sépage, France

Semantic Technologies Coordinators

Andrea Giovanni Nuzzolese	University of Bologna/STLab ISTC-CNR, Italy
Anna Lisa Gentile	University of Sheffield, UK
Maribel Acosta Deibe	Karlsruhe Institute of Technology, Germany
Luca Costabello	Inria, France

EU Project Networking Session Chairs

Mari Carmen Suárez-Figueroa	Universidad Politécnica de Madrid, Spain
Alessio Iabichella	STLab ISTC-CNR, Italy
Sergio Consoli	STLab ISTC-CNR, Italy

Publicity Chair

Silvio Peroni	University of Bologna/STLab ISTC-CNR, Italy

Proceedings Chair

Anna Tordai	Elsevier B.V., The Netherlands

Sponsor Chairs

Axel-Cyrille Ngonga Ngomo	University of Leipzig, Germany
Achim Rettinger	Karlsruhe Institute of Technology, Germany

Treasurer

Ioan Toma	STI International, Austria

Local Organization and Conference Administration

Martina Hartl	youvivo GmbH, Germany
Edith Leitner	youvivo GmbH, Germany

Web Site Administrator

Serge Tymaniuk	STI International, Austria

Program Committee

Program Chairs

Fabien Gandon	Wimmics, Inria, I3S, CNRS, University of Nice Sophia Antipolis, France
Claudia d'Amato	University of Bari Aldo Moro, Italy

Track Chairs

Maria Keet	University of KwaZulu-Natal, South Africa
Jérôme Euzenat	Inria and LIG, France

Thomas Lukasiewicz	University of Oxford, UK
Sebastian Rudolph	Technische Universität Dresden, Germany
Laura Hollink	VU University Amsterdam, The Netherlands
Vojtěch Svátek	University of Economics, Prague, Czech Republic
Matthew Rowe	Lancaster University, UK
Maria-Esthel Vidal	Universidad Simón Bolívar, Venezuela
Jacopo Urbani	VU University Amsterdam, The Netherlands
Elena Montiel-Ponsoda	Universidad Politécnica de Madrid, Spain
Diana Maynard	University of Sheffield, UK
Nicola Fanizzi	University of Bari Aldo Moro, Italy
Agnieszka Lawrynowicz	Poznan University of Technology, Poland
Payam Barnaghi	CCSR, University of Surrey, UK
Kerry Taylor	CSIRO, Australian National University and University of Melbourne, Australia
Matthias Klusch	German Research Center for Artificial Intelligence, DFKI, Germany
Freddy Lécué	IBM Research, Ireland
Aldo Gangemi	Université Paris 13 – Sorbonne Paris Cité – CNRS, FR/ISTC-CNR, Italy
Krzysztof Janowicz	University of California, Santa Barbara, USA
Renato Iannella	Semantic Identity, Australia
Pompeu Casanovas	Universitat Autònoma de Barcelona, Spain
Massimo Romanelli	Attensity Europe GmbH, Germany
Stefan Rüger	Knowledge Media Institute, The Open University, UK
Evelyne Viegas	Microsoft Research, USA
Milan Stankovic	Université Paris-Sorbonne, STIH and Sépage, France
Erik Cambria	National University of Singapore, Singapore
Diego Reforgiato Recupero	STLab ISTC-CNR, Italy
Iván Cantador	Universidad Autónoma de Madrid, Spain
Tommaso Di Noia	Polytechnic University of Bari, Italy
Angelo Di Iorio	University of Bologna, Italy
Christoph Lange	University of Birmingham, UK

Concept-Level Sentiment Analysis Challenge Program Committee

Newton Howard	MIT Media Lab, USA
ChengXiang Zhai	University of Illinois at Urbana-Champaign, USA
Rada Mihalcea	University of North Texas, USA
Ping Chen	University of Houston-Downtown, USA
Yongzheng Zhang	LinkedIn Inc., USA
Giuseppe Di Fabbrizio	Amazon Inc., USA
Rui Xia	Nanjing University of Science and Technology, China

Rafal Rzepka   Hokkaido University, Japan
Amir Hussain   University of Stirling, UK
Alexander Gelbukh   National Polytechnic Institute, Mexico
Björn Schuller   Technical University of Munich, Germany
Amitava Das   Samsung Research India, India
Dipankar Das   National Institute of Technology, India
Carlo Strapparava   Fondazione Bruno Kessler, Italy
Stefano Squartini   Marche Polytechnic University, Italy
Cristina Bosco   University of Turin, Italy
Paolo Rosso   Technical University of Valencia, Spain

Semantic Publishing Challenge Program Committee

Sören Auer   University of Bonn/Fraunhofer IAIS, Germany
Chris Bizer   University of Mannheim, Germany
Sarven Capadisli   University of Leipzig, Germany
Paolo Ciancarini   University of Bologna, Italy
Alexandru Constantin   University of Manchester, UK
Jeremy Debattista   University of Bonn/Fraunhofer IAIS, Germany
Alexander García Castro   Florida State University, USA
Leyla Jael García Castro   Bundeswehr University of Munich, Germany
Manfred Jeusfeld   University of Skövde/CEUR-WS.org, Sweden
Paul Groth   VU University Amsterdam, The Netherlands
Rinke Hoekstra   VU University Amsterdam, The Netherlands
Aidan Hogan   Universidad de Chile, Chile
Evangelos Milios   Dalhousie University, Canada
Lyubomir Penev   Pensoft Publishers, Bulgaria
Robert Stevens   University of Manchester, UK
Jun Zhao   Lancaster University, UK

Semantic Publishing Challenge Jury

Aliaksandr Birukou   Springer, Germany
Jeremy Debattista   University of Bonn/Fraunhofer IAIS, Germany
Laura Drägan   University of Southampton, UK
Eero Hyvönen   Aalto University, Finland
Sebastian Schaffert   Salzburg Research, Austria

Linked Open Data-Enabled Recommender System Challenge Program Committee

Pablo Castells   Universidad Autónoma de Madrid, Spain
Oscar Corcho   Universidad Politécnica de Madrid, Spain

Marco de Gemmis	University of Bari Aldo Moro, Italy
Frank Hopfgartner	Technische Universität Berlin, Germany
Andreas Hotho	Universität Würzburg, Germany
Dietmar Jannach	TU Dortmund University, Germany
Pasquale Lops	University of Bari Aldo Moro, Italy
Valentina Maccatrozzo	VU University Amsterdam, The Netherlands
Roberto Mirizzi	Polytechnic University of Bari, Italy
Vito Claudio Ostuni	Polytechnic University of Bari, Italy
Alexandre Passant	seevl.fm, Ireland
Francesco Ricci	Free University of Bozen-Bolzano, Italy
Giovanni Semeraro	University of Bari Aldo Moro, Italy
David Vallet	NICTA, Australia
Manolis Wallace	University of Peloponnese, Greece
Markus Zanker	Alpen-Adria-Universität Klagenfurt, Austria
Tao Ye	Pandora Internet Radio, USA

Steering Committee

Chair

John Domingue	Knowledge Media Institute, The Open University, UK and STI International, Austria

Members

Grigoris Antoniou	FORTH, Greece
Lora Aroyo	VU University Amsterdam, The Netherlands
Phillipp Cimiano	Bielefeld University, Germany
Oscar Corcho	Universidad Politécnica de Madrid, Spain
Marko Grobelnik	JSI, Slovenia
Eero Hyvönen	Aalto University, Finland
Axel Polleres	Siemens AG, Austria
Elena Simperl	University of Southampton, UK

Sponsoring Institutions

Contents

Concept Level Sentiment Analysis

ESWC'14 Challenge on Concept-Level Sentiment Analysis   3
   Diego Reforgiato Recupero and Erik Cambria

A Fuzzy System for Concept-Level Sentiment Analysis. 21
   Mauro Dragoni, Andrea G.B. Tettamanzi, and Célia da Costa Pereira

Unsupervised Fine-Grained Sentiment Analysis System Using Lexicons
and Concepts 28
   Nir Ofek and Lior Rokach

Semantic Lexicon Expansion for Concept-Based Aspect-Aware Sentiment
Analysis. 34
   Anni Coden, Dan Gruhl, Neal Lewis, Pablo N. Mendes,
   Meena Nagarajan, Cartic Ramakrishnan, and Steve Welch

Dependency Tree-Based Rules for Concept-Level Aspect-Based Sentiment
Analysis. 41
   Soujanya Poria, Nir Ofek, Alexander Gelbukh, Amir Hussain,
   and Lior Rokach

Sinica Semantic Parser for ESWC'14 Concept-Level Semantic
Analysis Challenge 48
   Shafqat Mumtaz Virk, Yann-Huei Lee, and Lun-Wei Ku

Polarity Detection of Online Reviews Using Sentiment Concepts: NCU IISR
Team at ESWC-14 Challenge on Concept-Level Sentiment Analysis 53
   Jay Kuan-Chieh Chung, Chi-En Wu, and Richard Tzong-Han Tsai

Semantic Publishing

Semantic Publishing Challenge – Assessing the Quality of Scientific Output . . . 61
   Christoph Lange and Angelo Di Iorio

ROHub — A Digital Library of Research Objects Supporting Scientists
Towards Reproducible Science 77
   Raúl Palma, Piotr Hołubowicz, Oscar Corcho, José Manuel Gómez-Pérez,
   and Cezary Mazurek

Semantify CEUR-WS Proceedings: Towards the Automatic Generation
of Highly Descriptive Scholarly Publishing Linked Datasets   83
   Francesco Ronzano, Gerard Casamayor del Bosque, and Horacio Saggion

A Template-Based Information Extraction from Web Sites
with Unstable Markup   89
   Maxim Kolchin and Fedor Kozlov

Linkitup: Semantic Publishing of Research Data   95
   Rinke Hoekstra, Paul Groth, and Marat Charlaganov

Understanding Research Dynamics   101
   Francesco Osborne and Enrico Motta

Semantic Facets for Scientific Information Retrieval   108
   Iana Atanassova and Marc Bertin

Extraction and Semantic Annotation of Workshop Proceedings in HTML
Using RML   114
   Anastasia Dimou, Miel Vander Sande, Pieter Colpaert,
   Laurens De Vocht, Ruben Verborgh, Erik Mannens,
   and Rik Van de Walle

Extraction and Characterization of Citations in Scientific Papers   120
   Marc Bertin and Iana Atanassova

Linked-Data Enabled Recommender Systems

Linked Open Data-Enabled Recommender Systems: ESWC 2014 Challenge
on Book Recommendation   129
   Tommaso Di Noia, Iván Cantador, and Vito Claudio Ostuni

Hybrid Recommending Exploiting Multiple DBPedia Language Editions   144
   Ladislav Peska and Peter Vojtas

A Hybrid Multi-strategy Recommender System Using Linked Open Data . . .   150
   Petar Ristoski, Eneldo Loza Mencía, and Heiko Paulheim

Exploring Semantic Features for Producing Top-N Recommendation Lists
from Binary User Feedback   157
   Nicholas Ampazis and Theodoros Emmanouilidis

Content-Based Recommender Systems + DBpedia Knowledge
= Semantics-Aware Recommender Systems   163
   Pierpaolo Basile, Cataldo Musto, Marco de Gemmis, Pasquale Lops,
   Fedelucio Narducci, and Giovanni Semeraro

SemStim at the LOD-RecSys 2014 Challenge...................... 170
  Benjamin Heitmann and Conor Hayes

Popular Books and Linked Data: Some Results for the ESWC'14 RecSys
Challenge.. 176
  Michael Schuhmacher and Christian Meilicke

A Semantic Pattern-Based Recommender.......................... 182
  Valentina Maccatrozzo, Davide Ceolin, Lora Aroyo, and Paul Groth

Increasing Top-20 Diversity Through Recommendation Post-processing..... 188
  *Matevž Kunaver, Tomaž Požrl, Štefan Dobravec, Uroš Droftina,
  and Andrej Košir*

Hybrid Model Rating Prediction with Linked Open Data
for Recommender Systems..................................... 193
  *Andrés Moreno, Christian Ariza-Porras, Paula Lago,
  Claudia Lucía Jiménez-Guarín, Harold Castro, and Michel Riveill*

Deep Learning of Semantic Word Representations to Implement
a Content-Based Recommender for the RecSys Challenge'14............ 199
  Omar U. Florez

Author Index 205

Concept Level Sentiment Analysis

ESWC'14 Challenge on Concept-Level Sentiment Analysis

Diego Reforgiato Recupero[1][(✉)] and Erik Cambria[2]

[1] CNR, Via Gaifami 18, 95028 Catania, Italy
`diego.reforgiato@istc.cnr.it`
[2] School of Computer Engineering, Nanyang Technological University,
50 Nanyang Ave, Singapore, Singapore
`cambria@ntu.edu.sg`

Abstract. With the introduction of social networks, blogs, wikis, etc., the users' behavior and their interaction in the Web have changed. As a consequence, people express their opinions and sentiments in a totally different way with respect to the past. All this information hinders potential business opportunities, especially within the advertising world, and key stakeholders need to catch up with the latest technology if they want to be at the forefront in the market. In practical terms, the automatic analysis of online opinions involves a deep understanding of natural language text, and it has been proved that the use of semantics improves the accuracy of existing sentiment analysis systems based on classical machine learning or statistical approaches. To this end, the Concept Level Sentiment Analysis challenge aims to provide a push in this direction offering the researchers an event where they can learn new approaches for the employment of Semantic Web features within their systems of sentiment analysis bringing to better performance and higher accuracy. The challenge aims to go beyond a mere word-level analysis of text and provides novel methods to process opinion data from unstructured textual information to structured machine-processable data.

1 Introduction

As the Web rapidly evolves, people are becoming increasingly enthusiastic about interacting, sharing, and collaborating through social networks, online communities, blogs, wikis, and so forth. In recent years, this collective intelligence has spread to many different areas, with particular focus on fields related to everyday life such as commerce, tourism, education, and health, causing the size of the social web to expand exponentially.

The opportunity to capture the sentiment of the general public about social events, political movements, company strategies, marketing campaigns, and product preferences has raised growing interest both within the scientific community, leading to many exciting open challenges, as well as in the business world, due to the remarkable benefits of marketing prediction. However, the distillation of knowledge from such a large amount of unstructured information is so difficult

V. Presutti et al. (Eds.): SemWebEval 2014, CCIS 475, pp. 3–20, 2014.
DOI: 10.1007/978-3-319-12024-9_1

that hybridizing different methods from complementary disciplines facing similar challenges is a key activity.

Various Natural Language Processing (NLP) techniques have been applied to process texts to detect subjective statements and their sentiment. This task is known as sentiment analysis, and overlaps with opinion mining. Sentiment analysis over social media faces several challenges due to informal language, uncommon abbreviations, condensed text, ambiguity, illusive context, etc. Much work in recent years focused on investigating new methods for overcoming these problems to increase sentiment analysis accuracy over Twitter and the other social networks [5].

Mining opinions and sentiments from natural language involves a deep understanding of most of the explicit and implicit, regular and irregular, syntactical and semantic rules proper of a language. Existing approaches mainly rely on identifying parts of text in which opinions and sentiments are explicitly expressed such as polarity terms, affect words and their co-occurrence frequencies. However, opinions and sentiments are often conveyed implicitly through latent semantics, which make purely syntactical approaches ineffective [6].

To this end, concept-level sentiment analysis aims to go beyond a mere word-level analysis of text and provide novel approaches to opinion mining and sentiment analysis that allow a more efficient passage from (unstructured) textual information to (structured) machine-processable data, in potentially any domain. Indeed, semantics can play an important role in enhancing our ability to accurately monitor sentiment over social media with respect to specific concept and topics. For example, using semantics will enable us to extract and distinguish sentiment about, say Berlusconi, in politics, business, criminal investigations, soccer, or for different events that involve him. When moving from one context to another, or from one event to another, opinions can shift from positive to negative, or neutral.

Semantics can capture this evolution and differentiate its results accordingly, whereas most existing sentiment analysis systems provide an analysis that can be too coarse-grained, due to missed contextualization.

Concept-level sentiment analysis focuses on a semantic analysis of text through the use of web ontologies or semantic networks, which allow the aggregation of conceptual and affective information associated with natural language opinions. By relying on large semantic knowledge bases, concept-level sentiment analysis steps away from blind use of keywords and word co-occurrence count, but rather relies on the implicit features associated with natural language concepts [4].

It has been proved that the quality of sentiment analysis algorithms improves when considering semantic features [8,12,18]. The natural direction is therefore to provide existing sentiment analysis systems and algorithms based on machine learning techniques with semantic capabilities in order to increase their accuracy.

The Concept-level sentiment analysis challenge[1] has provided breeding ground for this process. In particular, the challenge has focused on the introduction, presentation, and discussion of novel approaches to concept-level sentiment analysis. Participants had to design a concept-level opinion-mining engine that exploited

---

[1] http://challenges.2014.eswc-conferences.org/index.php/SemSA

common-sense knowledge bases, e.g., SenticNet[2], and/or Linked Data and Semantic Web ontologies, e.g., DBPedia[3], to perform multi-domain sentiment analysis.

Submitted and accepted systems had a semantics flavor (e.g., by making use of Linked Data or known semantic networks within their core functionalities) and authors showed how the introduction of semantics could be used to obtain valuable information, functionality or performance. Some of the submitted systems were based on natural language processing methods and statistical approaches and the authors pointed out how the embedded semantics played a main role within the core approach (engines based merely on syntax/word-count have been excluded from the challenge).

Concept-level sentiment analysis research benefited also from the First Workshop on Semantic Sentiment Analysis[4], held at ESWC2014 concurrently with the challenge. The workshop focused on the introduction, presentation, and discussion of novel approaches to semantic sentiment analysis even if the approaches were still at early stage and no evaluation had been conducted. The audience of the workshop included researchers from academia and industry as well as professionals and industrial practitioners to discuss and exchange positions on new hybrid techniques, which use semantics for sentiment analysis.

Similar initiatives and papers related to the semantic sentiment analysis are listed and mentioned in the Sect. 2. Section 3 describes in detail the five tasks of the Concept-level sentiment analysis challenge that the challengers' systems had to face. Details on the creation of the annotated dataset where the challengers' systems have been tested is explained in Sect. 4. Section 5 includes details on the evaluation measures performed on each submitted system and each task. Section 6 presents the submitted systems whereas Sect. 7 shows the results of each of them for each addressed task. Section 8 ends the paper with comments and experiences gained from this challenge.

2   Related Work

The 2014 edition was the first ESWC to include a challenge call and session within its program, and the first time for an event on semantic sentiment analysis at ESWC.

The concept of challenges related to the Semantic Web domain is not new within the most prestigious international conferences.

For example, SemEval (Semantic Evaluation) is an ongoing series of evaluations workshops of computational semantic analysis systems which evolved from the Senseval word sense evaluation series. The goal is to evaluate semantic analysis systems in a wide range of domains and in a different set of tasks. The semantic sentiment analysis task was introduced in SemEval2007 and had a presence in 2010 and 2013 editions (the reader notices that between 2007 and 2013 there were only four SemEval events; it was the 2012 edition where the

---

[2] http://sentic.net/

[3] http://dbpedia.org

[4] http://ontologydesignpatterns.org/wiki/SemanticSentimentAnalysis2014

sentiment analysis task was missed). Reflecting the importance of this problem in social media, the current edition, SemEval2014[5], includes two different tasks for semantic sentiment analysis: (i) the aspect-based sentiment analysis and (ii) sentiment analysis on Twitter.

One more example is constituted by the International Semantic Web Conference, ISWC[6], that with a slightly broader coverage than ESWC, each year hosts a Semantic Web challenge whose central idea is to extend the current human-readable web by encoding some of the semantics of resources in a machine-processable form. Its target is quite general and the goals are:

- to show to the society what the Semantic Web can provide,
- to give researchers an opportunity to showcase their work and compare it to others,
- and to stimulate current research to a higher final goal by showing the state-of-art every year.

Semantic Web challenge at ISWC has not detailed tasks but only an Open Track and a Big Data track. As a consequence, the overall evaluation of the submitted systems is not based on precision/recall analysis or similar but a group of judges decide the finalists and the winners according to a set of requirements that the systems have to fulfill.

The 2013 edition of the ISWC challenge call included 17 systems to be evaluated[7]. One of them, *Sentilo: Semantic Web-based Sentiment Analysis*, represents the first semantic sentiment analysis system ever submitted for a Semantic Web challenge at ISWC. The challenger system was based on a Sentic Computing[8] method called Sentilo, [9], to detect holders and topic of opinion sentences. This method implements an approach based on the neo-Davidsonian assumption that events and situations are the primary entities for contextualizing opinions, which makes it able to distinguish holders, main topics, and sub-topics of an opinion. Besides, it uses a heuristic graph mining approach that relies on FRED [16], a machine reader for the Semantic Web that leverages NLP and Knowledge Representation (KR) components jointly with cognitively-inspired frames. Finally it developed a model for opinion sentences that was used for annotating their semantic representation. A more recent extension of this work is [17], where the authors have extended *OntoSentilo*, the ontology for opinion sentences, created a new lexical resource called *SentiloNet* enabling the evaluation of opinions expressed by means of events and situations, and introduced a novel scoring algorithm for opinion sentences which uses a combination of two lexical resources, SentiWordNet [1] and SenticNet [7], used among others as background knowledge for sentiment analysis.

Besides SentiWordNet and SenticNet, current approaches for concept-level sentiment analysis use other affective knowledge bases such as ANEW [3], WordNet-Affect [19], and ISEAR [22]. In [20], a two step method integrates iterative regression

---

[5] http://alt.qcri.org/semeval2014/

[6] Check http://iswc2014.semanticweb.org/ for the current edition

[7] http://challenge.semanticweb.org/2013/submissions/

[8] http://sentic.net/sentics/

and random walk with in-link normalization to build a concept-level sentiment dictionary. The approach, based on the assumption that semantically related concepts share a common sentiment, uses ConceptNet [13] for the propagation of sentiment values.

A similar approach is adopted in [14], which presents a methodology to create a resource resulting from automatically merging SenticNet and WordNet-Affect. Authors trained a classifier on the subset of SenticNet concepts present in WordNet-Affect and used several concept similarity measures as well as various psychological features available in ISEAR.

One more recent work that exploits an existing affective knowledge base is [11], which extracts from SentiWordNet the objective words and assess the sentimental relevance of such words and their associated sentiment sentences. A support vector machines classifier is adopted for the classification of sentiment data. The resulting method outperforms the traditional sentiment mining approaches where the objectivity of opinion words in SentiWordNet is not taken into account.

In [2] the authors survey existing works related to the development of an opinion mining corpus. Moreover the authors present Senti-TUT, an ongoing Italian project where a corpus for the investigation of irony within the political and social media domain is developed.

Other existing works exploit the combined advantages of knowledge bases and statistical methods. For example, in [21], the authors introduced a hybrid approach that combines the throughput of lexical analysis with the flexibility of machine learning to cope with ambiguity and integrate the context of sentiment words. Ambiguous terms that vary in polarity are identified by the context-aware method and are stored in contextualized sentiment lexicons. These lexicons and semantic knowledge bases map ambiguous sentiment terms to concepts that correspond to their polarity.

Further works based on machine-learning include [10], which develops a new approach for extracting product features and opinions from a collection of free-text customer reviews about a product or service. The approach exploits a language-modeling framework that, using a seed set of opinion words, can be applied to reviews in any domain and language. The approach combines both a statistical mapping between words and a kernel-based model of opinion words learned from the seed set to approximate a model of product features from which the retrieval is performed.

3   Proposed Tasks of the Challenge

The Concept-Level Sentiment Analysis challenge was defined in terms of five different tasks (Elementary Task 0 Polarity Detection, Advanced Task 1 Aspect-Based Sentiment Analysis, Advanced Task 2 Semantic Parsing, Advanced Task 3 Topic Spotting, The Most Innovative Approach Task). Participants had to submit a description of their system indicating which tasks their system was going to target. One of the five tasks, the **most innovative approach task**, took into account all the submitted systems and gave a deep analysis on each of them. Within this task, a mixture of innovation and the employment of semantics were taken into account for the evaluation.

The first task was elementary whereas the second, third and fourth were more advanced. The input units of these four tasks were sentences. Sentences were assumed to be in grammatically correct American English and had to be processed according to the input format specified at http://sentic.net/challenge/sentence.

Following we will describe in detail each task.

3.1   Elementary Task 0: Polarity Detection

The main goal of task 0 was the classical polarity detection. The proposed systems were assessed according to precision, recall and F-measure of detected binary polarity values (1 = positive; 0 = negative) for each input sentence of the evaluation dataset, following the same format as in http://sentic.net/challenge/task0. As an example, considering the sentence of the above URL, *Today I went to the mall and bought some desserts and a lot of very nice Christmas gifts*, the correct polarity that a system should identify is positive (related to the Christmas gifts) and therefore it should write 1 in the polarity tag of the output. The problem of subjectivity detection was not addressed within this challenge, hence participants could assume that there were no neutral sentences. Participants were encouraged to use the Sentic API or further develop and apply sentic computing tools.

3.2   Advanced Task 1: Aspect-Based Sentiment Analysis

The output of this task was a set of aspects of the reviewed product and a binary polarity value associated to each of such aspects, in the format specified at http://sentic.net/challenge/task1. So, for example, while for the elementary task an overall polarity (positive or negative) was expected for a review about a mobile phone, this task required a set of aspects (such as speaker, touchscreen, camera, etc.) and a polarity value (positive or negative) associated with each of such aspects. Systems were assessed according to both aspect extraction and aspect polarity detection. As an example, the sentence *The touchscreen is awesome but the battery is too short* contains two aspects, *touchscreen* and *battery*, and a sentiment for each of them, positive for the former and negative for the latter.

3.3   Advanced Task 2: Semantic Parsing

As suggested by the title, the challenge focused on sentiment analysis at concept-level. This means that the proposed systems were not supposed to work at word/syntax level but rather work with concepts/semantics. Hence, this task evaluated the capability of the proposed systems to deconstruct natural language text into concepts, following the same format as in http://sentic.net/challenge/task2. SenticNet could be taken as a reference to test the efficiency of the extracted concepts of the proposed systems, but they did not necessary have to match SenticNet concepts. The proposed systems, for example, were supposed to be able to extract a multi-word expression like *buy christmas present* or *go mall* or *buy desserts* from sentences such as *Today I bought a lot of very nice Christmas presents*. The number of extracted concepts per sentence were assessed through precision, recall and F-measure against the evaluation dataset.

3.4   Advanced Task 3: Topic Spotting

Input sentences were about four different domains, namely: books, DVDs, electronics, and housewares. This task focused on the automatic classification of sentences into one of such domains, in the format specified at http://sentic.net/challenge/task3. All sentences were assumed to belong to only one of the above-mentioned domains. The proposed systems were supposed to exploit the extracted concepts to infer which domain each sentence belonged to. Classification accuracy was evaluated in terms of precision, recall and F-measure against the evaluation dataset. As an example, the sentence *The touchscreen is awesome but the battery is too short* should be classified in the domain of electronics.

3.5   The Most Innovative Approach Task

This task looked for the most innovative system, how the semantics was employed and the overall innovation brought by the adopted method.

4   Dataset Generation

4.1   Data Collection

We arbitrarily chose 50 *electronics*, *book*, *housewares* and *dvd* reviews from the Blitzer dataset[9]. Reviews were then split into sentences and each of these was labeled by a pool of four annotators (two native English speakers, 1 Chinese and 1 Indian). The dataset can be freely downloaded[10]; the compressed file contains the annotated dataset for each of the four tasks.

4.2   Task 0: Polarity Detection

Annotators were asked to label sentences according to their polarity, i.e., positive or negative (neutral sentences were removed). This yielded 2,322 sentences bearing either positive or negative sentiment. Specifically, annotators were asked to empathize with the speaker. So, in a sense, the polarity associated with each sentence does not reflect the conveyed emotions but rather is an inference about

---

[9] http://www.cs.jhu.edu/~mdredze/datasets/sentiment/
[10] http://sentic.net/eswc14.zip

the speaker's sentiments. This is key to disambiguate sentences that refer to more than one actor, e.g., "I love the movie that you hate". For each sentence, the polarity with the highest inter-annotator agreement was selected. We obtained 1,420 negative sentences and 902 positive (Table 1).

Table 1. Example sentences with polarity scores

Sentence	Polarity
The cheapest option I found at the time but an excellent pen drive	positive
What a useless thing	negative
They are very sharp and of high quality	positive
I've used this kettle for more than 1 year and it's still working perfectly	positive
The book is disproportionally focused on single and multilayer feedforward networks	negative
Its a shame to be forced to give this novel a one star rating	negative
Great product, I use it every day	positive

4.3   Task 1: Aspect Extraction

For the aspect extraction task, annotators were asked to infer aspects and label the sentiment associated with each of them. For this task, we liaised on majority voting for the selection of extracted aspects and their sentiment labels. It was notable that for most sentences the inter annotator agreement was greater than 2, i.e., most of the times, at least 3 annotators extracted same aspects and labeled them with the same sentiment. Sentences that did not have any aspect were removed from the final corpus. Table 2 shows the top 15 aspects extracted according to their occurrence in the corpus. 1725 sentences have been generated for such a task. The statistics on number of sentences having n number of aspects are shown in Table 3. Finally, Table 4 shows example sentences with aspects.

4.4   Task 2: Semantic Parsing

For semantic parsing task, we manually selected 2,398 sentences and asked annotators to extract the most useful concepts from them. Majority voting technique was applied on the extracted concepts to come up with a final list of concept for each sentence. The guideline was to choose multiword expressions richer in semantics so that in a sentence like "I went to the mall to buy food" the parsed concepts would be `go_mall` and `buy_food` rather than simply `go`, `mall`, `buy`, and `food`. Table 5 shows some statistics about the semantic parsing dataset.

4.5   Task 3: Topic Spotting

The topic spotting dataset was also built at sentence level. For each sentence, annotators labeled the topic and a majority voting technique determined the

Table 2. Top 15 aspects

Aspect	Frequency	Aspect	Frequency	Aspect	Frequency
player	188	camera	99	software	90
size	61	phone	54	picture	47
price	42	sound	41	battery	37
battery life	35	feature	34	use	31
weight	31	dvd	29	sound quality	29

Table 3. Number of sentence having n number of aspects

No. of aspects = 1	No. of aspects = 2	No. of aspects = 3	No. of aspects $\geq$ 4
1453	203	52	17

Table 4. Example sentences with aspects

Sentence	Aspects
but , if you 're looking for my opinion of the apex dvd player, i love it!	dvd player
for the price it is a well spent investment!	price
customer service and technical support are overloaded and nonresponsive - tells you about the quality of their products and their willingness to stand behind them.	customer service, technical service

Table 5. Number of sentence having n number of concepts

No. of concepts $\leq$ 5	No. of concepts > 5	No. of concepts $\leq$ 10	No. of concepts > 10
1037	1361	1845	553

final topic label for that sentence. It is notable that for almost every sentence annotator agreement was 4 (but this is mainly due to the fact that topics were predefined). The final dataset contains 1,122 sentences about *electronics*, 442 sentences about *books*, 1104 sentences about *dvds* and 1088 sentences about *housewares*. Table 6 shows example sentences and their topic.

5 Evaluation Measures

To evaluate the accuracy of the challenge tasks we analyzed each task and came up with a measure scheme for each of them. We wrote a Python script which automatically read the output of each system for each task and computed the accuracy according the scheme we adopted. In general, we followed

Table 6. Example sentences and their topic

Sentence	Topic
I love these speakers and the price was great	electronics
This dvd system is sweet and the sound system is off the hook its worth your Dollar	dvd
Nicely printed and bound - If you like James Allen you'll like this book	books
Though I have not tried the juicer yet, but i could not pass off the price	housewares

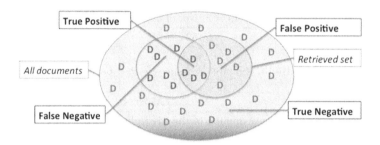

Fig. 1. Precision/Recall reference image.

the precision/recall study[11] with the observations and analysis defined in [15]. Figure 1 shows a general view of the precision/recall analysis where retrieved documents (true positive and false positive) are a subset of all the documents containing false negative and true negative. In general and where otherwise mentioned, the winner of a task was the resulting system with the highest F1 measure.

5.1 Evaluating Task 0

This task was pretty straightforward to evaluate. A precision/recall analysis was implemented to compute the accuracy of the output for this task. A true positive (tp) was defined when a sentence was correctly classified as positive. On the other hand, a false positive (fp) is a positive sentence which was classified as negative. Then, a true negative (tn) is detected when a negative sentence was correctly identified as such. Finally, a false negative (fn) happens when a negative sentence was erroneously classified as positive. With the above definitions, we defined the precision as

$$precision = \frac{tp}{tp + fp}$$

---

[11] http://en.wikipedia.org/wiki/Precision_and_recall

the recall as

$$recall = \frac{tp}{tp + fn}$$

and the F1 measure as

$$F1 = \frac{2 \times precision \times recall}{precision + recall}$$

5.2   Evaluating Task 1

Task 1 was a bit more tricky than the previous one as it hindered two different subtasks, the extraction of the aspects/features and the polarity of each of them. A precision/recall analysis, similar to the one adopted for Task 0, has first been applied to the extraction subtask. Therefore, when a system detected a correct feature we marked that as true positive (tp); if the detected feature was not into the annotation dataset, then that was classified as false negative (fn). All the features present into the annotation dataset but not retrieved by the system constituted the false positive (fp) set. The precision, recall and F1 measure were then straightforward computed by using the formulas above.

As we have not taken the polarity information into account yet, we had to perform one more step and we decided to implement another precision/recall analysis as follows. If the extracted feature was correct and its associated polarity was also rightly spotted then we counted it as a true positive (tp), otherwise we counted it as a false negative (fn). The false positive (fp) set remained unchanged as in the previous subtask. At the end, for Task 1, we had two different F1 measures for each system. We simply took the average of those in order to establish the winners.

5.3   Evaluating Task 2

For Task 2, the annotated dataset we built, provided a set of concepts for each sentence. A concept might be written in several ways, using prepositions, articles and so on. That is why, when we built the annotated dataset for Task 2, we tried to generate as many different grammatical forms of a concept as possible. When performing the precision/recall analysis for Task 2 we classified as true positive (tp) a given concept of a certain system that was also included into the annotation dataset. The false negative (fn) set was constituted by all the defined concepts that were not present into the annotation dataset; finally, the concepts present into the annotations but not included into the system output were classified as false positive (fp). The precision, recall and F1 measure were then computed with the formulas above. The reader notices that the recall for this task was much lower than the other tasks because the presence of a large amount of concepts we wrote in different forms in our annotated dataset that increased the size of the false negative set.

5.4 Evaluating Task 3

Task 3 was the easiest to measure. As each sentence of the output consisted of just one of the four possible domains (books, DVDs, electronics, and housewares), we simply counted the sentences with the correct detected domain and used this number as the final measure to identify the winners for this task. The system with the highest number of sentences whose domain was correctly identified was the winner.

5.5 Evaluating the Most Innovative Approach Task

A board of three judges, chosen among the challenge program committee, evaluated each system in more detail and gave their assessment on the employment of the semantics and the use of concept-level mechanisms of each system. In particular, an important aspect was related to the interaction between semantics and sentics and how the polarity was handled within the context. Minor points that were taken into account were the computational time and the easiness of utilization.

6   Submitted Systems

There were around 15 different intentional submissions to the Concept-Level Sentiment Analysis challenge. The challenge chairs had several discussions with many of the authors before the submission deadline about the requirements that the authors' systems had to satisfy. As each system had to have a semantic flavor using Linked Data, semantic resources, and so on, systems missing of semantics features were discouraged from the submission. Besides, the call for this challenge was launched at the end of December 2013 and the first deadline was for mid March 2014. Therefore time was not of help to authors with existing sentiment analysis systems for improving their systems with semantic resources and being able to satisfy the requirements of the challenge for the submission. However, six of them were able to ultimate their semantic sentiment analysis systems and those were submitted and accepted for the challenge. Participants were from very different countries: Italy, France, Israel, USA, Singapore, Mexico, UK, Taiwan. Only one system targeted and competed for all the tasks whereas the others participated for two, three or four tasks. Table 7 shows the title of the submitted systems, their authors and indicates the tasks that each of them targeted.

During the ESWC conference a poster and demo session was allocated for challengers to show their system by using either a poster or a demo (or both) to the public and explain the semantics their systems were based on. Table 8 shows a screenshot of the presented posters of four out of six systems participating to the Concept-Level Sentiment Analysis challenge whereas Table 9 shows a screenshot of five of them.

Table 7. The competing systems at the Concept-Level Sentiment Analysis challenge and the tasks they target.

System	Task 0	Task 1	Task 2	Task 3	Most Innovative
Mauro Dragoni, Andrea Tettamanzi and Celia Da Costa Pereira **A Fuzzy System For Concept-Level Sentiment Analysis**	X	X	X	X	X
Nir Ofek and Lior Rokach **Lechuzo: Weakly-Supervised System for** **Fine-Grained Sentiment Analysis**		X			X
Pablo Mendes, Anni Coden, Daniel Gruhl et al. **Semantic Lexicon Expansion for Concept-based** **Aspect-aware Sentiment Analysis**	X	X		X	X
Soujanya Poria, Nir Ofek **Sentic Demo: A Hybrid Concept-Level** **Aspect-Based Sentiment Analysis Toolkit**	X		X		X
Shafqat Mumtaz Virk, Yann-Huei Lee and Lun-Wei Ku **Sinica Semantic Parser for ESWC'14** **Concept-Level Semantic Analysis Challenge**			X		X
Jay Kuan-Chieh Chung, Chi-En Wu and Richard Tzong-Han Tsai **Improve Polarity Detection of Online Reviews** **with Bag-of-Sentimental-Concepts**	X				X

Table 8. Four poster screenshots of the participants' systems.

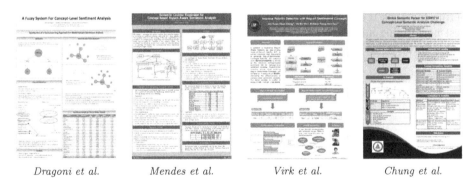

Dragoni et al.   *Mendes et al.*   *Virk et al.*   *Chung et al.*

7   Results

During the challenge days, the evaluation dataset was revealed to the participants and the output of their systems was sent to the challenge chairs according to the same RDF format mentioned for each task description. In two cases, many of the sentences present within the output provided by the participants contained format errors and therefore they were excluded from that specific task. Following, the winners of each task and the evaluation measures results will be shown.

Table 9. Five screenshots of the running systems.

Dragoni et al.   *Ofek et al.*   *Poria et al.*

Virk et al.   *Chung et al.*

7.1 Task 0

Table 10 shows the precision-recall analysis for the output of the systems competing for Task 0 and the related winners. The system of *Chung et al.* had the best performing approach for this task and it was the winner of 100 euros award and a Springer voucher of the value of 150 euros.

Table 10. Precision-recall analysis and winners for Task 0.

System	Prec	Rec	F1	Pos
Chung et al.	0.78	0.57	0.66	1
Mendes et al.	0.66	0.59	0.62	2
Dragoni et al.	0.42	0.47	0.44	3
Poria et al.	Excluded for formatting errors			

7.2 Task 1

Table 11 shows the precision-recall analysis for the output of the systems competing for Task 1 and the related winners. The system of *Dragoni et al.* had the highest precision recall analysis and got an award of 100 euros and a Springer voucher of the value of 150 euros.

Table **11.** Precision-recall analysis and winners for Task 1.

System	$Prec_1$	Rec_1	$F1_1$	$Prec_2$	Rec_2	$F1_2$	$F1_{avg}$	Pos
Dragoni et al.	0.25	0.26	0.26	0.12	0.11	0.11	0.19	1
Mendes et al.	0.24	0.15	0.18	0.12	0.06	0.09	0.14	2
Ofek et al.	0.12	0.06	0.08	0.09	0.04	0.06	0.07	3

7.3   Task 2

Table 12 shows the precision-recall analysis for the output of the systems competing for Task 2 and the related winners. The system of *Poria et al.* was the winner of an award of 100 euros and a Springer voucher of the value of 150 euros.

Table **12.** Precision-recall analysis and winners for Task 2.

System	Prec	Rec	F1	Pos
Poria et al.	0.87	0.0.37	0.0.52	1
Virk et al.	0.05	0.003	0.005	2
Dragoni et al.	Excluded for formatting errors			

7.4   Task 3

Finally, Table 13 shows the results for the output of the systems competing for Task 3 and the related winners. The reader notices that some sentences have been taken out of the count when formatting errors were present. In the system of *Mendes* 3501 sentences were correctly evaluated whereas in the system of *Dragoni* 879 sentences have been taken out for problems with RDF specifications. Therefore, the system of *Mendes et al.* was the winner and got an award of 100 euros and a Springer voucher of the value of 150 euros.

Table **13.** Results and winners for Task 3.

System	Number of sentences with correctly classified domain	Pos
Mendes et al.	1179 out of 3501	1
Dragoni et al.	458 out of 2622	2

7.5   The Most Innovative Approach Task

The Innovation Prize went to *Dragoni et al.* (a) for introducing the concept of fuzzy membership of multi-word expressions for dynamically detecting the polarity of natural language concepts according to different domains and contexts and

(b) for proposing the use of a two-level framework that nicely models the inter-action between semantics and sentics for aspect-based sentiment analysis. These are two key elements for the advancement of sentiment analysis research because (a) polarity is not a static thing but rather a dynamic context-dependent mea-sure and (b) semantic and affective relatedness are two different coefficients that need to be kept separate while used concomitantly. The most common mistakes in current sentiment analysis research, in fact, are (a) the a-priori definition of polarity, e.g., in the case of the "small" adjective which is neither positive nor negative but rather acquires a polarity according to the context, and (b) the (con)fusion of semantic and affective level, e.g., in the case of concepts like "joy" and "anger" which are highly semantically related (as they are both emotions) but have opposite affective relatedness.

8   Conclusions

The Concept-Level Sentiment Analysis challenge attracted several researchers mainly from two different domains: (i) those of the sentiment analysis area who have been pushed to explore the strengths and opportunities of the Semantic Web and tried to exploit it within their existing sentiment analysis systems which were based on traditional artificial intelligence, machine learning or nat-ural language processing approaches. (ii) Those involved within the Semantic Web area, showing them the domain of the sentiment analysis and attracted them to develop their own systems with a strong base of Semantic Web fea-tures to solve some of the tasks of the challenge mentioned above. Besides, the concurrent execution of the First Workshop on Semantic Sentiment Analysis at ESWC on similar topics brought a process of cross-pollination of ideas among the attendees: researchers, editors of prestigious international journals and mag-azines, people from industry and key stakeholders in general. It is to highlight the number of attendees of the workshop which was around 30 including sev-eral participants of the challenge which had been asked to held a small session within the workshop briefly showing their system and giving tips on their learned experience about the technical development. During the challenge, all the partic-ipants were really active and we did not experience problems during the normal conduction of the challenge and its evaluation. Among the learned lessons we had, one is particularly important and to be shared as it is related to several other challenge even in different domains. We have noticed that it would have been much better to provide the participants not only an evaluation dataset where they have tested their systems but also the very same script we used for the precision/recall analysis. This could have given the participants further tips on the reasons related to the performance of their systems (e.g. the wrong for-mat of the output of a few systems could have been spotted and fixed earlier). Overall, the Concept-Level Sentiment Analysis was successful and we aimed at reconsidering it again at the next edition of the ESWC.

References

1. Baccianella, A., Esuli, S., Sebastiani, F.: SentiWordNet 3.0: an enhanced lexical resource for sentiment analysis and opinion mining. In: Calzolari, N., Choukri, K., Maegaard, B., Mariani, J., Odijk, J., Piperidis, S., Rosner, M., Tapias, D. (eds.) Proceedings of the Seventh Conference on International Language Resources and Evaluation (LREC'10), Valletta, Malta (2010)
2. Bosco, C., Patti, V., Bolioli, A.: Developing corpora for sentiment analysis: the case of irony and Senti-TUT. IEEE Intell. Syst. **28**(2), 55–63 (2013)
3. Bradley, M., Lang, P.: Affective norms for English words (ANEW): stimuli, instruction manual and affective ratings. Technical report, The Center for Research in Psychophysiology, University of Florida (1999)
4. Cambria, E., Hussain, A.: Sentic Computing: Techniques, Tools, and Applications, vol. 2. Springer, Heidelberg (2012)
5. Cambria, E., Schuller, B., Xia, Y., Havasi, C.: New avenues in opinion mining and sentiment analysis. IEEE Intell. Syst. **28**(2), 15–21 (2013)
6. Cambria, E., White, B.: Jumping NLP curves: a review of natural language processing research. IEEE Comput. Intell. Mag. **9**(2), 48–57 (2014)
7. Cambria, E., Olsher, D., Rajagopal, D.: Senticnet 3: a common and common-sense knowledge base for cognition-driven sentiment analysis. In: Brodley, C.E., Stone, P. (eds.) Twenty-Eight AAAI Conference on Artificial Intelligence, pp. 1515–1521. AAAI Press, Palo Alto, July 2014
8. Chen, H., Wuand, Z., Cudré-Mauroux, P.: Semantic Web meets computational intelligence: state of the art and perspectives. IEEE Comput. Intell. Mag. **7**(2), 67–74 (2012)
9. Gangemi, A., Presutti, V., Reforgiato Recupero, D.: Frame-based detection of opinion holders and topics: a model and a tool. IEEE Comput. Intell. Mag. **9**(1), 20–30 (2014)
10. Garcia-Moya, L., Anaya-Sanchez, H., Berlanga-Llavori, R.: Retrieving product features and opinions from customer reviews. IEEE Intell. Syst. **28**(3), 19–27 (2013)
11. Hung, C., Lin, H.-K.: Using objective words in sentiwordnet to improve word-of-mouth sentiment classification. IEEE Intell. Syst. **28**(2), 47–54 (2013)
12. Johansson, R., Moschitti, A.: Relational features in fine-grained opinion analysis. Comput. Ling. **39**(3), 473–509 (2013)
13. Liu, H., Singh, P.: Conceptnet: a practical commonsense reasoning toolkit. BT Technol. J. **22**, 211–226 (2004)
14. Poria, S., Gelbukh, A.F., Hussain, A., Howard, N., Das, D., Bandyopadhyay, S.: Enhanced senticnet with affective labels for concept-based opinion mining. IEEE Intell. Syst. **28**(2), 31–38 (2013)
15. Powers, D.M.W.: Evaluation: from precision, recall and F-factor to ROC, informedness, markedness & correlation. Technical report SIE-07-001, School of Informatics and Engineering, Flinders University, Adelaide, Australia (2007)
16. Presutti, V., Draicchio, F., Gangemi, A.: Knowledge extraction based on discourse representation theory and linguistic frames. In: ten Teije, A., Völker, J., Handschuh, S., Stuckenschmidt, H., d'Acquin, M., Nikolov, A., Aussenac-Gilles, N., Hernandez, N. (eds.) EKAW 2012. LNCS, vol. 7603, pp. 114–129. Springer, Heidelberg (2012)
17. Reforgiato Recupero, D., Presutti, V., Consoli, S., Gangemi, A., Nuzzolese, A.: Sentilo: frame-based sentiment analysis. Cogn. Comput. (2014)

18. Saif, H., He, Y., Alani, H.: Semantic sentiment analysis of Twitter. In: Cudré-Mauroux, P., et al. (eds.) ISWC 2012, Part I. LNCS, vol. 7649, pp. 508–524. Springer, Heidelberg (2012)
19. Strapparava, C., Valitutti, A.: WordNet-affect: an affective extension of WordNet. In: LREC, Lisbon, pp. 1083–1086 (2004)
20. Tsai, A.C.-R., Wu, C.-E., Tsai, R.T.-H., Hsu, J.Y.-J.: Building a concept-level sentiment dictionary based on commonsense knowledge. IEEE Intell. Syst. **28**(2), 22–30 (2013)
21. Weichselbraun, A., Gindl, S., Scharl, A.: Extracting and grounding context-aware sentiment lexicons. IEEE Intell. Syst. **28**(2), 39–46 (2013)
22. Weigand, E. (ed.).: Emotion in Dialogic Interaction. Current Issues in Linguistic Theory, vol. 248. John Benjamins, Philadelphia (2004)

A Fuzzy System for Concept-Level Sentiment Analysis

Mauro Dragoni[1]([✉]), Andrea G.B. Tettamanzi[2], and Célia da Costa Pereira[2]

[1] FBK–IRST, Trento, Italy
dragoni@fbk.eu
[2] Université Nice Sophia Antipolis, I3S, UMR 7271,
Sophia Antipolis, France
{andrea.tettamanzi,celia.pereira}@unice.fr

Abstract. An emerging field within Sentiment Analysis concerns the investigation about how sentiment concepts have to be adapted with respect to the different domains in which they are used. In the context of the Concept-Level Sentiment Analysis Challenge, we presented a system whose aims are twofold: (i) the implementation of a learning approach able to model fuzzy functions used for building the relationships graph representing the appropriateness between sentiment concepts and different domains (Task 1); and (ii) the development of a semantic resource based on the connection between an extended version of WordNet, SenticNet, and ConceptNet, that has been used both for extracting concepts (Task 2) and for classifying sentences within specific domains (Task 3).

1 Introduction and Related Work

Sentiment Analysis is a kind of text categorization task that aims to classify documents according to their opinion (polarity) on a given subject [1]. This task has created a considerable interest due to its wide applications. However, in the classic Sentiment Analysis the polarity of each term of the document is computed independently with respect to domain which the document belongs to. Recently, the idea of adapting terms polarity to different domains emerged [2]. The rational behind the idea of such investigation is simple. Let's consider the following example concerning the adjective "small":

1. The sideboard is **small** and it is not able to contain a lot of stuff.
2. The **small** dimensions of this decoder allow to move it easily.

In the first text, we considered the Furnishings domain and, within it, the polarity of the adjective "small" is, for sure, "negative" because it highlight an issue of the described item. On the other side, in the second text, where we considered the Electronics domain, the polarity of such adjective can be considered "positive".

In literature, different approaches related to the Multi-Domain Sentiment Analysis has been proposed. Briefly, two main categories may be identified: (i) the transfer of learned classifiers across different domains [3,4], and (ii) the

© Springer International Publishing Switzerland 2014
V. Presutti et al. (Eds.): SemWebEval 2014, CCIS 475, pp. 21–27, 2014.
DOI: 10.1007/978-3-319-12024-9_2

use of propagation of labels through graphs structures [5,6]. Independently from the kind of approach, works using concepts rather than terms for representing different sentiments have been proposed.

Differently from the approaches already discussed in the literature, we address the multi-domain sentiment analysis problem by applying the fuzzy logic theory for modeling membership functions representing the relationships between concepts and domains. Moreover, the proposed system exploits the use of semantic background knowledge for propagating information represented by the learned fuzzy membership functions to each element of the network. As the best of our knowledge, the proposed approach is innovative with respect to the state of the art of the Multi-Domain Sentiment Analysis.

The paper is structured as follows. Section 2 introduces the background knowledge and tools used during the development of the system that is described in detail in Sect. 3. While, Sect. 4 provide a description about how the tasks of the challenge have been addressed and it concludes the paper.

2   Preliminaries

The system is implemented on top of a background knowledge used for representing the linguistic connections between "concepts" described in several resources. Below, it is possible to find the list of such resources and the links where further information about them may be found.

WordNet[1] [7] is one of the most important resource available to researchers in the field of text analysis, computational linguistics, and many related areas. In the implemented system, WordNet has been used as starting point for the construction of the semantic graph used by the system (see Sect. 3) However, due to some coverage limitations occurring in WordNet, it has been extended by linking further terms coming from the Roget's Thesaurus [8].

SenticNet[2] [9] is a publicly available resource for opinion mining that exploits both Artificial Intelligence and Semantic Web techniques to infer the polarity associated with common-sense concepts and represent it in a semantic-aware format. In particular, SenticNet uses dimensionality reduction to calculate the affective valence of a set of Open Mind concepts and represent it in a machine-accessible and machine-processable format.

All resources have been connected by exploiting links contained in Concept-Net[3] [10] in order to build a single graph for representing the entire background knowledge exploitable by the system.

3   System

The main aim of implemented system is the learning of fuzzy membership functions representing the belonging of a concept with respect to a domain in terms of both sentiment polarity as well as aboutness. The two pillars on which the

---

[1] https://wordnet.princeton.edu/

[2] http://sentic.net/

[3] http://conceptnet5.media.mit.edu/

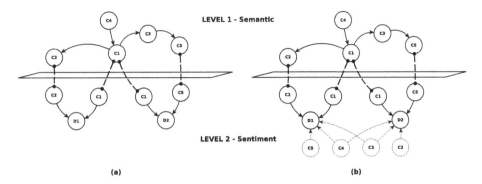

Fig. 1. The two-layer graph initialized during the Preliminary Learning Phase (a) and its evolution after the execution of the Information Propagation Phase (b).

system has been though are: (i) the use of fuzzy logic for modeling the polarity of a concept with respect to a domain as well as its aboutness, and (ii) the creation of a two-levels graph where the top level represents the semantic relationships between concepts, while the bottom level contains the links between all concept membership functions and the domains.

Figure 1 shows the conceptualization of the two-levels graph. Relationships between the concepts of the Level 1 (the Semantic Level) are described by the background knowledge exploited by the system as described in Sect. 2. The type of relationships are the same generally used in linguistic resource: for example, concepts C_1 and C_3 may be connected through an Is-A relationship rather than the Antonym one. Instead, each connection of the Level 2 (the Sentiment Level) describes the belonging of each concept with respect to the different domains taken into account.

The system has been trained by using the Blitzer dataset[4] in two steps: first, the fuzzy membership functions have been initially estimated by analyzing only the explicit information present within the dataset (Sect. 3.1); then, (ii) the explicit information have been propagated through the Sentiment Level graph by exploiting the connections defined in the Semantic Level.

3.1 Preliminary Learning Phase

The Preliminary Learning (PL) phase aims to estimated the starting polarity of each concept with respect to a domain. The estimation of this value is done by analyzing only the explicit information provided by the training set. This phase allows to define the preliminary fuzzy membership functions between the concepts defined in the Semantic Level of the graph and the domains that are defined in the Sentiment one. Such a value is computed by the Eq. 1

$$\text{polarity}_i^*(C) = \frac{k_C^i}{T_C^i} \in [-1, 1] \qquad \forall i = 1, \ldots, n, \tag{1}$$

---

[4] http://www.cs.jhu.edu/~mdredze/datasets/sentiment/

where C is the concept taken into account, index i refers to domain D_i which the concept belongs to, n is the number of domains available in the training set, k_C^i is the arithmetic sum of the polarities observed for concept C in the training set restricted to domain D_i, and T_C^i is the number of instances of the training set, restricted to domain D_i, in which concept C occurs. The shape of the fuzzy membership function generated during this phase is a triangle with the top vertex in the coordinates $(x, 1)$, where $x = \text{polarity}_i^*(C)$ and with the two bottom vertices in the coordinates $(-1, 0)$ and $(1, 0)$ respectively. The rationale is that while we have one point (x) in which we have full confidence, our uncertainty covers the entire space because we do not have any information concerning the remaining polarity values.

3.2   Information Propagation Phase

The Information Propagation (IP) phase aims to exploit the explicit information learned in the PL phase in order to both (i) refine the fuzzy membership function of the known concepts, as well as, (ii) to model such functions for concepts that are not specified in the training set, but that are semantically related to the specified ones. Figure 1 presents how the two-levels graph evolves before and after the execution of the IP phase. After the PL phase only four membership functions are modeled: C_1 and C_2 for the domain D_1, and C_1 and C_5 for the domain D_2 (Fig. 1a). However, as we may observe, in the Semantic Level there are concepts that are semantically related to the ones that were explicitly defined in the training set, namely C_3 and C_4; while, there are also concepts for which a fuzzy membership function has not been modeled for some domains (i.e. C_2 for the domain D_2 and C_5 for the domain D_1).

Such fuzzy membership functions may be inferred by propagating the information modeled in the PL phase. Similarly, existing fuzzy membership functions are refined by the influence of the other ones. Let's consider the polarity between the concept C_3 and the domain D_2. The fuzzy membership function representing this polarity is strongly influenced by the ones representing the polarities of concepts C_1 and C_5 with respect to the domain D_2.

The propagation of the learned information through the graph is done iteratively where, in each iteration, the estimated polarity value of the concept x learned during the PL phase is updated based on the learned values of the adjoining concepts. At each iteration, the updated values is saved in order to exploit it for the re-shaping of the fuzzy membership function associating the concept x to the domain i.

The resulting shapes of the inferred fuzzy membership functions will be trapezoids where the extension of the upper base is proportional to the difference between the value learned during the PL phase (V_{pl}) and the value obtained at the end of the IP phase (V_{ip}); while, the support is proportional to both the number of iterations needed by the concept x to converge to the V_{ip} and the variance with respect to the average of the values computed after each iteration of the IP phase.

3.3   Polarity Aggregation and Decision Phases

The fuzzy polarities of different concepts, resulting from the IP phase, are finally aggregated by a fuzzy averaging operator obtained by applying the extension principle (for the technical details see [11]) in order to compute fuzzy polarities for complex entities, like texts, which consist of a number of concepts and thus derive, so to speak, their polarity from them. When a crisp polarity value is needed, it may be computed from a fuzzy polarity by applying one of the defuzzification methods proposed in the literature [11].

Let $\mu_C : [-1,1] \rightarrow [0,1]$ be the fuzzy interval (i.e., a convex fuzzy set) representing the fuzzy polarity of concept C resulting from the IP phase. Let T be a text (or any other entity that may be regarded as a combination of concepts) related to concepts $C_1, \ldots, C_n$. The fuzzy polarity of T, $\mu_T : [-1,1] \rightarrow [0,1]$, may be defined as the average of the fuzzy polarities of concepts $C_1, \ldots, C_n$, by applying the extension principle, as follows, for all $x \in [-1,1]$:

$$\mu_T(x) = \sup_{x=\frac{1}{n}\sum_{i=1}^{n} x_i} \min_{i=1,\ldots,n} \mu_{C_i}(x_i). \tag{2}$$

The result of the polarity aggregation phase is a fuzzy polarity, whose membership function reflects the uncertainty of the available estimate obtained by the system. In this sense, μ_T may be regarded as a possibility distribution of the actual polarity of T. Given $x \in [-1,1]$, the membership degree $\mu_T(x)$ represent the degree to which it is possible that the polarity of T is x. Here, we are making the assumption that polarity is gradual, i.e., that a text may be more or less negative or positive.

At some point, if a decision must be made based on the polarity of T, some criterion has to be adopted, which takes the uncertainty of the estimate into account. The fact is a criterion can be defined only with reference to a given application scenario. For instance, if we can afford any desired number of texts and what we want is to pick a few of them whose polarity is certain, we can look for T such that either $d_T < 0$ or $a_T > 0$, i.e., the support of μ_T lies entirely on the left or on the right of zero, because in those cases it is certain that polarity is negative (in the former case) or positive (in the latter). In other scenarios, where what we want is to classify each and every text as either negative or positive as accurately as possible, we will have to be less picky and rely on a defuzzification method to transform μ_T into a crisp polarity value.

4   Challenge Tasks and Conclusion

In this paper, we have presented a fuzzy concept-based sentiment analysis system able to model fuzzy membership functions representing the polarities and the aboutness of concepts with respect to a particular domain. The system has been implemented in the context of the ESWC 2014 Concept-Level Sentiment Analysis Challenge. The Tasks proposed by the challenge have been addressed as follows.

Elementary Task: the polarity of each text is computed by aggregating the fuzzy membership functions associated with the extracted concepts. The aggregation operation is performed by applying the extension principle as described in Sect. 3.3.

Advanced Task #1 and #2: both aspects and concepts (simple and complex) are extracted by exploiting the built knowledge base (as explained in Sect. 2) and, concerning the Advanced Task #1, its polarity is computed by applying the approach used in the Elementary Task.

Advanced Task #3: similarly to the Elementary Task, the classification of each text is done by analyzing the associations between concepts and domains (independently from the polarity); therefore, the domain of each text is extracted by applying the extension principle of fuzzy sets.

Finally, the system have been preliminarily tested on the full version of the Blitzer dataset as shown in Table 1[5]. The system has been compared with three different baselines representing the most well-known machine learning techniques available today demonstrating the feasibility of the proposed approach for addressing the multi-domain sentiment analysis problem.

Table 1. Results obtained on the full version of the Blitzer dataset.

SVN [12]	Naive-Bayes [13]	Max-Entropy [13]	MDFSA Precision	MDFSA Recall
0.8068	0.8227	0.8275	**0.8617**	0.9987

References

1. Pang, B., Lee, L., Vaithyanathan, S.: Thumbs up? Sentiment classification using machine learning techniques. In: Proceedings of the Conference on Empirical Methods in Natural Language Processing (EMNLP), Philadelphia, Association for Computational Linguistics, pp. 79–86 (July 2002)
2. Blitzer, J., Dredze, M., Pereira, F.: Biographies, bollywood, boom-boxes and blenders: domain adaptation for sentiment classification. In: Carroll, J.A., van den Bosch, A., Zaenen, A. (eds.) ACL, The Association for Computational Linguistics (2007)
3. Bollegala, D., Weir, D.J., Carroll, J.A.: Cross-domain sentiment classification using a sentiment sensitive thesaurus. IEEE Trans. Knowl. Data Eng. **25**(8), 1719–1731 (2013)
4. Xia, R., Zong, C., Hu, X., Cambria, E.: Feature ensemble plus sample selection: domain adaptation for sentiment classification. IEEE Int. Syst. **28**(3), 10–18 (2013)
5. Ponomareva, N., Thelwall, M.: Semi-supervised vs. cross-domain graphs for sentiment analysis. In: Angelova, G., Bontcheva, K., Mitkov, R. (eds.) RANLP, RANLP 2011 Organising Committee/ACL, pp. 571–578 (2013)
6. Tsai, A.C.R., Wu, C.E., Tsai, R.T.H., Hsu, J.Y.: Building a concept-level sentiment dictionary based on commonsense knowledge. IEEE Int. Syst. **28**(2), 22–30 (2013)

---

[5] Detailed results and tool demo are available at http://dkmtools.fbk.eu/moki/demo/ mdfsa/mdfsa_demo.html.

7. Fellbaum, C.: WordNet: An Electronic Lexical Database. MIT Press, Cambridge (1998)
8. Kipfer, B.A.: Roget's 21st Century Thesaurus, vol. 3. Random House, New York (2005)
9. Cambria, E., Speer, R., Havasi, C., Hussain, A.: Senticnet: a publicly available semantic resource for opinion mining. In: AAAI Fall Symposium: Commonsense Knowledge. Volume FS-10-02 of AAAI Technical report, AAAI (2010)
10. Liu, H., Singh, P.: ConceptNet: a practical commonsense reasoning tool-kit. BT Technol. J. **22**(4), 211–226 (2004)
11. Zadeh, L.A.: The concept of a linguistic variable and its application to approximate reasoning - I. Inf. Sci. **8**(3), 199–249 (1975)
12. Chang, C.C., Lin, C.J.: LIBSVM: a library for support vector machines. ACM TIST **2**(3), 27 (2011)
13. McCallum, A.K.: Mallet: a machine learning for language toolkit (2002). http://mallet.cs.umass.edu

Unsupervised Fine-Grained Sentiment Analysis System Using Lexicons and Concepts

Nir Ofek[(✉)] and Lior Rokach

Ben-Gurion University of the Negev, Beersheba, Israel
{nirofek,liorrk}@bgu.ac.il

Abstract. Sentiment is mainly analyzed at a document, sentence or aspect level. Document or sentence levels could be too coarse since polar opinions can co-occur even within the same sentence. In aspect level sentiment analysis often opinion-bearing terms can convey polar sentiment in different contexts. Consider the following laptop review: "the big plus was a large screen but having a large battery made me change my mind," where polar opinions co-occur in the same sentence, and the opinion term that describes the opinion targets ("large") encodes polar sentiments: a positive for *screen*, and a negative for *battery*. To parse these differences, our approach is to identify opinions with respect to the specific opinion targets, while taking the context into account. Moreover, considering that there is a problem of obtaining an annotated training set in each context, our approach uses unlabeled data.

Keywords: Fine-grained sentiment analysis · Opinion mining · Lexicon

1 Introduction

The surging number of subjective information across the Web, in several forms such as of reviews, blogs, and bulletin board can be useful for decision-making and various applications. Since manual assessment is not feasible, not only because the high number, but also due to the fact that some opinioned-text are very long, automatically analyzing the sentiment becomes extremely useful. Traditional sentiment analysis approaches aim to extract sentiment at the document level [1–3]. However consider the following excerpt:

"(1) I bought an iPhone a few days ago. (2) It was such a nice phone. (3) The touch screen was really cool. (4) The voice quality was clear too. (5) Although the battery life was not long..." [4]

Notice that sentence (3) conveys a positive opinion of the *touch-screen*, whereas sentence (5) describes the *battery* negatively. Sentence (2) conveys a positive general opinion of the product.

More researchers have recognized that even if a document bears a negative classification, it can contain some positive indicators. Consequently, they have an increasing interest in applying opinion mining techniques at a more granular level—specifically, the phrase level or sentence level [5–7]. However, such approach is still limited when polar opinions co-occur in the same sentence. For example, in: *"the big*

© Springer International Publishing Switzerland 2014
V. Presutti et al. (Eds.): SemWebEval 2014, CCIS 475, pp. 28–33, 2014.
DOI: 10.1007/978-3-319-12024-9_3

plus was a large screen but still the price was too high," polar opinions are conveyed for two different opinion targets (screen, price).

Since there could be several opinions in the text, even within the same sentence, we would like to extract each opinion and to associate it with the corresponding opinion target. The suggested fine-grained system is designed to identify sentiment of opinion targets and therefore it can identify multiple, and possibly polar opinions for each occurrence of opinion target in the text. Opinion target are entities and their attributes which are also referred as aspects [8].

Labeled data is in shortage and for some aspects not available at all. For example, TripAdvisor suggests user rating for only seven aspects, in addition to the overall rating. Hence, some methods utilize the overall rating of a review, while assuming that it is generated based on a weighted combination of the ratings over all the aspects [9, 10]. Since not all websites provide overall rating in addition to the content, our method uses unlabeled data without any rating. Instead, our system uses conjunction patterns in order to infer the polarity of adjectives, with respect to each opinion target, that co-occur with known adjectives.

Adjectives are words that describe or modify other elements in a sentence, and are frequently used to directly convey facts and opinions about the nouns they modify. As such, they found as useful with sentiment identification [11–13] and are the backbones of our system; therefore, this paper elaborates mainly on disambiguating the polarity of adjectives across different opinion targets i.e., aspects. This process is iterative and differs from [13] since it is designed to produce polarity score for each adjective based on previously discovered adjectives, which can describe how positive (or negative) an adjective is, and is useful for sentiment summarization.

Since sentiment is not always conveyed by adjectives, the system is able to identify concepts by using SenticNet 3 [14], and to further disambiguate their polarity in the relevant context, i.e., opinion target, by using the adjective lexicons. For example, our system can successfully predict the sentiment in the excerpts "*the pool looks large*," and to associate it to the relevant aspect *pool*, although the adjective *large* does not modify it.

To summarize, our method has the following properties: (1) it can be trained with unsupervised data, (2) it can determine an adjective's polarity with respect to the target aspect, and (3) it is designed in a cascading approach to seamlessly support adding more modules.

2   Description

The system starts with discovering important aspects in the text. First, repeating nouns that often opinion-bearing adjectives are related to, are identified. In the next step these nouns are considered as aspects and are clustered to a single topical aspect, i.e., each topical aspect will be represented by a set of aspects. For example, the sentiment of the topical aspect *room* is calculated by averaging sentiment of the aspects: room, bed, bathroom and view. This is done in a similar way as described by [9], where a set of seed words are used to discover additional ones, however we are only using nouns.

Once aspects are identified, the system aims to learn the polarity score of adjectives associated with each aspect. This information (adjectives and their polarity per aspect) is used when adjectives are directly modifying the target aspect, and to derive the sentiment of more complex concepts identified by SenticNet 3. The process is illustrated by Fig. 1; we further elaborate mainly on learning the polarity of adjectives.

The process of generating aspect-specific lexicon is an iterative process that starts with a seed lexicon and expands it in constructing an aspect-specific sentiment lexicon. In each iteration we start with the current aspect-specific lexicon of known adjectives, and by processing a set of unlabeled reviews, we search for new adjectives that are not in the lexicon and modify (i.e., are connected to) the target aspect. The system uses a parser in order to determine for each aspect-adjective pair in a sentence whether they are connected, i.e., the adjective modifies the noun, or not. Recent works in sentiment analysis have focused utilizing dependency tree structure for rule-based concept extraction as well as for sentiment analysis [15–18]. Our system, however, uses dependency tree only in connecting nouns with adjectives as described by the work of [19] in their English baseline. A new adjective is added to the lexicon only if it is connected with a conjunction pattern to anther adjective which is already in the lexicon. In this case, the polarity of the new adjective is derived by considering the conjunction pattern and the polarity of the known adjective. The input to the algorithm includes the following:

- A seed lexicon (*SL*) - a set of adjectives paired with their corresponding polarity to reflect how positive/negative each adjective is (1 for positive and 0 for negative). The polarity paired with each adjective pertaining to this lexicon should not be dependent on the opinion target, i.e., the polarity of these adjectives is set as a-prior convention. For example, the polarity of the adjectives *excellent* and *amazing* should always be positive. Two classes of adjectives must be excluded from the seed lexicon: ambiguous adjectives (such as *great* which may be very good or big) and adjectives that are used to express polar sentiment in different contexts (such as *big* which can be negative to describe a device or positive in the context of the description of a meal).
- Reviews (*R*) - a set of opinioned text such as reviews which is relevant to the domain of the target aspects, i.e., they are likely to be discussed in. For example TripAdvisor.com is an adequate choice for aspects in the tourism domain.
- Conjunction patterns (*C*) - a set of conjunctions to be matches between a pair of adjectives that co-occur in the same sentence, and their polarity property, i.e., linear of shifter. For example, the conjunction *and* has a linear polarity property whereas the conjunction *but* indicates shift in polarity.

The main output of the learning phase is an extended set of aspect-specific lexicons which includes the seed as well as new adjectives with their sentiment scores.

The process of creating the aspect-dependent lexicon performed for each aspect separately. First, the extended lexicon of aspect A (EL_A) is initialized with the seed lexicon (*SL*). Then, the following steps are repeated n times (n is a configurable parameters). We identify all adjectives in each review $r_i \in R$. Then, for each identified adjective a and for each discovered aspect A we check whether a is modifying aspect A or not. Then, for each pair of adjectives a_1 and a_2 which both modify aspect A, we check whether this instance of two adjectives is connected with a conjunction pattern. If a_1 and a_2 are connected with a conjunction c, then, if one of the two adjectives (let's assume a_1 – without loss of generality) is in the current extended lexicon EL_A, and the second adjective a_2 is not in EL_A, we compute the polarity score (pol) of a_2, which is determined according to the conjunction pattern c and adjective a_1; for example, if pol $(a_1) = 0.9$ and $c =$ shifter then $pol(a_2) = 1\text{-}pol(a_1) = 0.1$. At the end of each iteration, the polarity score of each new adjective a_2 is computed as the average of the polarity scores that were computed for each instance. Finally, a_2 is added to the extended lexicon of A (EL_A) with its corresponding polarity score.

To this end, the polarity of the adjectives that are modifying the target aspect can be used to calculate its sentiment score in all of its instances, i.e., in each time it appears in the text. This lexical approach can obtain a relatively high precision rate. As a result, in some cases still the target aspect does not have any modifying adjectives, or the modifying adjective does not include in the aspect's lexicon. Aiming to increase recall, we use SenticNet 3, a semantic source that contains 14,000 common sense-knowledge concepts labeled by their polarity scores, in a cascading approach. If the lexical approach returns no answer for aspect A which still appears in the text, we retrieve concepts by using SenticNet 3. If an adjective a_1 appears in one of the concepts, and it pertains to A's lexicon, the aspect's sentiment score is determined by the score of a_1 in the lexicon. Otherwise, the sentiment of that concept is determined by SenticNet 3. It is to mention that at any time a polarity of an adjective is computed or used, negation, if recognized, is taken into consideration by using a dependency parser.

The final score of an aspect is the average of all of its instances' scores in the text. The system can output an overall sentiment for a given sentence, based on averaging the calculated sentiment for each aspect in the sentence.

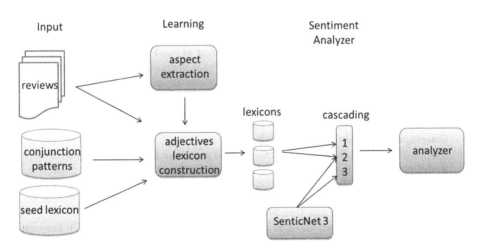

Fig. 1. Illustration of learning and prediction processes.

3 Conclusion

The represented system is using unlabeled set of opinioned text to construct sentiment lexicons of adjectives. Each adjective is given with a score that is computed for a specific aspect and can be used in various of ways since adjectives are frequently used to convey sentiment. Methods that use the overall score may be too coarse. Consider the following review taken from Tripadvisor.com, rated as *'terrible'* (1 of 5 points): *"Nice kitchenette, good location next to Museum station. Aircon unit is standalone and controls fully adjustable"*. No doubt that the overall rating is not in accordance with the text. A conclusive overall score cannot take into consideration divergent opinions. The cascading approach makes the system capable of adding more methods while high precision methods will be employed first. Thus, it is configurable, and users can achieve high precision rates on the expense of lower recall, according to their needs.

References

1. Dave, K., Lawrence, S., Pennock, D.: Mining the peanut gallery: opinion extraction and semantic classification of product reviews. In: Proceedings of the 12th International Conference on World Wide Web, Budapest, Hungary, pp. 519–528, 20–24 May 2003
2. Turney, P.D.: Thumbs up or thumbs down? Semantic orientation applied to unsupervised classification of reviews. In: Proceedings of the 40th Annual Meeting of the Association for Computational Linguistics (ACL'02), pp. 417–424 (2002)
3. Yang, K., Yu, N., Zhang, H.: WIDIT in TREC 2007. Blog track: combining lexicon-based methods to detect opinionated blogs. In: Proceedings of TREC 2007 (2007)
4. Liu, B.: Sentiment analysis and subjectivity. Handbook of Natural Language Processing, 2nd edn. (2010)
5. Xu, R., Wong, K.F., Lu, Q., Xia, Y., Li, W.: Learning knowledge from relevant webpage for opinion analysis. In: Proceedings of the 2008 IEEE/WIC/ACM International Conference on Web Intelligence and Intelligent Agent Technology, Sydney, Australia, pp. 307–313, 9–12 December 2008
6. Agarwal, A., Biadsy, F., Mckeown, F.: Contextual phrase-level polarity analysis using lexical affect scoring and syntactic N-Grams. In: Proceedings of the 12th Conference of the European Chapter of the Association for Computational Linguistics, pp. 24–32 (2009)
7. Wilson, T., Wiebe, J., Hoffmann, P.: Recognizing contextual polarity in phrase-level sentiment analysis. In: Proceedings of the Human Langugae Technology Conference and Conference on Empirical Methods in Natural Language Processing. The Association for Computational Linguistics, pp. 347–354 (2005)
8. Qiu, G., Liu, B., Bu, J., Chen, C.: Opinion word expansion and target extraction through double propagation. Comput. Linguist. **37**(1), 9–27 (2011)
9. Wang, H., Lu, Y., Zhai, C.: Latent aspect rating analysis on review text data: a rating regression approach. In: Proceedings of the 16th ACM SIGKDD International Conference on Knowledge Discovery and Data Mining, pp. 783–792. ACM, July 2010
10. Wang, H., Lu, Y., Zhai, C.: Latent aspect rating analysis without aspect keyword supervision. In: Proceedings of the 17th ACM SIGKDD international conference on Knowledge discovery and data mining, pp. 618–626. ACM, 2011 August

11. Kamps J., Marx, M., Mokken, R.J., De Rijke M.: Using WordNet to measure semantic orientation of adjectives. In: Proceedings of LREC-04, 4th International Conference on Language Resources and Evaluation, Lisbon, PT, vol. 4, pp. 1115–1118 (2004)
12. Blair-Goldensohn, S., Hannan, K., McDonald, R., Neylon, T., Reis, G.A., Reynar, J.: Building a sentiment summarizer for local service reviews. In: WWW Workshop on NLP in the Information Explosion Era (NLPIX). ACM, New York (2008)
13. Qiu, G., Liu, B., Bu, J., Chen, C.: Expanding Domain Sentiment Lexicon through Double Propagation. In: IJCAI, vol. 9, pp. 1199–1204 (2009)
14. Cambria, E., Olsher, D., Rajagopal, D.: SenticNet 3: A common and common-sense knowledge base for cognition-driven sentiment analysis. In: Twenty-Eighth AAAI Conference on Artificial Intelligence, June 2014
15. Poria, S., Gelbukh, A., Cambria, E., Yang, P., Hussain, A., Durrani, T.: Merging SenticNet and WordNet-Affect emotion lists for sentiment analysis. In: 2012 IEEE 11th International Conference on Signal Processing (ICSP), vol. 2, pp. 1251−1255. IEEE (2012)
16. Poria, S., Agarwal, B., Gelbukh, A., Hussain, A., Howard, N.: Dependency-based semantic parsing for concept-level text analysis. In: Gelbukh, A. (ed.) CICLing 2014, Part I. LNCS, vol. 8403, pp. 113–127. Springer, Heidelberg (2014)
17. Poria, S., Cambria, E., Winterstein, G., Huang, G.-B.: Sentic patterns: dependency-based rules for concept-level sentiment analysis. Knowl.-Based Syst. (2014). doi:10.1016/j.knosys.2014.05.005
18. Poria, S., Cambria, E., Ku, L.-W., Gui, C., Gelbukh, A.: A Rule-based approach to aspect extraction from product reviews. In: COLING, Dublin (2014)
19. Ofek, N., Rokach, L., Mitra, P.: Methodology for Connecting nouns to their modifying adjectives. In: Gelbukh, A. (ed.) CICLing 2014, Part I. LNCS, vol. 8403, pp. 271–284. Springer, Heidelberg (2014)

Semantic Lexicon Expansion for Concept-Based Aspect-Aware Sentiment Analysis

Anni Coden[1]($\boxtimes$), Dan Gruhl[2], Neal Lewis[2]($\boxtimes$), Pablo N. Mendes[2]($\boxtimes$),
Meena Nagarajan[2], Cartic Ramakrishnan[2], and Steve Welch[2]

[1] Thomas J. Watson Research Center, Hawthorne, NY, USA
anni@us.ibm.com
[2] IBM Research Almaden, 650 Harry Rd, San Jose, CA, USA
{dgruhl,nrlewis,pnmendes,MeenaNagarajan,carticramakrishnan}@us.ibm.com

Abstract. We have developed a prototype for sentiment analysis that is able to identify aspects of an entity being reviewed, along with the sentiment polarity associated to those aspects. Our approach relies on a core ontology of the task, augmented by a workbench for bootstrapping, expanding and maintaining semantic assets that are useful for a number of text analytics tasks. The workbench has the ability to start from classes and instances defined in an ontology and expand their corresponding lexical realizations according to target corpora. In this paper we present results from applying the resulting semantic asset to enhance information extraction techniques for concept-level sentiment analysis. Our prototype(Demo at http://bit.ly/1svngDi) is able to perform SemSA's Elementary Task (Polarity Detection), Advanced Task #1 (Aspect-Based Sentiment Analysis), and Advanced Task #3 (Topic Spotting).

1 Introduction

Detecting the sentiment expressed in text is a challenging task riddled by the inherent ambiguity and contextual nature of human languages. Consider, for a moment, what is the sentiment expressed by the sentence "I had a cold beer in a cold dining room." Based on common knowledge (which can be location specific), beer is best enjoyed cold, which implies a positive sentiment. But is a cold dining room good or bad? This determination depends on the context of the sentence - e.g. on a very hot and humid summer day one may enjoy a cold room, however when coming into the house from shoveling snow, a warm room would be more desirable.

The above example illustrates that background knowledge and contextual information are important pieces in trying to solve the sentiment analysis puzzle. We propose a core ontology enriched by semantic lexicon expansion to tackle the most trivial sentiment analysis tasks, while alleviating more complex problems such as the aforementioned sentence. The domain model allows the association of concepts and *a priori* polarity information - such as 'beer' (a food concept) and 'cold temperature' (a temperature concept). Is a 'cold' glass of white wine good

© Springer International Publishing Switzerland 2014
V. Presutti et al. (Eds.): SemWebEval 2014, CCIS 475, pp. 34–40, 2014.
DOI: 10.1007/978-3-319-12024-9_4

or should it be served at room temperature? In order to help discover concept mentions in text for extending the ontology, we used a Semantic Asset Management Workbench to create and expand semantic lexicons. The workbench allows users to expand the ontology's coverage of concept and opinion mentions in text, easing and speeding up the creation of resources to aid in the interpretation of the same text through the eyes of different cultures and contexts.

This paper is organized as follows. Section 2 provides an overview of related work. Section 3 describes the core ontology developed and knowledge bases used. Section 4 describes the semantic lexicon expansion. Section 5 presents the sentiment analysis module. Section 6 presents evaluation results. Finally, Sect. 7 presents conclusions and future work.

2   Related Work

Sentiment Analysis and Aspect Detection have gained much attention over the last several years - see [6] for a survey. With the growth of social media and various review sites, rich data sources are becoming more accessible, and industrial use cases increasingly apparent. We find that most approaches rely on semantic lexicons, stressing the need for methods to create and maintain high quality lexical information per category.

Related work in aspect extraction and sentiment analysis has generally had a narrower focus as compared to ours. Blinov and Kotelnikov [1] perform sentiment analysis on verbs and adjectives only, restricting sentiment to narrow descriptive semantics, excluding contextual queues (e.g. "A burger and fries for $25"). Furthermore, it relies on linguistic features (e.g. POS tagging) that are known to be harder to accurately extract in informal text (e.g. Twitter). Schouten, Frasincar and de Jong [7] present a method that relies heavily on training corpus and co-occurrence based algorithms, restricting aspect terms to training corpus exposing a risk of over-fitting. Wagner et al. [8] presents a method that performs well with a combination of rules sets that account for domain specific sentiment terms and multiple distance metrics, combined with machine learning to boost their rule sets. However, the approach does not account for conflicting sentiment cases, as well as non-obvious expressions of negation (e.g. "The management was less than accommodating"). They do note that rule based systems will suffer in accuracy when encountering unforeseen terms.

Our work is related to recent advances in concept-level sentiment analysis [2] and relies on techniques ranging from keyword spotting, through endogenous NLP, to noetic NLP [9]. Our model captures entities and aspects, as well as opinions about these aspects or entities. Our focus is on rapidly expanding the model's lexical coverage to new domains and languages.

3   Ontology and Knowledge Bases

We designed an ontology to model online reviews – i.e. textual comments provided by a customer with opinions about some entity or aspect of that entity.

Each `Review` contains potentially multiple sentences, and each sentence contains 0 to N item reviews (`ItemReview`) and associated opinions (`Opinion`). For example, one review could state that a customer likes the food but dislikes the service. Another might state that the customer likes one food item and dislikes another item in the same category. It is also possible that reviewers provide item reviews with both positive and negative opinions about the same item, in which case we consider that review item as having a polarity `conflict`. Moreover, when contextual knowledge is needed but not present, the system may classify the sentiment as `vague`.

Each `ReviewItem` refers to a mention of an RDF resource in a sentence – i.e. it represents a surface form or the `rdfs:label` of a resource appearing in a certain position in the textual content of a review. The model is able to include review items that are aspects of other items. Aspects include parts-of, containment, or other characteristics of items. For example, a review may target a shop's floorplan, and offer opinions about the outside seating space (a part of the shop's floorplan). An opinion may also be directed at the review target resource itself, in which case the aspect is the resource itself – e.g. 'the restaurant was great'.

The RDF resources included as instances of our model may come from any number of knowledge bases (KBs). In the current prototype, we have imported instances from DBpedia 3.9 [4], and lexicalizations from the DBpedia Lexicalizations Dataset [5]. We focused on instances relating to Books, DVDs, Electronics, Restaurants, and Kitchen&Housewares. We expanded the lexicalizations through our Semantic Asset Management Workbench (see Sect. 4). Besides identifying new lexicalizations for existing concepts, this expansion enables the system to detect items or aspects that are in a known category, but that do not have a URI in the imported knowledge bases. Consequently, the system may produce blank (skolemized) nodes when it cannot find a suitable URI in the current KB. This allows for an incremental approach to maintaining and evolving the core ontology used by the system, as new terms can be later added to the KB or new lexicalizations can be associated to their corresponding URIs[1] (Fig. 1).

4   Semantic Asset Management Workbench

We have developed a Semantic Asset Management Workbench (SAMW) that allows an analyst to draw on a number of techniques for developing, expanding and refining lexical entries in an ontology. Starting with a seed set of terms (usually anywhere between 3 and 30), the system finds all occurrences of these terms in a corpus and collects a set of patterns composed of the 0–6 tokens on the left and right of each occurrence of terms in the corpus. It then examines the corpus to find other words that match these patterns. The results are scored for confidence, support and prevalence. The users are then prompted to examine the top (up to 100) candidates and select which results to add to the lexicon. The system then iterates, taking these new terms, creating an even larger set of patterns and reprocessing the corpus to find more potential matches. Having

---

[1] This process is currently handled manually, but algorithmic support is possible.

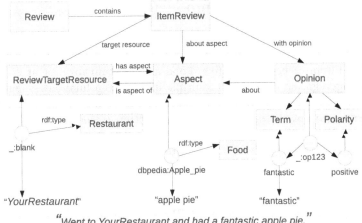

Fig. 1. Concept-based aspect-aware sentiment analysis ontology with examples.

the human in the loop helps to contain conceptual drift (e.g. is water a food?) and focus the lexicon on the concepts as necessary for the task at hand. Thus one key characteristic of SAMW is mutual discovery: it draws from user input to discover more terms, and provides output back to the users that prompts them to make new discoveries.

We started by defining a set of semantic classes of interest and adding them to the core ontology, namely Books, DVDs, Electronics, Restaurants, and Kitchen & Housewares. For the types that existed in DBpedia, we bootstraped SAMW with entity names from DBpedia. Since the main objective in this particular task is to understand user opinions, we also included classes for positive, negative and neutral valence opinion terms. For those classes, we seeded SAMW with 3–5 manually created examples. For each semantic class, we can also define a set of aspect categories. For example, restaurants have aspects categories in ambience, food, price and service[2]. Additionally, valence lexicons were created, negative, positive and true neutral opinions in a food context (which is somewhat suggestive - e.g. is so-so really neutral?).

We ran 5 to 50 iterations per lexicon on a variety of 'open' and 'closed' corpora and acquired between 29 and 1126 terms per category. This let us find rarer terms such as 'sopaipillas' or 'mole sauce' in food, more esoteric opinion terms such as 'exquisite' or 'viable' for positives in food. We note that SAMW identified opinion terms that have the potential to differ by domain. For example, you wouldn't say a food is very compact or blazing fast, nor would you say a laptop is 'flavorful' or 'intimate'. Valence varies by domain too, a 'small' camera is usually a positive opinion while a small car might not be, and SAMW is able to make such distinctions.

---

[2] We used the same categories as the SemEval'14 Task 4.

5   Sentiment Analysis Component

We have developed a sentiment analysis component that extracts sentiment at the item level (e.g. 'MyRestaurant'), at the aspect level (e.g. 'MyRestaurant's rice'), at the item category level (e.g. Food and Restaurant), or at the review level – i.e. aggregating opinions of multiple items into a final assessment of the overall sentiment in the review. It computes the sentiment of a sentence based on the sentiments of the concepts expressed within a that sentence. Inference across multiple sentences is planned for our future work.

In our prototype, each sentence is processed to produce constituency and dependency parses using OpenNLP[3] and ClearNLP[4] [3]. In addition, we use the aforementioned semantic lexicons from our core ontology, therefore considering concepts under the following categories: **1.** Aspects and ReviewTarget Resources (AR) – e.g. beer, wine, dining room; **2.** Positive Opinion Terms (Pos) express in general a positive sentiment – e.g. like, good, happy; **3.** Negative Opinion Terms (Neg) express in general a negative sentiment – e.g. death, bad, unhappy; **4.** Polarity Inversion Terms (Inv) used to invert the polarity of a sentiment – e.g. not, cannot, will not, but, however; **5.** Association concepts AC(concept, opinion, sentiment) describing the prior polarity for an opinion term given a concept, where concept and opinion are instances in one of the above lexicons – e.g. (beer, cold, positive). Clearly "negative concepts" can be used in a positive sense; for instance, the phrase "death by chocolate" is used to refer to very rich chocolate desserts delighting many people. Our model is able to capture these cases through the association concepts.

Our algorithm performs the following steps: **1.** Extract the concepts and opinion terms discussed in each sentence based on our semantic lexicons AR, Pos, and Neg; **2.** Identify the syntactical association between concepts based on the parse of the sentence. **3.** Query our knowledge base for semantic/sentiment (AC) associations. **4.** Special processing is done to identify lists, parenthesized expressions and hyphened expressions. **5.** Polarity inversion: a. Identify the concepts specified in Inv; b. Identify the part of the sentence the polarity inversion applies using syntactic parsing constructs and rules;

6   Results

We evaluated our system's performance on SemSA's Elementary Task (Polarity Detection), Advanced Task #1 (Aspect-Based Sentiment Analysis), and Advanced Task #3 (Topic Spotting). Precision (P), Recall (R) and F1 results are shown in Tables 1, 2 and 3.

We also performed a preliminary evaluation on the SemEval'14 Task 4 (Restaurants) dataset[5] and obtained good results for aspect term extraction of non-composed terms of length 1 (72 % of the dataset, with F1=0.829) and length 2

---

[3] http://opennlp.apache.org

[4] http://clearnlp.com

[5] http://alt.qcri.org/semeval2014/task4/

Table 1. Task 0.

Team	P	R	F1
NCU	0.78	0.57	**0.66**
ours	0.66	0.59	0.62
FBK	0.42	0.47	0.44

Table 2. Task 1.

Team	P	R	F1
FBK	0.25	0.26	**0.25**
ours	0.24	0.14	0.18
UNI-NEGEV	0.12	0.05	0.07

Table 3. Task 3.

Team	P
ours	**0.33**
FBK	0.17

(19 % of the data, F1=0.655). In future work we plan to address term compositionality and reevaluate terms that are longer than 3 tokens (9 % of the dataset, current F1=0.389).

7 Conclusion

We have presented a prototype for concept-based aspect-aware sentiment analysis. Our system relies on a core ontology of the task that allows us to model reviews based on the resources that they target, aspects of these resources as well as opinion terms related to these aspects or target resources. The ontology allows the definition of *a priori* concept-based opinion polarity to account for differences in expected polarity when one says 'cold beer' (positive) versus 'cold room' (negative). In order to expand the lexical forms in our ontology, we employed a Semantic Asset Management Workbench that empowers users to discover new terms and learns from the discoveries to improve its discovery process. This workbench allowed us to acquire new terms, name variations, as well as specialized opinion terms to particular categories that may not make sense for other categories (e.g. 'flavorful' for food and 'blazing fast' for a laptop).

Our system was the best performing system in SemSA's Task 3, and second best in Tasks 0 and 1, ranking highest of all systems if considering the 3 tasks.

References

1. Blinov, P., Kotelnikov, E.: Distributed representations of words for aspect-based sentiment analysis at SemEval. In: Proceedings of the 8th International Workshop on Semantic Evaluation (SemEval 2014), pp. 140–144 (2014)
2. Cambria, E., Schuller, B., Xia, Y., Havasi, C.: New avenues in opinion mining and sentiment analysis. IEEE Intell. Syst. **28**(2), 15–21 (2013)
3. Choi, J.D.: Optimization of Natural Language Processing Components for Robustness and Scalability. Ph.D thesis, Boulder, CO, USA (2012). AAI3549172
4. Lehmann, J., Isele, R., Jakob, M., Jentzsch, A., Kontokostas, D., Mendes, P., Hellmann, S., Morsey, M., van Kleef, P., Auer, S.: DBpedia - a large-scale. multilingual knowledge base extracted from wikipedia. Seman. Web J. (2014)
5. Mendes, P., Jakob, M., Bizer, C.: DBpedia for NLP: A Multilingual Cross-domain Knowledge Base. In: Calzolari, N., Choukri, K., Declerck, T., Uan, M., Maegaard, B., Mariani, J., Odijk, J., Piperidis, S. (eds) Proceedings of the Eight International Conference on Language Resources and Evaluation (LREC'12), Istanbul, Turkey, May 2012. European Language Resources Association (ELRA) (2012)

6. Pang, B., Lee, L.: Opinion mining and sentiment analysis. Found. Trends Inf. Retr. **2**(1–2), 1–135 (2008)
7. Schouten, K., Frasincar, F., de Jong, F.: Commit-p1wp3: A co-occurrence based approach to aspect-level sentiment analysis. In: Proceedings of the 8th International Workshop on Semantic Evaluation (SemEval 2014), pp. 203–207 (2014)
8. Wagner, J., Arora, P., Cortes, S., Barman, U., Bogdanova, D., Foster, J., Tounsi, L.: Dcu: Aspect-based polarity classification for semeval task 4. In: Proceedings of the 8th International Workshop on Semantic Evaluation (SemEval 2014), pp. 223–229 (2014)
9. White, B., Cambria, E.: Jumping NLP curves: a review of natural language processing research. IEEE Comput. Intell. Mag. **9**(2), 20–30 (2014)

Dependency Tree-Based Rules for Concept-Level Aspect-Based Sentiment Analysis

Soujanya Poria[1,4], Nir Ofek[2(✉)], Alexander Gelbukh[3], Amir Hussain[4],
and Lior Rokach[2]

[1] School of Electrical and Electronic Engineering, Nanyang Technological University,
Singapore, Singapore
sporia@ntu.edu.sg, soujanya.poria@cs.stir.ac.uk
[2] Department of Information Systems Engineering, Ben Gurion University,
Beersheba, Israel
{nirofek,liorrk}@bgu.ac.il
[3] Centro de Investigación En Computación, Instituto Politécnico Nacional,
Mexico, Mexico
http://www.gelbukh.com
[4] Department of Computing Science and Mathematics, University of Stirling,
Stirling, UK
ahu@cs.stir.ac.uk

Abstract. Over the last few years, the way people express their opinions
has changed dramatically with the progress of social networks, web communities, blogs, wikis, and other online collaborative media. Now, people
buy a product and express their opinion in social media so that other
people can acquire knowledge about that product before they proceed
to buy it. On the other hand, for the companies it has become necessary to keep track of the public opinions on their products to achieve
customer satisfaction. Therefore, nowadays opinion mining is a routine
task for every company for developing a widely acceptable product or
providing satisfactory service. Concept-based opinion mining is a new
area of research. The key parts of this research involve extraction of
concepts from the text, determining product aspects, and identifying
sentiment associated with these aspects. In this paper, we address each
one of these tasks using a novel approach that takes text as input and
use dependency parse tree-based rules to extract concepts and aspects
and identify the associated sentiment. On the benchmark datasets, our
method outperforms all existing state-of-the-art systems.

1 Introduction

For each sentence, our system generates a list of aspects (Sect. 3) and the polarity of the sentiment expressed in the sentence (Sect. 4). Our sentiment analysis
process relies on extraction of concepts (Sect. 2). Online demos of concept and
aspect parsing and the sentiment analysis are available on http://www.sentic.
net/demo.

© Springer International Publishing Switzerland 2014
V. Presutti et al. (Eds.): SemWebEval 2014, CCIS 475, pp. 41–47, 2014.
DOI: 10.1007/978-3-319-12024-9_5

2 Concept Parser

Concept parsing is crucial for such tasks as concept-based opinion mining [1,2], big social data analysis [3], and crowd validation [4]. The proposed concept parser deconstructs input sentences into multi-word expressions. For this, it extracts concepts from the dependency parse tree of the sentence[1] basing on hand-crafted rules. Examples of such rules are given below; see more details in [5].

Subject Noun Rule. If the active token h is in a subject noun relationship with a verb t, then the concept t-h is extracted. E.g., in (1), *movie* is the subject of *boring*; the concept `boring-movie` is extracted.

(1) The movie is boring.

Joint Subject Noun and Adjective Complement Rule. If the active token h is in a subject noun relationship with a verb t and t is in adjective complement relationship with an adverb w, then the concept w-h is extracted. E.g., in (2), *flower* is the subject of *smells*, which is in adjective complement relationship with *bad*; the concept `bad-flower` is extracted.

(2) The flower smells bad.

Experiments and Results. To calculate the performance, we selected 300 sentences from the *Stanford Sentiment Dataset* [6] and extracted the concepts manually, which gave 3204 concepts. On these sentences, our parser achieved 92.01 % accuracy.

3 Aspect Parser

Aspect-based opinion mining aims to model relations between the polarity of a document and its opinion targets, or aspects. Our system is able to extract both implicit and explicit aspects; see [7] for more details on our aspect parser.

Compilation of an Implicit Aspect Lexicon. We used the product review dataset described in [8,9] to create the implicit aspect lexicon. We selected from the dataset the sentences that had implicit aspects. From those sentences, we extracted the implicit aspect clues and manually labeled them with suitable categories. For example, from the sentence *The car is expensive* we extracted the implicit aspect clue *expensive* and labeled it with the category *price*. We identified in this corpus the following categories: *functionality, weight, price, appearance, behavior, performance, quality, service,* and *size*. For each identified implicit aspect clue, we also retrieved its synonyms from WordNet. This gave us a lexicon of 1128 implicit aspect clues labeled by aspect categories listed above.

---

[1] We used the Stanford Dependency parser, http://nlp.stanford.edu/software/lex-parser.shtml.

Opinion Lexicon. We used SenticNet 3.0 [10–13] as an opinion lexicon. It contains 14,000 common sense-knowledge concepts labeled by their polarity scores.

Algorithm. We used the Stanford Dependency parser to obtain the dependency tree of each sentence. Then we employed a complex system of hand-crafted rules on these parse trees to extract the aspects. Examples of such rules are given below. Some of our rules block the application of other rules, so the rules given below are not always applied.

Subject Noun Rule. If the active token h is in a subject noun relationship with a word t, then:

1. If t has an adverbial or adjective modifier that exists in the SenticNet, then we extract t as an aspect. E.g., in (3), according to Stanford parser, *it* is in a subject noun relationship with *camera*, which has an adjective modifier *nice*, so *camera* is extracted.

   (3) It is a nice camera.
2. If the sentence has no auxiliary verb (*is*, *was*, *would*, *should*, *could*, etc.), then:
   - If t is a verb modified by an adjective or adverb or it is in *adverbial clause modifier* relation with another token, then both h and t are extracted as aspects. E.g., in (4), *battery* is in a subject relation with *lasts*, so the aspects *last* and *battery* are extracted.

     (4) The battery lasts little.
   - If t has a noun n as a direct object, n is in SenticNet, and n is in a prepositional relation with another noun m, then both n and m are extracted as aspects. E.g., in (5), *like* is in direct object relation with *beauty*, which is connected to *screen* via a preposition relation. So the aspects *screen* and *beauty* are extracted.

     (5) I like the beauty of the screen.
3. Copula is the relation between the complement of a copular verb and the copular verb. If the token h existing in the implicit aspect lexicon is in a copula relation with a couplar verb, then we extract h as an aspect. E.g., in (6) *expensive* is extracted as an aspect.

   (6) The car is expensive.

Sentences with no subject noun relation in the parse tree. We extracted the aspects from such sentences using the following rules:

1. If an adjective or adverb h is in infinitival or open clausal complement relation with a token t and h exists in the implicit aspect lexicon, then we extract h as an aspect. E.g., in (7) we extract *big* as an aspect, since it is connected to *hold* via a clausal complement relation.

   (7) Very big to hold.
2. If a token h is connected to a noun t via a prepositional relation, then we extract both h and t as aspects. E.g., in (8), *sleekness* is extracted as an aspect.

   (8) Love the sleekness of the player.

Obtaining Implicit Aspect Categories. After obtaining the aspects using these rules, we retrieved the categories of the implicit aspects from the implicit aspect lexicon.

Experiments and Results. We experimented on the Semeval 2014 aspect-based sentiment analysis data.[2] On this dataset, we obtained 91.25 % precision and 88.12 % recall.

4   Common Sense Knowledge-Based Sentiment Analysis

This section describes the algorithm we used to compute the polarity score of a sentence. We have introduced a novel paradigm for concept-level sentiment analysis that merges linguistics, common-sense computing, and machine learning for improving the accuracy of tasks such as polarity detection [14]. By allowing sentiments to flow from concept to concept based on the dependency relation of the input sentence, in particular, we achieve a better understanding of the contextual role of each concept within the sentence. With this, our polarity detection engine outperforms the state-of-the-art statistical methods. Below we describe some rules we used and the ensemble classification process; see [14] for more details on our concept-level sentiment analysis algorithm.

Dependency Rules. We used rules based on specific dependency patterns to drive the way concepts were searched in SenticNet. Below are some examples of such rules.

Subject nouns. This rule is applied when the active token h is the syntactic subject of a word t. If the complex concept t-h was found in SenticNet, then it was used to calculate the polarity of the relation (otherwise, other rules are activated later). E.g., in (9), *movie* is in a subject relation with *boring* and (`boring-movie`) is in SenticNet, so its corresponding polarity was used.

(9) The movie is boring.

Adjective and clausal complements. These rules deal with verbs having as complements either an adjective or a closed clause (i.e. a clause, usually finite, with its own subject).

1. If the active token is head verb of one of the complement relations, then first the algorithm looks for the binary concept h d. If it is found, the relation inherits its polarity properties. If it is not found:
   – if both elements h and d are independently found in SenticNet, then we take sentiment of the d as the sentiment of the relation.

---

[2] http://alt.qcri.org/semeval2014/task4/index.php?id=data-and-tools

- if the dependent *d* alone is found in SenticNet, its polarity is attributed to the relation

E.g., in (10), *smells* is the head of a dependency relation with *bad* as the dependent; the relation inherits the polarity of *bad*.

(10) This meal smells bad.

2. If the active token is modified by a relative clause, restrictive or not, and the dependent is the verb of the relative clause (usually it is), then if the binary concept *h d* is found in SenticNet, then it assigns polarity to the relation, otherwise the polarity is assigned (in order of preference):
    - By the value of the dependent verb *d* if it can be found;
    - By the value of the active token *h* if it is found in SenticNet.

E.g., in (11) *movie* is in relation with *love* which acts as a modifier in the relative clause.

(11) I saw the movie you love.

Assuming *love movie* is not in SenticNet and that *love* is, then the latter will contribute the polarity score of the relation. If neither of these two is in SenticNet, then the dependency will receive the score associated with *movie*.

Machine Learning Technique. For each sentence, we extracted concepts from it as explained in Sect. 2 and looked them up in SenticNet. If we found at least one concept in SenticNet, then we used our knowledge-based method to detect sentiment. Otherwise, we resorted to our machine learning-based technique. The Machine Learning module was trained on the Blitzer dataset. Below we describe some of the features we used for training.

Sentic feature. The polarity scores of each concept extracted from the sentence were obtained from the SenticNet and summed up to produce a single scalar feature. This feature was used for training, but was not available in testing.

Part-of-speech features. This feature was defined by the total numbers of adjectives, adverbs, and nouns in the sentence, which gave three distinct features.

Modification feature. This binary feature was set to 1 if we found any modification relation in the sentence; otherwise it was set to 0.

Results on the Blitzer-Derived Dataset. At the sentence level, on the Blitzer dataset 87.00 % accuracy was achieved.

5   Conclusion

We gave examples of dependency tree-based rules to extract concepts, aspects, and sentiment polarity from natural language texts. In our future work, we aim to extend this work by adding more rules or using existing rules to find new rules based on association-based rules. We also aim to use extend the algorithm so that it can be applied to other languages. Techniques based on recognizing textual entailment [15, 16] will help us to achieve multilingual application of our algorithm. For aspect extraction, we will explore the role of adjectives [17] which are often used to modify the aspects in the opinionated text. Thus, identifying the role of adjectives will help us to extract the aspects from the text with a higher precision.

References

1. Poria, S., Gelbukh, A., Hussain, A., Howard, N., Das, D., Bandyopadhyay, S.: Enhanced SenticNet with affective labels for concept-based opinion mining. IEEE Intell. Syst. **28**(2), 31–38 (2013)
2. Poria, S., Gelbukh, A., Cambria, E., Hussain, A., Huang, G.B.: EmoSenticSpace: A novel framework for affective common-sense reasoning. Knowl.-Based Syst. (2014)
3. Cambria, E., Rajagopal, D., Olsher, D., Das, D.: Big social data analysis. Big Data Computing. Chapman and Hall/CRC, Boca Raton (2013)
4. Cambria, E., Hussain, A., Havasi, C., Eckl, C., Munro, J.: Towards crowd validation of the UK national health service. In: WebSci10 (2010)
5. Poria, S., Agarwal, B., Gelbukh, A., Hussain, A., Howard, N.: Dependency-based semantic parsing for concept-level text analysis. In: Gelbukh, A. (ed.) CICLing 2014, Part I. LNCS, vol. 8403, pp. 113–127. Springer, Heidelberg (2014)
6. Socher, R., Perelygin, A., Wu, J.Y., Chuang, J., Manning, C.D., Ng, A.Y., Potts, C.: Recursive deep models for semantic compositionality over a sentiment treebank. In: Conference on Empirical Methods in Natural Language Processing (EMNLP) (2013)
7. Poria, S., Cambria, E., Ku, L.W., Gui, C., Gelbukh, A.: A rule-based approach to aspect extraction from product reviews. In: Workshop Proceedings of the 25th International Conference on Computational Linguistics, COLING 2014 (2014)
8. Cruz-Garcia, I.O., Gelbukh, A., Sidorov, G.: Implicit aspect indicator extraction for aspect-based opinion mining (2014) (Submitted)
9. Qiu, G., Liu, B., Bu, J., Chen, C.: Opinion word expansion and target extraction through double propagation. Comput. Linguist. **37**(1), 9–27 (2011)
10. Cambria, E., Olsher, D., Rajagopal, D.: Senticnet 3: A common and common-sense knowledge base for cognition-driven sentiment analysis. In: AAAI (2014)
11. Poria, S., Gelbukh, A., Cambria, E., Yang, P., Hussain, A., Durrani, T.: merging SenticNet and wordnet-affect emotion lists for sentiment analysis. In: 11th International Conference on Signal Processing (ICSP 2012), vol. 2, pp. 1251–1255. IEEE (2012)
12. Poria, S., Gelbukh, A., Cambria, E., Das, D., Bandyopadhyay, S.: Enriching SenticNet polarity scores through semi-supervised fuzzy clustering. In: 12th International Conference on Data Mining Workshops (ICDMW 2012), pp. 709–716. IEEE (2012)
13. Castro-Manzano, J.M.: A defeasible logic of intention. In: Batyrshin, I., González Mendoza, M. (eds.) MICAI 2012, Part I. LNCS, vol. 7629, pp. 321–333. Springer, Heidelberg (2013)
14. Poria, S., Cambria, E., Winterstein, G., Huang, G.B.: Sentic patterns: Dependency-based rules for concept-level sentiment analysis. Knowl.-Based Syst. (2014). doi:10.1016/j.knosys.2014.05.005
15. Pakray, P., Pal, S., Poria, S., Bandyopadhyay, S., Gelbukh, A.: JU_CSE_TAC: Textual entailment recognition system at TAC RTE-6. In: System Report, Text Analysis Conference Recognizing Textual Entailment Track (TAC RTE), Notebook (2010)

16. Pakray, P., Neogi, S., Bhaskar, P., Poria, S., Bandyopadhyay, S., Gelbukh, A.: A textual entailment system using anaphora resolution. In: System Report. Text Analysis Conference Recognizing Textual Entailment Track (TAC RTE), Notebook (2011)
17. Ofek, N., Rokach, L., Mitra, P.: Methodology for connecting nouns to their modifying adjectives. In: Gelbukh, A. (ed.) CICLing 2014, Part I. LNCS, vol. 8403, pp. 271–284. Springer, Heidelberg (2014)

Sinica Semantic Parser for ESWC'14 Concept-Level Semantic Analysis Challenge

Shafqat Mumtaz Virk$^{(\boxtimes)}$, Yann-Huei Lee, and Lun-Wei Ku

Institute of Information Science (IIS), Academia Sinica, Taipei, Taiwan
{virk.shafqat,ycyrus}@gmail.com, lwku@iis.sinica.edu.tw

Abstract. We present a semantic parsing system to decompose a sentence into *semantic-expressions/concepts* for ESWC'14 semantic analysis challenge. The proposed system has a pipeline architecture, and is based on syntactic parsing and semantic role labeling of the candidate sentence. For the former task, we use Stanford English parser; and for the later task, we use an in-house developed semantic role labeling system. From the syntactically and semantically annotated sentence, the *concepts* are formulated using a set of hand-build concept-formulation patterns. We compare the proposed system's performance to SenticNet with the help of few examples.

Keywords: Syntactic parsing · Semantic parsing · Semantic role labeling · Concept formulation templates

1 Introduction

Natural languages are both complex and ambiguous. Unless machines are capable of handling these issues in an intelligent way, building smart natural language processing (NLP) applications is a tough and challenging task. Maybe, one way to ease this toughness is to try to make computers understand natural language text. For the same purpose, the trend in NLP is shifting from exploring 'What it is?' to 'What it means?' (i.e. from syntax to semantics).

During the last couple of decades, a number of sub-fields have emerged under the umbrella term *computational semantics* including but not limited to sentiment analysis, textual entailment, question answering, and semantic parsing. These are among rapidly growing areas of NLP, and the research community has recognized their worth in recent times. This can be realized by the fact that their are many workshops and/or special tracks/challenges in conferences dedicated to these tasks. The ESWC'14 challenge on semantic analysis is one among those special challenges, and is scheduled to be held together with the 11th European Semantic Web Conference 2014 (ESWC'14). The challenge has a number of advanced tasks in addition to an elementary task on polarity detection. The advanced task#2 is titled "Semantic Parsing", and refers to the task of de-constructing natural language text into a number of *semantic-expressions/concepts*. Though the term

© Springer International Publishing Switzerland 2014
V. Presutti et al. (Eds.): SemWebEval 2014, CCIS 475, pp. 48–52, 2014.
DOI: 10.1007/978-3-319-12024-9_6

semantic-expression/concept is very general in itself, and is hard to define clearly, we take it to be a single-word/multi-word expression for which we have semantics.

In this paper, we propose a system for semantic parsing in the context of task#2 of the challenge. The system has a pipeline architecture and relies on syntactic and semantic analysis of a candidate sentence. We use Stanford English parser [3] for syntactic parsing, and an in-house built semantic role labeling system for semantic interpretations. To formulate the concepts into desired format, we propose a set of hand-build concept formulation templates.

2   Proposed System

The architecture of the proposed system is shown in Fig. 1. It has three major components: a syntactic parsing, a semantic role labeling, and a concept formulation component. The purpose and importance of each component is explained in the following paragraphs.

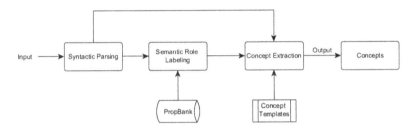

Fig. 1. System architecture

Syntactic Parsing: As a preliminary step, the input sentence is syntactically analyzed to get a syntactic parse tree. This step is necessary for the major reason that almost all automatic semantic role labeling system rely on a preliminary syntactic parsing step [10].

Semantic Role Labeling: Semantic role labeling (SRL), also known as shallow semantic parsing, is the task of semantically annotating natural language text. Conventionally, a syntactically parsed sentence is taken as input, and semantic arguments associated with predicate of the sentence are identified and classified to a particular semantic class. The first automatic SRL systems was reported by Gildea and Jurafsky in 2002 [5], and since then, their ideas have been dominating the field. In their approach, they emphasized on selection of appropriate lexical and syntactical features for SRL, use of statistical classifiers and their combinations, and ways to handle the data sparseness issue. Researchers have tried to build on that by augmenting and/or altering the feature set [9], by experimenting with various classification approaches [6,11], and by attempting different ways to handle data sparseness [1]. For this challenge, we developed a SRL system, which is based largely on previously explored features and maximum entropy classifiers. The classifiers were trained using English Penn Treebank [8], and Propbank [7] data. However, we have proposed a number of additional features to enhance its performance. The details of the SRL system are beyond the scope of this paper, and are supposed to be covered in another planned article.

Table 1. Concept templates

#	Concept template	#	Concept template
1	ARG0_Pred	10	Pred_in_the_direction_ARGM-DIR
2	Pred_ARG1	11	Pred_because_ARGM-ARGM-CAU
3	Pred_ARG1_ARG2	12	Pred_when_ARGM-TMP
4	Pred_ARG1_ARG2_ARG3	13	Pred_ARGM-GOL
5	Pred_ARG1_ARG2_ARG3_ARG4	14	Pred_by_ARGM-EXT
6	Pred_ARG1_ARG2_ARG3_ARG4_ARG5	15	Pred_ARGM-MNR
7	Pred_with_ARGM-COM	16	Pred_ARGM-NEG
8	Pred_in_ARGM-LOC	17	ARGX's
9	Pred_in_order_to_ARGM-PRP	18	ARGM's

Concept Formulation: Once the sentence has been annotated syntactically and semantically, the concepts can be formulated using a set of hand-build concept templates. Table 1 lists few of the templates used in our experiments. Here, Pred and ARG1, ARG2, ARGM-LOC, ARGM-GOL, etc. refer to the predicate, and to the semantic role classes used in the prop-bank labeling scheme (see [2] for details on these classes).

3   An Example

To explain how our proposed system works at different levels, lets take an example sentence: *This film served as great entertainment for young people.*, and go through all the steps that the proposed system will perform to extract *concepts*. As a first step the sentence is syntactically parsed, which is semantically annotated by the SRL system as the second step. The resulting syntactically and semantically annotated tree is shown in Fig. 2. From the semantically annotated tree, the extractable predicate-argument information is given in Table 2. Using this information and the templates given in Table 1, the following concepts can be formulated:

```
(1) This_film_serve (2) serve_as_great_entertainment
(3) serve_for_young_people (4) great_entertainment
(5) This_film (6) young_people
```

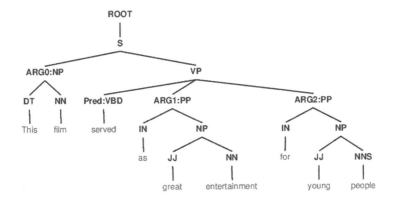

Fig. 2. Syntactically and semantically annotated parse tree

Table 2. Predicate-argument information

Predicate	Arguments
serve	Arg0: This film
	ARG1: as great entertainment
	ARG2: for young people

4 Comparison to SenticNet

At the current stage of our experiments, we did not perform any automatic comparison or performance measurement leaving it to the official evaluation during the challenge days. However to give an idea to the reviewers, Table 3 lists a couple of example sentences together with the extracted[1] concepts both by the proposed system[2], and SenticNet [4]. We leave it to the reviewers to compare the outputs.

Table 3. Example sentences and extracted concepts

Sentence	Proposed System's Output	SenticNet's Output
I went to the market, bought fresh fruits and vegetables, and came back	(1)bought_fresh_fruits (2)I_went (3)I_bought (4)vegetables (5)bought_vegetables (6)the_market (7)fresh_fruits (8)went_to_the_market (9)came_{in_the_direction}_ back (10)came_I	(1)go_to_market (2)market (3)buy_fruit (4)buy_vegetable (5)fresh_fruit (6)back_come
We also ordered the bedding and got the pillow	(1)got_the_pillow (2)the_pillow (3)We_got (4)the_bedding (5)We_order (6)order_also (7)order_the_bedding	(1)also_order (2)order_bed (3)bed (4)get_pillow (5)pillow

---

[1] The SenticNet concepts were extracted using its web-demo version available at (http://sentic.net/demo/).

[2] A web-demo of the proposed system is available at (http://andycyrus.github.io/ESCW2014-challenge).

Acknowledgment. We would like to acknowledge that this work was partially supported by National Science Council, Taiwan, under the contract NSC 102-2221-E-001-026.

References

1. Zapirain, B., Agirre, E., Màrquez, L.: Ubc-upc: sequential srl using selectional preferences: an approach with maximum entropy markov models. In: Proceedings of the 4th International Workshop on Semantic Evaluations, Stroudsburg, PA, USA, pp. 354–357. Association for Computational Linguistics (2007)
2. Bonial, C., Hwang, J., Bonn, J., Conger, K., Babko-Malaya, O., Palmer, M.: English PropBank Annotation Guidelines, Center for Computational Language and Education Research Institute of Cognitive Science University of Colorado at Boulder, November 2012
3. Klein, D., Manning, C.D.: Accurate unlexicalized parsing. In: Proceedings of the 41st Meeting of the Association for Computational Linguistics, pp. 423–430 (2003)
4. Cambria, E., Olsher, D., Rajagopal, D.: SenticNet 3: a common and commonsense knowledge base for cognition-driven sentiment analysis. In: Association for the Advancement of Artificial Intelligence (2014)
5. Daniel, G., Jurafsky, D.: Automatic labeling of semantic roles. Comput. Linguist. **28**(3), 245–288 (2002)
6. Park, K.-M., Rim, H.-C.: Maximum entropy based semantic role labeling. In: Proceedings of the Ninth Conference on Computational Natural Language Learning, CONLL ?05, Stroudsburg, PA, USA, pp. 209–212. Association for Computational Linguistics (2005)
7. Palmer, M., Gildea, D., Kingsbury, P.: The proposition bank: a corpus annotated with semantic roles. Comput. Linguist. J. **31**, 1 (2005)
8. Mitchell, P., Santorini, B., Marcinkiewicz, M.A.: Building a large annotated corpus of english: the penn treebank. Comput. Linguist. **10**(2), 313–330 (1993)
9. Xue, N.: Calibrating features for semantic role labeling. In: Proceedings of EMNLP 2004, pp. 88–94 (2004)
10. Johansson, R., Nuges, P.: The effect of syntactic representation on semantic role labeling. In: Proceedings of the 22nd International Conference on Computational Linguistics (Coling 2008), pp. 393–400, Manchester, August 2008
11. Pradhan, S., Ward, W., Haciuglu, K., Martin, J., Jurafsky, D.: Shallow semantic parsing using support vector machines. In: Proceedings of HLT/NAACL-2004 (2004)

Polarity Detection of Online Reviews Using Sentiment Concepts: NCU IISR Team at ESWC-14 Challenge on Concept-Level Sentiment Analysis

Jay Kuan-Chieh Chung[3], Chi-En Wu[2], and Richard Tzong-Han Tsai[1(✉)]

[1] Department of Computer Science and Information Engineering,
National Central University, Jhongli, Taiwan, R.O.C.
thtsai@csie.ncu.edu.tw
[2] Department of Computer Science and Information Engineering,
National Taiwan University, Taipei, Taiwan, R.O.C.
[3] Department of Computer Science and Engineering, Yuan Ze University,
Jhongli, Taiwan, R.O.C.

Abstract. In this paper, we present our system that participated in the Polarity Detection task, the elementary task in the ESWC-14 Challenge on Concept-Level Sentiment Analysis. In addition to traditional Bag-of-Words features, we also employ state-of-the-art Sentic API to extract concepts from documents to generate Bag-of-Sentiment-Concepts features. Our previous work SentiConceptNet serves as the reference concept-based sentiment knowledge base for concept-level sentiment analysis. Experimental results on our development set show that adding Bag-of-Sentiment-Concepts can improve the accuracy by 1.3 %, indicating the benefit of concept-level sentiment analysis. Our demo website is located at http://140.115.51.136:5000.

Keywords: Concept-level sentiment analysis · Sentiment concepts · Polarity detection of online reviews

1 Introduction

The growth in social media use has altered the role of users from information receivers to information providers. As snowballing numbers of people share their ideas, experiences, and opinions on the Web, sentiment analysis has become a key tool for those who wish to understand public opinion in online data.

A fundamental task in sentiment analysis [1] is classifying the polarity of a given text at the document level—whether the expressed opinion in a document is positive, negative, or neutral. Early work in this area includes Turney [2] and Pang [3] who developed different methods to detect the polarity of product reviews and movie reviews, respectively. Such existing approaches primarily rely on text in which opinions and sentiments are explicitly expressed, such as terms with negative/positive polarity and their co-occurrence frequencies. However, sentiments are often implied through underlying

© Springer International Publishing Switzerland 2014
V. Presutti et al. (Eds.): SemWebEval 2014, CCIS 475, pp. 53–58, 2014.
DOI: 10.1007/978-3-319-12024-9_7

semantics, which makes purely syntactical approaches ineffective [4]. Concept-level sentiment analysis, on the other hand, aims to go beyond traditional word-level analysis of text. By relying on large semantic knowledge bases, concept-level sentiment analysis steps away from blind use of keywords and word co-occurrence counts, relying instead on the implicit features associated with natural language concepts.

In this paper, we present the system that we submitted to the ESWC-14 Challenge on Concept-Level Sentiment Analysis Polarity Detection task. In addition to traditional Bag-of-Words features, we also extract concepts from documents to generate Bag-of-Sentiment-Concepts features. Our paper is organized as follows: Sect. 2 describes the system overview and our method. Section 3 presents the experimental results. Section 4 contains discussion of the results, and Sect. 5 gives the concluding remarks.

2   Method

2.1   Formulation and Term Weighting Schemes

In this paper, polarity detection is formulated as a classification problem. Each document is transformed to a feature vector and then classified as either positive or negative. We adopt support vector machines (SVM) model as our classification model because its efficacy has been demonstrated for binary classification tasks, and it allows non-binary values in feature vectors.

Following the classical Bag-of-Words feature representation, a document d is represented as a term vector $\mathbf{v}$, in which each dimension v_i corresponds to a term t_i. v_i is calculated by a term-weighting function. In this task, we use t_i's term frequency (TF) in d as v_i's value.

2.2   SentiConceptNet

SentiConceptNet [5, 6] is a concept-level sentiment dictionary built through a two-step method combining iterative regression and random walk with in-link normalization using ConceptNet 5 [7]. We exploit ANEW [8] and SenticNet 2 [9] to propagate sentiment values based on the assumption that semantically related concepts share common sentiments. Currently, SentiConceptNet contains 265,353 concepts with sentiment values, ranging from −1 to 1.

2.3   Bag of Sentiment Concept Features

In addition to the Bag-of-Words features introduced in Sect. 2.1, we also explore the sentiment concepts contained in review texts. We adopt the graph-based approach proposed by Rajagopal et al. [10] to extract concepts from the review articles and represent each review as a bag of concepts (Bag-of-Sentiment-Concepts). The reference sentiment dictionary is SentiConceptNet. Each dimension v_i corresponds to a concept c_i. v_i is calculated by a term-weighting function. In this task, we use c_i's term frequency (TF) in d or TF(c_i)*Sentiment_value(c_i) as v_i's value.

3   Experiments

In this experiment, we use the Blitzer review dataset[1], which contains online reviews of 25 domains. The statistics of the Blitzer dataset is listed in the following table. It contains three xml files, positive, negative and all reviews. We use the positive.review and negative.review files as our development set. To train the final model for online testing, we use the all.review file. The numbers of reviews in these three files are shown in Table 1.

Table 1.   Statistics of the used files in the Blitzer dataset.

File name	# of reviews
positive.review	21,972
negative.review	16,576
all.review	148,718

Our system is evaluated in terms of precision (P), recall (R), F-measure (F), and accuracy (ACC). We perform 10-fold cross-validation on the development set with five configurations of our polarity detection system. The details of these five configurations are shown in Table 2.

Table 2.   Details of all configurations.

Configuration	Abbreviation
Bag-of-Words	BoW
Bag-of-Sentiment-Concepts (TF(c_i))	BoSC_{TF}
Bag-of-Sentiment-Concepts (TF(c_i)*Sentiment_value(c_i))	$\text{BoSC}_{\text{TF}*\text{S}}$
Bag-of-Words+Bag-of-Sentiment-Concepts (TF(c_i))	$\text{BoW+BoSC}_{\text{TF}}$
Bag-of-Words+Bag-of-Sentiment-Concepts (TF(c_i)*Sentiment_value(c_i))	$\text{BoW+BoSC}_{\text{TF}*\text{S}}$

As shown in Table 3, BoSC_{TF} achieves closer accuracy to BoW. After adding sentiment value information ($\text{BoSC}_{\text{TF}*\text{S}}$), BoSC outperforms BoW. Further adding Bag-of-Sentiment-Concepts features to BoW (denoted as $\text{BoW+BoSC}_{\text{TF}}$) achieves even greater accuracy than BoW due to the larger vocabulary size and higher sentiment unit level (word-level vs. concept-level). When we multiply the concept's term frequency by its sentiment value (denoted as $\text{BoW+BoSC}_{\text{TF}*\text{S}}$), we achieve the best performance (0.8803 in F and 0.8622 in ACC). Our demo website is located at http://140.115.51.136:5000.

Table 4 shows the results of the top three participants in the Polarity Detection Task at ESWC2014. The evaluation is carried out on the test set, which is composed of 2,429 sentences constructed in the same way and from the same sources as the Blitzer dataset. Our system achieved the best performance on precision and F-measure, finishing first

---

[1] http://www.cs.jhu.edu/~mdredze/datasets/sentiment/

Table 3. Performance comparison.

Configuration	P	R	F	ACC
BoW	0.8685	0.8666	0.8675	0.8492
BoSC$_{TF}$	0.8705	0.8662	0.8665	0.8485
BoSC$_{TF*S}$	0.8668	0.8856	0.8761	0.8572
BoW+BoSC$_{TF}$	0.8757	0.8712	0.8734	0.8561
BoW+BoSC$_{TF*S}$	0.8712	0.8897	0.8803	0.8622

Table 4. Results of Polarity Detection Task at ESWC2014

Participant	P	R	F	Final position
Our system (NCU)	0.78	0.57	0.66	1
IBM	0.66	0.59	0.62	2
FBK	0.42	0.47	0.44	3

overall. Our system outperforms the second best team by 4 % in F-measure. The significant performance drop from the development set to the test set may be due to the difference between the development set and the test set.

4   Discussion

4.1   Advantages of BoW+BoSC$_{TF}$ Over BoW

As expected, adding BoSC$_{TF}$ features can help identify sentiments contributed by phrases or idioms rather than words. Take the following sentence for example:

Snapping up the shoes makes me cry tears of joy.

The words "cry" and "tear" often appear in negative reviews. Therefore, this sentence is classified as negative by BoW. However, because the idiomatic phrase "cry tears of joy" appears in positive reviews, the "cry tears of joy" sentiment concept feature is included in BoW+BoSC$_{TF}$, allowing the model to correctly classify the sentiment as positive.

4.2   Advantages of BoW+BoSC$_{TF*S}$ Over BoW+BoSC$_{TF}$

Even though sentiment concepts are used as features in BoW+BoSC$_{TF}$, some reviews are still classified incorrectly. After the inclusion of sentiment values in SentiConceptNet as feature values, some of the above reviews can be correctly classified. Take the following sentence for example:

The camera can be taken with you anywhere by putting it in your pocket.

We can see that the frequency of "put it in your pocket" in negative reviews is slightly higher than in positive reviews; therefore, it is incorrectly classified as negative. After its sentiment value in SentiConceptNet (0.198) is included, its polarity can be correctly predicted.

4.3   Error Analysis

SentiConceptNet contains 250,000 sentiment concepts, which are helpful for polarity classification. Due to the nature of its automatic construction, it contains some incorrect sentiment values, which result in polarity classification errors. Take the following sentence for example:

For these prices you do not get the quality of Neiman's, Sak's, or Bloomie's.

In SentiConceptNet, "you do not" has positive sentiment value (0.023). Therefore, our best configuration (BoW+BoSC$_{TF*S}$) classifies it as positive. However, this concept should have a little bit negative sentiment value. If we give the concept a negative value, the sentence can be correctly classified as negative.

5   Conclusion

In this paper, we present our system that participated in the Polarity Detection task, which is the elementary task in the ESWC-14 Challenge on Concept-Level Sentiment Analysis. In addition to traditional Bag-of-Words features, we also employ state-of-the-art Sentic API to extract sentiment concepts from documents to generate Bag-of-Sentiment-Concepts features. Our previous work SentiConceptNet serves as our reference concept-based sentiment knowledge base for concept-level sentiment analysis. Experimental results on our development set show that adding Bag-of-Sentiment-Concepts can improve the accuracy by 1.3 %, indicating the benefit of concept-level sentiment analysis.

References

1. deHaaff, M.: Sentiment Analysis, Hard But Worth It!, customer THINK (2010)
2. Turney, P.D.: Thumbs up or thumbs down?: semantic orientation applied to unsupervised classification of reviews. In: Proceedings of the 40th Annual Meeting on Association for Computational Linguistics, Philadelphia, Pennsylvania, pp. 417–424. Association for Computational Linguistics (2002)
3. Pang, B., Lee, L., Vaithyanathan, S.: Thumbs up?: sentiment classification using machine learning techniques. In: Proceedings of the ACL-02 Conference on Empirical Methods in Natural Language Processing, vol. 10, pp. 79–86. Association for Computational Linguistics (2002)
4. Cambria, E., Hussain, A.: Sentic Computing: Techniques, Tools, and Applications. SpringerBriefs in Cognitive Computation, vol. 2. Springer, Holland (2012)

5. Tsai, A., Tsai, R.T.-H., Hsu, J.Y.-j.: Building a concept-level sentiment dictionary based on commonsense knowledge. IEEE Intell. Syst. **28**, 22–30 (2013)
6. Wu, C.-E., Tsai, R.T.-H.: Using relation selection to improve value propagation in a ConceptNet-based sentiment dictionary. Knowl.-Based Syst. (2014, in Press)
7. Speer, R., Havasi, C.: ConceptNet 5: a large semantic network for relational knowledge. In: Gurevych, I., Kim, J. (eds.) The People's Web Meets NLP, pp. 161–176. Springer, Berlin Heidelberg (2013)
8. Bradley, M.M., Lang, P.J.: Affective norms for English words (ANEW): stimuli, instruction manual, and affective ratings (1999)
9. Cambria, E., Havasi, C., Hussain, A.: SenticNet 2: a semantic and affective resource for opinion mining and sentiment analysis. In: Youngblood, G.M., McCarthy, P.M. (eds.) FLAIRS Conference. AAAI Press (2012)
10. Rajagopal, D., Cambria, E., Olsher, D., Kwok, K.: A graph-based approach to commonsense concept extraction and semantic similarity detection. In: Proceedings of the 22nd International Conference on World Wide Web companion, Rio de Janeiro, Brazil, pp. 565–570. International World Wide Web Conferences Steering Committee (2013)

Semantic Publishing

Semantic Publishing Challenge – Assessing the Quality of Scientific Output

Christoph Lange[1]([⊠]) and Angelo Di Iorio[2]

[1] University of Bonn and Fraunhofer IAIS, Bonn, Germany
math.semantic.web@gmail.com
[2] Università di Bologna, Bologna, Italy
diiorio@cs.unibo.it

Abstract. Linked Open Datasets about scholarly publications enable the development and integration of sophisticated end-user services; however, richer datasets are still needed. The first goal of this Challenge was to investigate novel approaches to obtain such semantic data. In particular, we were seeking methods and tools to extract information from scholarly publications, to publish it as LOD, and to use queries over this LOD to assess quality. This year we focused on the quality of workshop proceedings, and of journal articles w.r.t. their citation network. A third, open task, asked to showcase how such semantic data could be exploited and how Semantic Web technologies could help in this emerging context.

1 Introduction: Scholarly Publishing and the Semantic Web

Scholarly publishing is increasingly driven by a new wave of applications that better support researchers in disseminating, exploiting and evaluating their results. The huge potential of publishing scientific papers enriched with semantic information has been proved, e.g., by Elsevier's Grand Challenges of 2009 and 2011 [10,11] and by the yearly SePublica [2] and Linked Science workshop series [1][1], both taking place for the fourth time in 2014. The semantic publishing community believes that semantics will help to improve the way users access, share, exploit and evaluate research results, and it will help to advance services such as search, expert finding, or visualisation, and even further applications not yet envisioned. Semantic Web technologies play a central role in this context, as they can help publishers to make scientific results available in an open format the whole research community can benefit from. New ways of publishing scientific results, as presented at the events mentioned above, include:

- machine-comprehensible experimental data,
- linking machine-comprehensible datasets to research papers,
- machine-comprehensible representations of scientific methods and models,
- alternative publication channels (e.g. social networks and micro-publications),

---

[1] http://linkedscience.org/category/workshop/

© Springer International Publishing Switzerland 2014
V. Presutti et al. (Eds.): SemWebEval 2014, CCIS 475, pp. 61–76, 2014.
DOI: 10.1007/978-3-319-12024-9_8

- alternative metrics for scientific impact ('altmetrics' [18]), e.g., taking into account the scientist's social network, user-generated micro-content such as discussion post, and recommendations.

Scientific data published using Semantic Web technology not only solves isolated problems, but generates further value in that datasets can be shared, linked to each other, and reasoned on.

Section 2 explains how we developed the definition of this year's Semantic Publishing Challenge, Sect. 3 explains the evaluation procedure for the two information extraction tasks, Sects. 4–6 explain the definitions and outcomes of the three tasks in detail, and Sect. 7 discusses overall sessions learnt.

2   The Challenge of Defining a Publishing Challenge

In the other two challenges in the ESWC Semantic Web Evaluation Challenges track, it seemed straightforward to objectively measure the performance of a solution, as suitable, curated datasets existed – the Blitzer dataset for the Concept-Level Sentiment Analysis Challenge [19] – or were relatively straightforward to obtain – the DBbook dataset for the Linked Open Data-enabled Recommender Systems Challenge [8].

Existing datasets on scholarly publishing mainly contain basic bibliographical metadata (such as DBLP [22]), or research data specific to one scientific domain, as can, e.g., be seen from the 'life science' section of the LOD Cloud [14]. In preparing the challenge, we judged that basic bibliographical author/title/year metadata did not have a sufficiently challenging semantics, whereas advanced publishing applications could be built on top of richer semantic data; we also judged that existing research datasets were too domain-specific to design relevant and feasible challenge tasks around them. We concluded that the semantic publishing community had so far lacked datasets adequate for evaluation challenges and therefore designed our *first* challenge[2] to *produce, by information extraction, an initial collection of data that would be useful for future challenges and that the community can experiment on.* This data collection should, of course, be produced in an objectively measurable way.

Technically, we focused on producing data *going beyond basic bibliographical metadata* in terms of structure and complexity, and in that some of the information covered would not be available from existing structured databases, but only by full-text analysis; consider, e.g., authors' affiliations, or references to funding bodies. As 'producing data to base future challenges on' is not an appealing objective in itself, we identified *quality* as a key concern of relevance to the whole scientific community: *how can one assess the quality of scientific production* by automated data analysis? This time, we focused on analysing (extended)metadata of publications, not yet on research data or on linked data representations of the full text of publications. The objective of Task 1 of 3 was to assess the quality of workshops by computing metrics from data extracted

---

[2] http://challenges.2014.eswc-conferences.org/index.php/SemPub/

from their proceedings, also considering information about persons and events. The objective of Task 2 was to assess the quality of journal articles by characterising citations and identifying, e.g., their context, their function and their position in the citing papers.

After calling for submissions to Tasks 1 and 2, we received feedback from the community that mere information extraction, even if motivated by quality assessment, was not the most exciting task related to the future of scholarly publishing, as it assumed a traditional publishing model where results are mainly disseminated through papers, and the quality of scientific production is assessed from these papers. We therefore added a third, *open task*.

3 Common Procedures for the Extraction Tasks

The extraction tasks 1 and 2 followed a common procedure similar to the other evaluation challenges:

1. For each task, we initially published a *training dataset* (TD) on which the participants could test and train their extraction tools.
2. We specified the basic structure of the linked data to be extracted from these source data, without prescribing a vocabulary.
3. We provided natural language queries and their expected results on TD.
4. A few days before the submission deadline, we published an *evaluation dataset* (ED), a superset of TD, which was the input for the final evaluation.
5. We asked the participants to submit their extracted linked data (under an open license to permit reuse), SPARQL implementations of the queries, as well as their extraction tools, as we reserved the right to inspect them.
6. We awarded prizes for the best-performing (w.r.t. precision/recall) and for the most innovative approach (to be determined by an expert jury).
7. Both before and after the submission we maintained transparency. Prospective participants were invited to ask questions, e.g. about the expected query results, which we answered publicly. After the evaluation, we made the scores and the gold standard (see below) available to the participants.

The given queries contained placeholders, e.g. 'all authors of the paper titled T'. For training, we specified the results expected after substituting certain values from TD for the variables. We evaluated by substituting further values, mostly values that were only available in ED. We had intentionally chosen easy as well as challenging queries, all weighted equally, to help participants get started, without sacrificing our ability to clearly distinguish the best-performing approach. The evaluation was automated with a collection of PHP scripts: they compared a CSV form of the results of the participants' SPARQL queries over their data against a gold standard of expected results, and compiled a report with precision/recall measures and a list of false positives and false negatives (see Figs. 1 and 2).

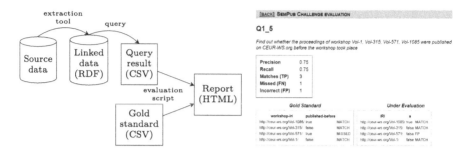

Fig. 1. Precision/recall evaluation   **Fig. 2.** Report for one query

4   Task 1: Extraction and Assessment of Workshop Proceedings Information

4.1   Motivation and Objectives

Common questions related to the quality of a scientific workshop or conference include whether a researcher should submit a paper to it, whether a researcher should accept an invitation to its programme committee, whether a publisher should publish its proceedings, and whether a company should sponsor it [5]. Moreover, knowing the quality of a scientific event helps to assess the quality of papers that have been accepted there. Quality indicators include[3] a long history and growth over time, attracting high-quality sub-events, a high ratio of contributed over invited papers (unless there are high-profile invited speakers), a low ratio of submissions (co-)authored by the event's chairs (and thus a high diversity in schools of thought), a fast publication turnaround (proceedings published quickly after, or even before the workshop – giving an impression of professional organisation).

   Producing data that would help to answer such questions was the first objective of Task 1, from the perspective of the Semantic Publishing Challenge. There was a second motivation, owed to Christoph Lange's role of technical editor of CEUR-WS.org. CEUR-WS.org is an open access publishing website which enjoys great popularity among the organisers of computer science workshops and has published more than 1,200 proceedings volumes since 1995. CEUR-WS.org has recently started discussing innovations[4], and a linked data representation of the workshop proceedings would certainly facilitate the implementation of innovative services. As the CEUR-WS.org volumes also provide sufficient information for answering quality-related questions such as those listed above, we chose them as the data source for Task 1. Note that DBLP also covers most of the workshops published with CEUR-WS.org, but it does not cover certain quality-related

---

[3] Some of these indicators have been suggested by Manfred Jeusfeld, the founder and publisher of CEUR-WS.org.

[4] http://ceurws.wordpress.com

information, such as what series a workshop is part of, the affiliations of the editors, the exact dates of a workshop and the publication of its proceedings, and a distinction between invited and contributed papers.

4.2 Data Source

The input dataset for Task 1 consists of documents in different formats and different levels of encoding quality and semantics:

– one HTML 4 index page linking to *all* workshop proceedings volumes (http://ceur-ws.org/; invalid, somewhat messy but still uniformly structured)
– the HTML tables of contents of selected volumes. They link to the individual workshop papers. Their format is largely uniform but has gained more structure and more semantics over time, while old volumes remained unchanged. Microformat annotations were introduced with volume 559 in 2010 and subsequently extended. RDFa (in addition to microformats) was introduced with volume 994 in 2013, but its use is optional, and therefore it has been used in less than 5 % of all volumes since then. Valid HTML5 has been mandatory since volume 1059 in 2013; before, hardly any volume was completely valid.
– the full text (PDF or PostScript) of the papers of *some* volumes

Challenges in processing tables of contents include the lack of standards for marking up editors' affiliations, for separating multiple workshops in joint volumes, for referring to invited talks[5], or for linking to all-in-one proceedings PDFs.

The training and evaluation datasets, TD1 and ED2 were chosen to comprise a fair balance of different document formats. To enable reasonable quality assessment, the training data already comprised all volumes of several workshop series, including, e.g., Linked Data on the Web, and for some conferences, such as WWW 2012, it comprised all those of its workshops that were published with CEUR-WS.org. In the evaluation dataset ED2, some more workshop series and conferences were completed. The datasets are available at http://challenges.2014.eswc-conferences.org/index.php/SemPub/Task1 (Table 1).

Table 1. Task 1 data sources

	Training dataset (TD1)	Evaluation dataset (ED1)
Proceedings volumes	54	91
... including metadata of	689 papers	1645 papers
Full text of	46 papers	88 papers
Volumes using RDFa	3	4
... using microformats only	48	71

---

[5] Possible keywords include 'invited paper', 'invited talk', or 'keynote'.

4.3   Queries

The queries were roughly ordered by increasing difficulty. The initial queries were basic ones to help the participants get started, whereas most queries from Q1.5 onward correspond to quality indicators discussed in Sect. 4.1:

Q1.1 List the full names of all **editors of the proceedings of workshop** W.[6]

Q1.2 Count the **number of papers in workshop** W.[7]

Q1.3 List the full names of all **authors who have (co-)authored a paper** in workshop W.

Q1.4 Compute the **average length of a paper** (in numbers of pages) in workshop W.[8]

Q1.5 (publication turnaround) Find out whether the proceedings of workshop W were published on CEUR-WS.org before the workshop took place.[9]

Q1.6 (previous editions of a workshop) Identify all editions that the workshop series titled T has published with CEUR-WS.org.

Q1.7 (chairs over the history of a workshop) Identify the full names of those chairs of the workshop series titled T that have so far been a chair in every edition of the workshop that was published with CEUR-WS.org.

Q1.8 (all workshops of a conference) Identify all CEUR-WS.org proceedings volumes in which papers of workshops of conference C in year Y were published.[10]

Q1.9 Identify those papers of workshop W that were **(co-)authored by at least one chair** of the workshop.

Q1.10 List the full names of all **authors of invited papers** in workshop W.

Q1.11 Determine the **number of editions** that the workshop series titled T has had, regardless of whether published with CEUR-WS.org.

Q1.12 (change of workshop title) Determine the title (without year) that workshop W had in its first edition.[11]

Q1.13 (workshops that have died) Of the workshops of conference C in year Y, identify those that did not publish with CEUR-WS.org in the following year (and that therefore probably no longer took place).

Q1.14 (papers of a workshop published jointly with others) Identify the papers of the workshop titled T (which was published in a joint volume V with other workshops).

---

[6] We did not ask the participants to disambiguate names. In the relatively small set of CEUR-WS.org workshop editors and authors, names are rarely ambiguous. We believe that cases of ambiguity can easily be fixed manually.

[7] Counting can be hard, as some workshops comprise multiple sessions, and as pre-microformat volumes do not always properly distinguish prefaces or all-in-one proceedings volumes from proper papers.

[8] Page numbers in tables of contents are optional and do not always start from 1.

[9] For old proceedings volumes, the date of publication is not listed in the table of contents, but only in the main index.

[10] Conferences may be abbreviated, e.g., as 'CCCCYYYY' or 'CCCC'YY'.

[11] Here, we assumed that the 'see also' links in the main index always point to previous editions of a workshop. In reality, they sometimes point to closely related but different workshops.

Q1.15 (editors of one workshop published jointly with others) List the full names of all editors of the proceedings of the workshop titled T (which was published in a joint volume V with other workshops).

Q1.16 Of the workshops that had editions at conference C both in year Y and $Y+1$, identify the **workshop(s) with the biggest percentage of growth** in their number of papers.

Q1.17 (change of conference affiliation) Return the acronyms of those workshops of conference C in year Y whose previous edition was co-located with a different conference series.

Q1.18 (change of workshop date) Of the workshop series titled T, identify those editions that took place more than two months later/earlier than the previous edition that was published with CEUR-WS.org.

Q1.19 (internationality of a workshop) Identify all countries that the authors of all regular papers in workshop W were from.

Q1.20 (institutional diversity of a workshop) Identify those papers in workshop W that were (co-)authored by people from the same institution as one of the chairs (including papers by chairs).[12]

Q1.5 (partly), Q1.12, Q1.13, Q1.16 and Q1.17 relied on the main index; Q1.19 and Q1.20 relied on the full-text PDF.

As Task 1 also aimed at producing linked data that we could eventually publish at CEUR-WS.org, the participants were additionally asked to follow a uniform URI scheme: http://ceur-ws.org/Vol-NNN/ for volumes, and http://ceur-ws.org/Vol-NNN/#paperM for a paper having the filename `paperM.pdf`.

4.4 Accepted Submissions and Winners

We received and accepted three submissions that met the requirements.

Ronzano et al. [20] solved the problem of annotating old proceedings volumes without any semantic markup by using the ones with microformat markup to train an automated annotation system that would retrofit microformat annotations to the old volumes. The system consults dumps of DBLP and WikiCFP data to more reliably identify author names and conference titles and acronyms. Using several external web services, the extracted data are enriched with further bibliographical information from BibSonomy and linked to the external datasets DBLP and DBpedia. This submission won the award for the *most innovative approach*.

Kolchin/Kozlov [15] defined templates for the typical structures of proceedings volumes, e.g., with or without RDFa or microformats. These templates extract the required data from the HTML pages using XPath and regular expressions. Countries (from authors' affiliations) are linked to DBpedia, using a SPARQL query against the DBpedia endpoint. Despite (or because of?) its relative simplicity, this submission won the *best precision/recall award*.

---

[12] Names of institutions require normalisation. English papers may, e.g., use the unofficial name 'University of Bonn'. German papers often prefer the short 'Universität Bonn' over the full official name Rheinische Friedrich-Wilhelms-Universität Bonn.

Table 2. Task 1 evaluation results

Authors	Overall average precision	Overall average recall	Queries attempted	Average precision on these	Average recall on these
Ronzano et al. [20]	0.335	0.313	1–12, 14, 15	0.478	0.447
Kolchin/Kozlov [15]	0.707	0.639	1–20	0.707	0.639
Dimou et al. [9]	0.138	0.092	1–9, 11–13, 16	0.212	0.142

Dimou et al. [9] took the template approach a step further, implementing them in the declarative language RML. RML, which has so far been capable of mapping CSV, XML and JSON to RDF, was extended to process non-XML HTML input. HTML elements with microformat annotations were accessed using CSS3 selectors. This submission focused on those proceedings volumes that used microformats, using a separate RML mapping definition for each proceedings volume. While sharing most code, many of them were manually adapted to the specific structures of certain volumes.

4.5   Lessons Learnt

From the perspective of running the challenge, Task 1 was successful, in that it led to three submissions, which were not only technically quite different, but whose performances could also be distinguished clearly – even when only taking into account the queries that the participants addressed at all (cf. Table 2). Two solutions primarily consisted of code specific to this task [15,20], whereas Dimou et al. wrote task-specific mappings in the otherwise generic RML language [9]. While proving the versatility of RML, this approach had the drawback of neglecting all steps RML had not been designed for, such as cleaning up messy input. Malformed literals remaining in the LOD stopped three queries from working. While it seems striking that the most innovative approach did not perform best, note that poor precision/recall results are partly owed to the participants focusing on a subset of the datasets for lack of time. For example, only one tool processed the main index and the full-text PDF [15]. Therefore, and because of its good performance and its relatively few technical requirements, we are currently rolling it out at CEUR-WS.org to become part of the publication process.[13] Only time will, however, tell the maintenance effort required for adapting to subsequent changes of the template for a proceedings volume table of contents.

---

[13] For a proof of concept, request RDF/XML from http://ceur-ws.org/Vol-1191/.

5 Task 2: Extraction and Characterisation of Citations

5.1 Motivation and Objectives

The importance of citations for the scientific community is undeniable: researchers cite works that investigated the same problem they are facing, or papers that proposed a similar (or contrasting) solution, and so on.

Citations are also being increasingly used to evaluate the impact of a given research, under the assumption that if a paper A cites another paper B then B had some impact on A. The impact factor is a measure of the quality of a journal obtained by averaging the impacts of the papers published by that journal in a given time interval. Citations are also used to evaluate the quality of the work of single researchers or teams or even universities. Just think about the h-index [12] and its diffusion.

Mere citation counting, however, is not enough to evaluate the quality of research. Citations are not all equal. Is it fair, e.g., to give the same relevance to a citation of a paper that introduced a ground-breaking theory, compared to a citation of a paper that contains a lot of errors? Also, should self-citations have the same relevance as others? How should a citation be evaluated if grouped with many others in a generic list?

These and other questions inspired us in the design of Task 2: our objective was to investigate methods and tools to characterise citations *automatically*, so that the tasks of linking, sharing and evaluating research through citations could be done in a more precise way. Participants were asked to process a set of XML-encoded research papers and to build an annotated network of citations. There are many different ways of annotating a citation, for instance by making explicit its type (is it a self-citation?), its structural information (where is it placed in the citing paper?) or even its function (why a paper is being cited?).

Participants were asked to make such information explicit, so that it could be exploited to answer a given set of queries. They were free to use their own ontological model, provided that the given queries could be translated and run on their dataset. The queries are described in the following section, after presenting the dataset on which they were launched.

5.2 Data Source

The construction of the input datasets was driven by the idea of covering a wide spectrum of cases. We collected papers encoded in XML JATS[14], a language for encoding journal articles derived from the NLM Archiving and Interchange DTD, and its TaxPub extension for taxonomic treatments. The papers were selected from two sources:

– *PubMedCentral Open Access Subset*[15], a subset of the PubMedCentral full-text archive of biomedical and life sciences articles from different journals and publishers; some of these are freely available for redistribution and reuse.

---

[14] http://dtd.nlm.nih.gov
[15] http://www.ncbi.nlm.nih.gov/pmc/tools/openftlist/

– *Pensoft Biodiversity Data Journal and ZooKeys archive*, open access archives of XML documents owned by Pensoft[16] and freely available for redistribution and reuse. Pensoft publishes scientific books on natural history. Some years ago they launched their first open access journal (ZooKeys), implementing several innovations in digital publishing and dissemination. Recently, they launched the Biodiversity Data Journal (BDJ) and the associated Pensoft Writing Tool (PWT) as the first workflow that puts authoring, peer-review, publication, and dissemination into a single online collaborative platform.

The selected papers are structurally very different from each other. First of all, they use different elements to encode citations: some citations are organised in complete records, others are contained in mixed structures, others are completely unstructured and stored as plain text. Also, different elements are used to encode data about the authors (that in some cases are listed with their full names, or with their initials, or with different abbreviation styles) and about the publication types (stored as attributes or elements). Furthermore the papers use different content structures (this information is useful to identify the position of citations) and different forms to express acknowledgements (useful to extract data about grants and fundings). Finally, some citation sentences make explicit the reasons why a paper is being cited, but these sentences have different forms.

The datasets TD2 (training) and ED2 (evaluation) are available at http:// challenges.2014.eswc-conferences.org/index.php/SemPub/Task2. Table 3 reports some statistics about these datasets. TD2 is a subset of ED2, composed of *randomly* chosen papers. The final evaluation was performed on a randomly chosen subset of ED2 too. To cover all queries and balance results, we clustered input papers around each query and selected some of them from each cluster. Each cluster was in fact composed of papers containing enough information to answer each query, and structuring that information in different ways.

Table 3. Task 2 data sources

	Training dataset (TD2)	Evaluation dataset (ED2)
Papers	150	400
Journals	15	70
Citations	>10000	>25000
Citations per paper	>70	>66
Bibliographic references	5419	16626

5.3 Queries

The community has proposed many research quality indicators; the discussion about them is open. We asked participants to extract some qualitative information about citations. The queries are not meant to be exhaustive but they

---

[16] http://www.pensoft.net

were selected to provide a quite large spectrum of information. We selected 10 queries, covering different aspects of citations. The first two are very basic and are meant to check if the produced network of citations was complete and if the cited resources were classified correctly:

Q2.1 Identify **all papers cited** by the paper X.
Q2.2 Identify **all journal papers cited** by the paper X.

In order to extract such information participants were basically asked to parse input files covering all possible cases: highly-structured citations, semi-structured and unstructured ones.

The second group of queries was meant to check if the produced dataset contained enough information to identify authors and to find self-citations:

Q2.3 Identify **all authors cited by the author** whose surname is X.
Q2.4 (auto-citations) Identify all papers cited by the paper X and written by the same authors (or some of them).

The correct identification of the authors is tricky and opens complex issues of content normalisation and management of homonymity. A simplified approach was adopted for this task: participants were required to extract all information available in the input dataset and to normalise it by providing surname, first-name and first-name-initials. These data were all normalised in lowercase – stripping spaces and punctuations – in the final evaluation.

The following two queries covered the position and context of citations:

Q2.5 Identify all **papers cited multiple times** by the paper X.
Q2.6 Identify all **papers cited multiple times in the same paragraph** by the paper X.

The idea behind these queries is that knowing the position of citations and their co-presence with others could give more information about their value (for instance, giving less relevance to multiple citations of the same work from the same paper, or even from the same paragraph).

The last four queries required additional processing of the textual content of the papers. First, we added a query about grants and funding agencies:

Q2.7 (grants and funding agencies) Identify the grant (or more than one) that supported the research presented in the paper X, along with the funding agency that funded it.

The basic idea was to make such information explicit, so that it can be used to investigate how fundings were connected to, or even influenced, a given research. Information about fundings are examples of *research context data*. Many more contextual data could be extracted, for instance about the institutions involved in a research project or partial works, etc. At this stage, we wanted to investigate some of these dimensions and to study how such structured data can be extracted from unstructured ones.

The last queries was meant to check how the tools characterised citations and to what extent they were able to identify the reasons why a work was cited:

Q2.8 Identify the **"literature review" section** of the paper X.

Q2.9 (using methods of a paper) Identify all papers of which paper X declares to use methodologies or theories.

Q2.10 (extending results of a paper) Identify all papers of which paper X declares to provide an extension of the results.

Automatic characterisation of citation has previously been approached with CiTalO [7], a chain of tools based on Semantic Web technologies, and by machine learning [21]. In both of these cases, however, the agreement between human annotators and automatic processes was quite low. Such a characterisation is actually an extremely difficult task for humans too: the experiments in [6] confirmed that the opinions about citation functions are often disaligned, and rarely match among users. To avoid this problem we selected some simple cases and unambiguous forms of citations. Nonetheless these queries still ended up being too difficult and only a few were answered correctly (see below for details).

5.4   Accepted Submissions and Winner

We received fewer submissions than expected. Some were incomplete and could not be considered for the evaluation. Eventually only one submission was completed and unfortunately we had to cancel the competition. Bertin and Atanassova [4] presented a novel approach combining machine-learning techniques and rule-based transformation, which produced good results. We evaluated their tool as explained in Sect. 3 even if they could not win an award. They also provided us with a lot of feedback, useful to better shape such a task in the future.

5.5   Lessons Learnt

The spirit of the challenge, and in particular of task 2, was to explore a large number of aspects in order to have a clearer picture of the state-of-the-art and to identify the most interesting and challenging issues.

In retrospect, this choice led us to defining a quite difficult task and we could have structured it in a slightly different way. In fact the questions we were asking are logically divided in two groups: queries Q2.1–Q2.7 required participants to basically map data from XML to RDF, while the last three required additional processing on the content. These two blocks required different skills and some people were discouraged to participate as they only felt strong in one of them. We could have split them in two tasks: one on data conversion and publishing and another one on textual processing.

These two blocks also differ for the quality of the results. The proposed solution, in fact, showed that very good results can be achieved in producing *semantically-annotated networks of citations*, that also include information about authors and about citation contexts. The automatic analysis of content and characterisation of citations, on the other hand, still has several open and fascinating issues to address.

6   In-Use Task 3: Semantic Technologies in Improving Scientific Production

6.1   Motivation and Objectives

The goal of task 3 was to investigate novel approaches to exploit semantic publications. We invited demos that showcased the potential of Semantic Web technology for enhancing and assessing the quality of scientific production. The task was open: participants could use their own datasets and were not required to connect to other tasks. We followed the tradition of open challenges established in the community: in 2009 and 2011, e.g., Elsevier ran two Grand Challenges, for which challengers were asked to '1. improve the process/methods/results of creating, reviewing and editing scientific content; 2. interpret, visualize or connect the knowledge more effectively, and/or 3. provide tools/ideas for measuring the impact of these improvements' [11] and to 'improve the way scientific information is communicated and used' [10]. Task 3 is also similar to the open track of the ISWC Semantic Web Challenge[17] (yearly since 2003) and the AI Mashup challenge[18] (yearly since 2009), though focused on semantic publishing.

6.2   Accepted Submissions

We accepted 4 out of 5 submissions. Each got 3 reviews and presented a sophisticated application for supporting researchers in their activities.

Linkitup [13] is a Web-based application for integrating research articles with semantic data retrieved from multiple heterogeneous sources. The platform enriches data available in existing repositories in many different ways: for instance, it finds terms, categories, entities (people, institutions, projects, etc.) related to a given work and shows them in an intuitive interface.

ROHub [17] is a digital library for Research Objects (ROs) that supports their management, dissemination and preservation. ROs are defined as aggregations of scientific resources, not only papers but also experimental data, reports, slides, and so on. Particularly interesting is the support for the lifecycle of these objects, even in their drafting stage.

Rexplore [16] is a sophisticated Web-based platform for exploring and making sense of scientific data. It integrates multiple sources and exploits data mining and semantic technologies to identify trends in research communities, to mine relations between researchers, to evaluate their performance, and to identify research trajectories. These data are shown in a rich interactive interface where users can search data, access them in personalised views and easily customise the overall dashboard by activating/deactivating the modules of the platform.

Atanassova and Bertin [3] presented an information retrieval system for enhancing publications by automatically identifying semantic relations between the components of these publications, for instance the methods, definitions and

---

[17] http://challenge.semanticweb.org/2014/criteria.html
[18] http://aimashup.org

hypotheses. The system is based on a rule engine and offers a user-friendly interface that allows users to search, browse and filter results by using facets.

6.3   Evaluation and Winners

In contrast to Tasks 1 and 2, the evaluation of Task 3 was carried out by an expert jury, taking into account the reviews and comments from the PC and applying five criteria: *potential impact* (the ability of the tool to make an impact on a large audience, with different background and expertise), *originality* (its innovative nature compared to related work), *breakthrough* (to what extent the tool is groundbreaking and visionary, and opens new perspectives and challenges for researchers), *quality of the Demo* (clarity and usability of the demo), and *appropriateness for ESWC* (to what extent Semantic Web technologies play a prominent role in the tool). The jury finally decided to award Francesco Osborne and Enrico Motta for *Understanding Research Dynamics*. Both the robustness of the tool and its potential applications were appreciated: the ability to mine new unexpected information from existing data was considered a key success factor, together with the ability to integrate multiple resources, to identify research trends and to evaluate research results in an innovative way.

7   Overall Lessons Learnt for Future Challenges

The first lesson we learnt is that is challenging to define appealing tasks that bridge the gap between building up initial datasets and exploring possibilities for innovative semantic publishing. As this first challenge has produced linked data about the CEUR-WS.org workshops (currently being published) and subsets of the PMC Open Access and the PenSoft archives (not yet published, but reusable under an open license), we now have a foundation to build on. Possible tasks for future challenges could focus on linking these initial datasets, each extracted from a single source, to *further* relevant datasets, e.g., to link CEUR-WS.org workshops to co-located conferences in Springer's conference proceedings data [5], to identify the DBLP counterparts of articles and authors in the PMC and PenSoft datasets, or to link publications to related social websites such as SlideShare or Twitter. Instead of a completely open task, one could call for applications that make innovative use of the data produced by the previous challenge. Task suggestions from our participants addressed practical needs of researchers, such as finding high-profile venues for publishing a work, summarising publications, or helping early career researchers to find relevant papers.

Acknowledgements. We would like to thank our reviewers, judges and sponsors, whose names are mentioned in the preface of this overall proceedings volume, as well as our participants for their hard work, creative solutions and useful suggestions. We would also like to thank Silvio Peroni for his suggestions on the overall challenge structure and, in particular, on the definition of task 2.

References

1. 3th Workshop on Linked Science (LISC). CEUR-WS 1116 (2014)
2. 4th Workshop on Semantic Publishing (SePublica). CEUR-WS 1155 (2014)
3. Atanassova, I., Bertin, M.: Semantic facets for scientific information retrieval. In: Presutti, V., et al. (eds.) SemWebEval 2014. CCIS, vol. 457, pp. 108–113. Springer, Heidelberg (2014)
4. Bertin, M., Atanassova, I.: Hybrid approach for the semantic processing of scientific papers. In: Presutti, V., et al. (eds.) European Semantic Web Conference (ESWC 2014). CCIS, vol. 457, Springer, Heidelberg (2014)
5. Bryl, V., et al.: What's in the proceedings? Combining publisher's and researcher's perspectives. In: 4th SePublica Workshop. CEUR-WS 1155 (2014)
6. Ciancarini, P., Di Iorio, A., Nuzzolese, A.G., Peroni, S., Vitali, F.: Evaluating citation functions in CiTO: cognitive issues. In: Presutti, V., d'Amato, C., Gandon, F., d'Aquin, M., Staab, S., Tordai, A. (eds.) ESWC 2014. LNCS, vol. 8465, pp. 580–594. Springer, Heidelberg (2014)
7. Di Iorio, A., Nuzzolese, A.G., Peroni, S.: Identifying functions of citations with CiTalO. In: Cimiano, P., Fernández, M., Lopez, V., Schlobach, S., Völker, J. (eds.) ESWC 2013. LNCS, vol. 7955, pp. 231–235. Springer, Heidelberg (2013)
8. Di Noia, T., Cantador, I., Ostuni, V.C.: Linked open data-enabled recommender systems: ESWC 2014 challenge on book recommendation. In: Presutti, V., et al. (eds.) SemWebEval 2014. CCIS, vol. 457, pp. 129–143. Springer, Heidelberg (2014)
9. Dimou, A., et al.: Extraction and semantic annotation of workshop proceedings in HTML using RML. In: Presutti, V., et al. (eds.) SemWebEval 2014. CCIS, vol. 457, pp. 114–119. Springer, Heidelberg (2014)
10. Elsevier, ed. Executable Paper Grand Challenge. Knowledge enhancement in the computational sciences (2011). http://www.executablepapers.com
11. Elsevier, ed. The Elsevier Grand Challenge. Knowledge enhancement in the life sciences (2009). http://www.elseviergrandchallenge.com
12. Hirsch, J.E.: An index to quantify an individual's scientific research output. PNAS **102**(46), 6569–16572 (2005)
13. Hoekstra, R., Groth, P., Charlaganov, M.: Linkitup: semantic publishing of research data. In: Presutti, V., et al. (eds.) SemWebEval 2014. CCIS, vol. 457, pp. 95–100. Springer, Heidelberg (2014)
14. Jentzsch, A., Cyganiak, R., Bizer, C.: State of the LOD Cloud (2011). http://lod-cloud.net/state/ (visited on 2014–08-06)
15. Kolchin, M., Kozlov, F.: A template-based information extraction from web sites with unstable markup. In: Presutti, V., et al. (eds.) SemWebEval 2014. CCIS, vol. 457, pp. 89–94. Springer, Heidelberg (2014)
16. Osborne, F., Motta, E.: Understanding research dynamics. In: Presutti, V., et al. (eds.) SemWebEval 2014. CCIS, vol. 457, pp. 101–107. Springer, Heidelberg (2014)
17. Palma, R., et al.: ROHub – a digital library of research objects supporting scientists towards reproducible science. In: Presutti, V., et al. (eds.) SemWebEval 2014. CCIS, vol. 457, pp. 77–82. Springer, Heidelberg (2014)
18. Priem, J., et al.: altmetrics: a manifesto (2011). http://altmetrics.org/manifesto/ (visited on 2014–08-06)
19. Recupero, D.R., Cambria, E.: ESWC 14 challenge on concept-level sentiment analysis. In: Presutti, V., et al. (eds.) SemWebEval 2014. CCIS, vol. 457, pp. 3–20. Springer, Heidelberg (2014)

20. Ronzano, F., Del Bosque, G.C, Saggion, H.: Semantify CEUR-WS proceedings: towards the automatic generation of highly descriptive scholarly publishing linked datasets. In: Presutti, V., et al. (eds.) SemWebEval 2014. CCIS, vol. 457, pp. 83–88. Springer, Heidelberg (2014)

21. Teufel, S., Siddharthan, A., Tidhar, D.: Automatic classification of citation function. In: Empirical Methods in Natural Language Processing, ACL (2006)

22. The DBLP Computer Science Bibliography. http://dblp.uni-trier.de

ROHub — A Digital Library of Research Objects Supporting Scientists Towards Reproducible Science

Raúl Palma[1]([✉]), Piotr Hołubowicz[1,4P], Oscar Corcho[2],
José Manuel Gómez-Pérez[3], and Cezary Mazurek[1]

[1] Poznan Supercomputing and Networking Center, Poznań, Poland
{rpalma,mazurek}@man.poznan.pl, piotrhol@google.com
[2] Ontology Engineering Group,
Universidad Politécnica de Madrid, Madrid, Spain
ocorcho@fi.upm.es
[3] ISOCO, Madrid, Spain
[4] Google, Mountain View, CA, USA
jmgomez@isoco.com

Abstract. Research Objects (ROs) are semantic aggregations of related scientific resources, their annotations and research context. They are meant to help scientists to refer to all the materials supporting their investigation. ROHub is a digital library system for ROs that supports their storage, lifecycle management and preservation. It provides a Web interface and a set of RESTful APIs enabling the sharing of scientific findings via ROs. Additionally, ROHub includes different features that help scientists throughout the research lifecycle to create and maintain high-quality ROs that can be interpreted and reproduced in the future. For instance, scientists can assess the conformance of an RO to a set of predefined requirements and create RO Snapshots, at any moment, to share, cite or submit to review the current state of research outcomes. ROHub can also generate nested ROs for workflow runs, exposing their content and annotations, and includes monitoring features that generate notifications when changes are detected.

Keywords: Research objects · Scientific workflows · Digital library · Sharing · Preservation

1 Introduction

Scientific publications have played a key role in the expansion of the vast body of human knowledge. From the traditional paper-based to the more recent digital publication, they have proved to be an effective dissemination channel of scientific findings. However, as stated in [8], a key idea that underpins science is *trust, but verify*. Verification is a step necessary to ensure the quality of the

© Springer International Publishing Switzerland 2014
V. Presutti et al. (Eds.): SemWebEval 2014, CCIS 475, pp. 77–82, 2014.
DOI: 10.1007/978-3-319-12024-9_9

published results, and in order to do so, scientists should be able to reproduce the experiments.

As research is increasingly being conducted in digital environments new types of content and artefacts are emerging [11], including computational methods like scientific workflows that encapsulate the research processes used to manipulate data and produce results in experimental science. Consequently, publication of results may not be enough to reproduce them. We need also the data used and produced, the methods employed, and the research context in which these artefacts were conceived. Similarly, in order to enable the reusability of scientific results, they should be published along with the set of all the resources associated to the enclosing investigation, including the research context and descriptions about the usage and provenance of these resources.

Research objects provide such container. They are aggregating objects that bundle together experimental resources that are essential to a computational scientific study or investigation, along with annotations on the bundle or the resources needed for the understanding and interpretation of the scientific outcomes. The resources aggregated can include the data used or results produced in an experiment study, the (computational) methods employed to produce and analyse that data, and the people involved in the investigation. The annotations can include provenance and evolution information, descriptions of the computational methods, dependency information and settings about the experiment executions. The RO model, introduced in [9], provides the means for capturing and describing such objects, their provenance and lifecycle, facilitating the reusability, reproducibility and better understanding of scientific experiments. The model consists of the core ro ontology, which provides the basic structure for the description of aggregated resources and annotations on those resources, and extensions for describing evolution aspects and experiments involving scientific workflows.

Hence, research objects can help scientists in sharing research outcomes that are more reusable and reproducible. However, scientists will need the appropriate technological support that assists them in creating research objects that satisfy certain requirements so that they can be easily understood, validated, reused and extended, thereby enhancing the quality of scientific production.

In this paper we present ROHub digital library system. ROHub enables the sharing of research outcomes via research objects and includes features that help scientists throughout the research lifecycle to create and maintain research objects satisfying predefined requirements so that they can be interpreted and reproduced in the future, to collaborate along this process, to publish and search these objects, and to monitor and preserve them to ensure that they will remain accessible and reproducible.

2   ROHub

ROHub is a digital library system for research objects that supports their storage, lifecycle management and preservation. It provides a Web interface and a set of RESTful APIs defining resources and representations according to the RO model, which expose a number of functionalities and possibilities for extension.

2.1 The Interfaces

ROHub provides a set of REST APIs, being the two primary ones the RO API [5] and the RO Evolution API [6]. The RO API defines the formats and links used to create and maintain ROs in the digital library. It is aligned with the RO model, hence recognising concepts such as aggregations, annotations and folders. The RO model ontology [10] is used to specify relations between different resources. ROHub supports content negotiation for metadata, including formats like RDF/XML, Turtle and TriG. The RO Evolution API defines the formats and links used to change the lifecycle stage of a RO, to create an immutable snapshot or archive from a mutable Live RO, as well as to retrieve their evolution provenance. The API follows the RO evolution model [9]. Additionally, ROHub provides a SPARQL endpoint, a Notification API [4], a Solr REST API, and a User Management API [7]. ROHub also provides a Web interface, which exposes all functionalities to the users. This is the main interface for scientists and researchers to interact with ROHub. A running instance of ROHub is accessible from http://www.rohub.org/portal/.

2.2 The Implementation

Internally, ROHub[1] has a modular structure that comprises access components, longterm preservation components and the controller that manages the flow of data (see Fig. 1). ROs are stored in the access repository once created, and periodically the new and/or modified ROs are pushed to the longterm preservation repository.

The access components are the storage backend and the semantic metadata triplestore. The storage backend can be based on dLibra [3], which provides file storage and retrieval functionalities, including file versioning and consistency checking. It has a built-in text search engine and allows organising stored objects into hierarchical structures and

Fig. 1. ROHub internal component diagram

associating metadata at the aggregation level. Alternatively, storage backend can use a built-in module for storing ROs directly in the filesystem.

---

[1] Source code available at: https://github.com/wf4ever/rodl and https://github.com/wf4ever/portal

The semantic metadata are additionally parsed and stored in a triplestore backed by Jena TDB [1]. Jena TDB provides good support for transactions, querying, cacheing and using named graphs. The use of a triplestore offers a standard query mechanism for clients. It also provides a flexible mechanism for storing metadata about any component of a RO that is identifiable via a URI.

The longterm preservation component is built on dArceo [2]. dArceo stores ROs, including resources and annotations, and monitors their quality, alerting administrators if necessary. Standard monitoring activities include file format decay alerts and fixity checking but ROHub also monitors the RO quality through time against a predefined set of requirements. If a change is detected, notifications are generated as Atom feeds according to the Notification API.

2.3 Functionalities Supporting Scientists Towards Reproducible Science

Create, manage and share ROs. There are different methods for creating ROs in ROHub. They can be created from (i) scratch, adding resources progressively; (ii) by importing pack of resources from other systems (currently myExperiment); and (iii) from a ZIP file aggregating files and folders. Resources can be added and annotated from the content panel, which also shows the folder structure. Also, as in daily practice it is sometimes common to work with local resources (scripts, data, etc.), users can use the RO-Manager tool (https://github.com/wf4ever/ro-manager) to create local ROs and push/pull them to/from ROHub. ROHub also provides different access modes to share the ROs: open, public or private. In open mode, anyone with an account can visualise and edit the RO. In public mode, everyone can visualise the RO, but only users with correct permissions can edit it. In private mode, only users with correct permissions can visualise and/or edit the RO. ROHub provides a faceted search interface, in addition to a simple keyword search mode, to find stored ROs. Additionally, scientists and other applications can use the provided SPARQL endpoint to query the RO metadata.

Assessing RO quality. During the RO creation, users can visualise a progress bar on the RO overview panel (see Fig. 2), which shows its quality based on set of predefined basic RO requirements. When clicked, a preview of the requirements and their compliance is displayed. Users can also get more information about the quality of the RO from the Quality panel, where they can choose the template used to evaluate the RO.

Fig. 2. ROHub - research object overview panel

There are a number of templates available, each specifying particular set of RO requirements for certain purpose or task. Users can create their own templates for their particular domain or standards. Internally, this feature calls a Restful service for the evaluation.

Managing RO evolution. At any point in time, users may want to create a snapshot (or release) of the current state of their RO for sharing the current outcomes with colleagues, get feedback, send it to review, or to cite them. Also, when the research has concluded, they would like to release and preserve the outcomes for future references. In ROHub this can be easily done from the RO overview panel. ROHub keeps the versioning history of these snapshots, and even calculates the changes between one snapshot and the subsequent one. Users can visualise the evolution of the RO from the History panel, where they can see a diagram with nodes the live RO and its associated snapshots/archives, and arrows showing the versioning relations between the latter. Users can click on the nodes to navigate the RO history.

Navigation of workflow run. Scientists can aggregate any type of resource, including links to external resources and RO bundles, which are structured ZIP files representing self-contained ROs that facilitate their transfer and integration with 3rd party tools. Taverna, for example, can export provenance of workflow runs as RO Bundles. In ROHub, these bundles are unpacked into a nested RO, exposing its full content and annotations. Hence, scientists are able to navigate through the inputs, outputs and intermediate values of the run, something potentially useful for future reproducibility.

Monitoring ROs. ROHub includes monitoring features, such as fixity checking and RO quality, which generate notifications when changes are detected. This can help to detect and prevent, for instance, workflow decay, occurring when an external resource or service used by a workflow becomes unavailable or behaves differently. Users can visualise changes in the RO regarding content and quality monitoring in the notification panel and they can subscribe to the atom feed to get automatic notifications.

3   Conclusions

We have introduced in this paper ROHub, a digital library enhanced with semantic technologies that assists users in the generation and publication of research outcomes which are more reusable and reproducible, thus facilitating the assessment of the results quality. To this end, ROHub implements a set of APIs and a web interface for management of ROs, exposing functionalities according the RO model and related ontologies. Currently, the running instance of ROHub stores more than 1150 research objects. The future plans of ROHub include an enhanced interface of the evolution history that shows also the changes between different versions, customisation of snapshotting process, interface to facilitate the generation of quality templates, improved notification and access control panel, as well as improvements in the performance of RO loading.

Acknowledgements. This work was supported by Wf4Ever EU project (http://www.wf4ever-project.org, FP7–270129). We acknowledge Filip Wisniewski for his contribution to ROHub, Graham Klyne and Stian Soiland-Reyes for their inputs to APIs, and Wf4Ever users for their feedback, especially Julián Garrido, Enrique Ruiz, Eleni Mina and Kristina Hettne.

References

1. Apache Jena. http://jena.apache.org/. Accessed 20 Mar 2014
2. dArceo. http://dlab.psnc.pl/darceo/. Accessed 20 Mar 2014
3. dLibra. http://dlab.psnc.pl/dlibra/. Accessed 20 Mar 2014
4. Notification API. http://www.wf4ever-project.org/wiki/display/docs/Notification+API. Accessed 20 Mar 2014
5. RO API. http://www.wf4ever-project.org/wiki/display/docs/RO+API+6. Accessed 20 Mar 2014
6. RO Evolution API. http://www.wf4ever-project.org/wiki/display/docs/RO+evolution+API. Accessed 20 Mar 2014
7. User Management API. http://www.wf4ever-project.org/wiki/display/docs/User+Management+2. Accessed 20 Mar 2014
8. How science goes wrong. http://econ.st/1hYoAaN (Oct 2013), The Economist Newspaper Limited. Accessed 20-Mar-2014
9. Belhajjame, K., Corcho, O., Garijo, D., Zhao, J., Missier, P., Newman, D., Palma, R., Bechhofer, S., García-Cuesta, E., Gómez-Pérez, J.M., Klyne, G., Page, K., Roos, M., Ruiz, J.E., Soiland-Reyes, S., Verdes-Montenegro, L., De Roure, D., Goble, C.A.: Workflow-centric research objects: First class citizens in scholarly discourse. In: ESWC2012 Workshop on Semantic Publication (SePublica2012) (2012)
10. Belhajjame, K., Klyne, G., Garijo, D., Corcho, O., García Cuesta, E., Palma, R.: Wf4ever Research Object Model (2013). http://wf4ever.github.io/ro/
11. De Roure, D., Belhajjame, K., Missier, P., Gómez-Prez, J.M., Palma, R., Ruiz, J.E., Hettne, K., Roos, M., Klyne, G., Goble, C.: Towards the preservation of scientific workflows. In: 8th International Conference on Preservation of Digital Objects (iPRES 2011) (2011)

Semantify CEUR-WS Proceedings: Towards the Automatic Generation of Highly Descriptive Scholarly Publishing Linked Datasets

Francesco Ronzano$^{(\boxtimes)}$, Gerard Casamayor del Bosque, and Horacio Saggion

TALN Research Group, Universitat Pompeu Fabra,
C/Tanger 122, 08018 Barcelona, Spain
{francesco.ronzano,gerard.casamayor,horacio.saggion}@upf.edu

Abstract. Rich and fine-grained semantic information describing varied aspects of scientific productions is essential to support their diffusion as well as to properly assess the quality of their output. To foster this trend, in the context of the ESWC2014 Semantic Publishing Challenge, we present a system that automatically generates rich RDF datasets from CEUR-WS workshop proceedings. Proceedings are analyzed through a sequence of processing phases. SVM classifiers complemented by heuristics are used to annotate missing CEUR-WS markups. Annotations are then linked to external datasets like DBpedia and Bibsonomy. Finally, the data is modeled and published as an RDF graph. Our system is provided as an on-line Web service to support on-the-fly RDF generation. In this paper we describe the system and present its evaluation following the procedure set by the organizers of the challenge.

Keywords: Semantic Web · Information extraction · Scholarly publishing · Open Linked Data

1 Information Extraction and Knowledge Modeling Approach: Motivation and Overview

The enhancement of scholarly publishing data by better structuring, interlinking and semantically modeling is one of the core objectives of **semantic publishing** [1–3]. Semantic Web technologies are an enabling factor towards this vision [4]. They provide the means to structure and semantically enrich scientific publications so as to support the generation of Linked Data from them [5,6]. In this context, recently, a few scientific publication repositories including DBLP[1],

---

The work described in this paper has been funded by the European Project Dr Inventor (FP7-ICT-2013.8.1 - Grant no: 611383) and the project SKATER-UPF-TALN (TIN2012-38584-C06-03) funded by Ministerio de Economía y Competitividad, Secretaría de Estado de Investigación, Desarrollo e Innovación, Spain.

[1] http://dblp.l3s.de/d2r/

V. Presutti et al. (Eds.): SemWebEval 2014, CCIS 475, pp. 83–88, 2014.
DOI: 10.1007/978-3-319-12024-9_10

ACM[2] and IEEE[3] have been also published as Open Linked Data. In general, however, only basic bibliographic information is exposed that is too generic to properly support the diffusion and the assessment of the quality of scientific publications.

With the purpose of experimenting with new approaches to generate rich and highly descriptive scholarly publishing Open Linked datasets, and in the context of the Task 1 of the ESWC2014 Semantic Publishing Challenge (SemPub Task 1), we present a system that automatically mines contents from the workshop proceedings of CEUR-WS Web portal and exports them as an RDF graph. SemPub Task 1 aims at enabling the computation of indicators of the quality of workshops. For this purpose participants are provided with a dataset of HTML documents with information about workshop proceedings indexed at CEUR-WS together with the PDF documents of the related papers. Microformats[4] and RDFa[5] annotations are available for some of these documents, and missing in others. The task requires extracting pieces of information from these textual and unstructured sources and model these contents as an RDF graph so as to enable the computation of the indicators of the quality of a workshop by means of SPARQL queries.

Our approach to Sem Pub Task 1 is based on the following core observations:

– Since 2010, HTML pages detailing the contents of individual proceeding volumes have been annotated with 20 microformat classes (CEURVOLEDITOR, CEURTITLE, CEURAUTHORS, etc.). The occurrences of each class provide a set of examples of relevant kinds of information that need to be extracted and modelled in SemPub Task 1. **This data can be exploited to train an automatic text annotation system**.
– There are several scholarly publishing resources accessible on-line where part of the information published by CEUR-WS proceedings is linked and partially replicated in a structured or semi-structured format. Some examples are Bibsonomy[6], DBLP, and Wiki CFP[7]. These resources can be exploited **to support the information extraction process and to make the RDF contents generated by our system strongly linked with related datasets**.

Starting from these observations, we have designed and implemented a data processing workflow to convert the CEUR-WS proceeding documents into rich RDF datasets.

2   System Description

This section describes in detail each phase of the processing workflow outlined in Fig. 1. This workflow was implemented using the text processing pipeline

---

[2] http://acm.rkbexplorer.com/

[3] http://ieee.rkbexplorer.com/

[4] A semantic markup approach that conveys metadata and other attributes in Web pages by existing HTML/XHTML tags.

[5] A semantic markup useful to embed RDF triples within XHTML documents.

[6] http://www.bibsonomy.org/

[7] http://www.wikicfp.com/cfp/

provided by GATE Text Engineering Framework[8] [7], and complemented by external tools and interactions with on-line Web services and knowledge repositories[9].

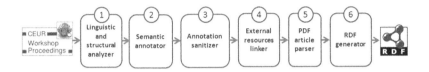

Fig. 1. CEUR-WS Proceeding to RDF: data processing work-flow

PHASE 1: Linguistic and structural analyzer: given a set of CEUR-WS proceeding Web pages, their contents are characterized by means of both linguistic features and structural information derived from HTML markup so as to support the execution of the following processing steps. Texts are split into lines containing homogeneous information according to a set of heuristics, then tokenized and POS-tagged using the information extraction framework ANNIE[10]. Names of paper authors, conference titles and acronyms are identified using gazetteers that were derived from the XML dump of DBLP and WikiCFP.

PHASE 2: Semantic annotator: this component automatically adds semantic annotations to the textual contents of HTML documents without semantic markups. The semantic annotator is based on a set of chunk-based and sentence-based Support Vector Machine (SVM) classifiers [8] trained with microformat annotations of the documents of 562 proceeding volumes that do have annotations. Considering the 14 most frequent microformat classes adopted by CEUR-WS, we compiled 14 training corpora. Each corpus includes all the documents that are annotated with the corresponding microformat class. Since editor affiliations constitute relevant information for SemPub Task 1 that is not marked by CEUR-WS microformat classes, we introduced a new dedicated type of annotation, CEURAFFILIATION. We created an additional training corpus by randomly choosing 75 proceedings among the previous set of volumes. We manually annotated these proceedings with editor affiliations, thus generating 252 training examples. The set of features used to characterize chunks and sentences are the linguistic and structural information added to each proceeding by PHASE 1. For each annotation type we trained a chunk-based and a sentence-based SVM classifier, evaluated both classifiers using 10-fold cross-validation over the related training corpus and chose the one with the best F1 score. Chunk-based classifiers perform better with annotation types covering a small number of consecutive tokens that are characterized by an highly distinctive set of

---

[8] https://gate.ac.uk/

[9] The system described in this paper can be accessed on-line at: http://sempub.taln. upf.edu/eswc2014sempub/ (password: ceurrdf2014).

[10] http://gate.ac.uk/sale/tao/splitch6.html

features and can be easily discriminated from preceding and following sets of tokens. Examples of this kinds of annotation types are CEURVOLACRONYM, CEURURN, CEURVOLNR, CEURPAGE and CEURVOLTITLE. On the contrary, sentence-based classifiers obtain better results with annotation types that can be better characterized by sentence level features rather than token level ones. We achieved F1 values of 0.9 or greater for all annotation types.

PHASE 3: Annotation sanitizer: a set of heuristics are applied to fix cases when the annotation borders are incorrectly identified or to delete annotations that are not compliant with the normal sequence of annotations of a proceeding (e.g. editor affiliations annotated after the list of paper titles and authors). In addition, links between pairs of related annotations are created (e.g. editors and affiliations by means of their markups).

PHASE 4: External resources linker: existing annotations are enriched with additional information not covered internally by CEUR-WS and useful to calculate the workshop quality indicators. The Bibsonomy REST API is used to associate annotations of paper titles to Bibsonomy entries and to import the related BibTeX metadata and links to external repositories like DBLP. DBpedia Spotlight Web service [9] is used to identify the DBpedia resources corresponding to mentions of states, cities and organizations.

PHASE 5: PDF article parser: this component retrieves the PDF files of the papers of a proceeding and parses them by means of the Apache PDFBox Java library. The number of pages of each paper is extracted and mentions of states, cities and organizations in the PDF document are identified using the DBpedia Spotlight Web service.

PHASE 6: RDF generator: all the information gathered by the previous processing steps is aggregated and normalized so as to generate an Open Linked RDF dataset that is informative enough to compute the quality indicators defined in SemPub Task 1. The contents of each Proceeding are modeled by reusing and extending two widespread semantic publishing ontologies: the *Semantic Web for Research Communities Ontology* (prefix swrc) and the *Publishing Role Ontology* (prefix pro).

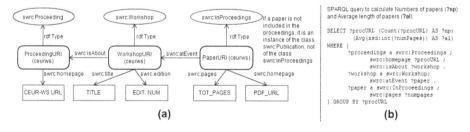

Fig. 2. (a) RDF model of papers presented at a workshop, included in a proceeding volume; (b) SPARQL query for **Numbers of papers** and **Average length of papers**

We defined - in a ceur-ws namespace - a few new classes and properties that were required to fully model the annotations produced by our system. For all these new resources we subclassed existing classes and properties in the ontologies before mentioned. The resulting RDF dataset imports the reused vocabularies and asserts all pertinent T-BOX axioms for the new concepts and properties.

In Fig. 2 we provide an example of the SPARQL query formulated to compute two of the workshop quality indicators of SemPub Task 1, starting from the proceeding information modelled by the RDF graph shown in the same figure.

3 Lessons Learned

Our system design has been motivated by the need of flexibility and robustness in the face of different ways in which information is written, structured or annotated in the input dataset. Despite that, we found that **customized and often laborious information extraction and post processing steps are essential to correctly deal with borderline information structures that are difficult to generalize**, like unusual markups, infrequent ways to link authors and affiliations, etc. For instance, our analysis detects when multiple workshops are published jointly in the same volume, yet it often fails to associate the right information to each individual workshop. This is caused by the lack of semantic annotations and structural mark-ups, as well as by a high variability in the linguistic expressions used to introduce each workshop contents in the text. In the face of this difficulty, in this specific context, our approach adopts a fall-back strategy by which papers, editors, sessions, etc. are linked directly to the proceeding volume rather to individual workshops. In general, all these irregularities greatly limit our ability to calculate quality indicators for workshops published jointly with others by means of SPARQL queries.

Although relying on external Web services provides us with useful information, **the responsiveness of our Web interface to generate on-the-fly an RDF graph from one or more proceeding volumes is compromised by the lag-times introduced by the access to these external services**. Overall, however, we think that the benefits outweigh the problems and that reusing existing datasets and services is good practice.

When we formulated the set of SPARQL queries to aggregate relevant information from our RDF graph, we realized that some of the queries required changes in the modeling of data for their formulation. This showed **the importance of keeping well present the information needs of a dataset before deciding how to model the data**.

4 Future Work

We described a system that extracts structured information from CEUR-WS on-line proceedings, modeling their contents as Linked Datasets.

As future work, we plan on increasing the flexibility of the information extraction procedure by doing further experimentation with statistical and trainable methods. Another venue of research is to increase the role of external services and datasets to inform and complement the content extraction process, specially in the face of missing annotations, ambiguous text or unstructured documents. Finally, we would like to generalize our approach so as to be able to extract and merge RDF datasets mined from distinct on-line Web Portals of academic documents and data.

In general, we hope that the increasing availability of structured and rich scientific publishing Linked Datasets will enable larger communities to easily discover and reuse research outcomes as well as to propose and test new metrics to better understand and evaluate research outputs. In this context we believe that, in parallel to the investigation of approaches to automate the creation of semantic datasets by mining partially structured inputs, it is also essential to push scientific communities towards standardized, shared and opened procedures to expose their outcomes in a structured way.

References

1. Shotton, D.: Semantic publishing: the coming revolution in scientific journal publishing. Learn. Publ. **22**(2), 85–94 (2009)
2. Shotton, D., Portwin, K., Klyne, G., Miles, A.: Adventures in semantic publishing: exemplar semantic enhancements of a research article. PLoS Comput. Biol. **5**(4), e1000361 (2009)
3. Smit, E., Van Der Graaf, M.: Journal article mining: the scholarly publishers' perspective. Learn. Publ. **25**(1), 35–46 (2012)
4. Bizer, C.: Linking data & publications expert report. Global Research Data Infrastructure of European Union (2012)
5. Ciancarini, P., Di Iorio, A., Nuzzolese, A.G., Peroni, S., Vitali, F.: Semantic annotation of scholarly documents and citations. In: Baldoni, M., Baroglio, C., Boella, G., Micalizio, R. (eds.) AI*IA 2013. LNCS, vol. 8249, pp. 336–347. Springer, Heidelberg (2013)
6. Attwood, T.K., Kell, D.B., McDermott, P., Marsh, J., Pettifer, S.R., Thorne, D.: Utopia documents: linking scholarly literature with research data. Bioinformatics **26**(18), 568–574 (2010)
7. Cunningham, H., Maynard, D., Bontcheva, K., Tablan, V.: GATE: a framework and graphical development environment for robust NLP tools and applications. In: Proceedings of the 40th Anniversary Meeting of the Association for Computational Linguistics, ACL (2002)
8. Li, Y., Bontcheva, K., Cunningham, H.: Adapting SVM for data sparseness and imbalance: a case study on information extraction. Nat. Lang. Eng. (Cambridge University Press) **15**, 241–271 (2009)
9. Mendes, P.N., Jakob, M., Garca-Silva, A., Bizer, C.: DBpedia spotlight: shedding light on the web of documents. In: Proceedings of the 7th International Conference on Semantic Systems, pp. 1–8. ACM (2011)

A Template-Based Information Extraction from Web Sites with Unstable Markup

Maxim Kolchin and Fedor Kozlov[✉]

ITMO University, St. Petersburg, Russia
kolchinmax@niuitmo.ru, kozlovfedor@gmail.com

Abstract. This paper presents results of a work on crawling CEUR Workshop proceedings(CEUR Workshop proceedings web site, URL: http://ceur-ws.org) web site to a Linked Open Data (LOD) dataset in the framework of ESWC 2014 Semantic Publishing Challenge 2014(ESWC 2014 Semantic Publishing Challenge, URL: http://2014.eswc-conferences.org/semantic-publishing-challenge). Our approach is based on using an extensible template-dependent crawler and DBpedia for linking extracted entities, such as the names of universities and countries.

Keywords: Information extraction · Semantic publishing · Linked open data · Semantic web

1 Introduction

The work that is presented in this paper aims to provide a solution for Task 1 of ESWC 2014 Semantic Publishing Challenge[1]. The task is to crawl CEUR Workshop proceedings web site[2] and create a LOD dataset containing detailed information about workshops, proceedings volumes, papers and their authors and etc.

The source code and instructions to run the crawler are located at our Github repository[3].

1.1 Challenges

At first glance, the task looks a pretty straightforward, but there are several challenges that need to be solved:

- the web site has a quite unstable and in some cases invalid HTML markup because of absence of a standardised and strict template for creation of pages

---

[1] ESWC 2014 Semantic Publishing Challenge, URL: http://2014.eswc-conferences.org/semantic-publishing-challenge.

[2] CEUR Workshop proceedings web site, URL: http://ceur-ws.org

[3] The source code and instructions, URL: https://github.com/ailabitmo/sempub-challenge2014-task1.

© Springer International Publishing Switzerland 2014
V. Presutti et al. (Eds.): SemWebEval 2014, CCIS 475, pp. 89–94, 2014.
DOI: 10.1007/978-3-319-12024-9_11

for proceedings volumes, so it makes it harder to crawl such pages, because usually crawlers are written for web sites with fixed markup;

- only a small percentage of proceedings volumes uses RDFa markup and microformats are used only for volumes starting from 559th one, so at the time of writing around 49 % of volume pages don't have any metadata that could help in crawling;
- according to the rules of the web site, proceedings should comply with some requirements regarding numbers of invited and regular papers, therefore there are joint proceedings of several workshops. Such workshop and proceedings should be represented in the dataset accordingly;
- the web site includes proceeding not only in English, but also in German. In addition it's quite common practise for authors of papers written in English to use names of their universities or companies in a native language;

2 Our Approach

We developed an extensible template-dependent crawler that uses sets of special predefined templates for each type of entity. The main aim of this templates is to cover entire variety of entity representations in HTML format. Some of templates used for extracting papers from workshops pages are:

- a template based on RDFa metadata,
- a template based on Microformats,
- and two templates specific to some similar HTML markups.

When HTML page parsing begins, the crawler consecutively runs predefined templates till one of the templates returns the valid data. Validation based on template's structure. Template's parsing process extracts data from HTML page using XPath Language and regular expressions. XPath Language is used for searching text data by elements and properties in HTML markup. Regular expressions is used for extracting entity tokens from plain text. When data is extracted template parsing process converts data into ontology instances and properties. The templates are completely independent from each other and the crawler uses a mapping of the templates to the types of contents where they are applied to such as the index page, a workshop page and a publication, which makes the crawler easily extensible. More about the extensibility in the next section.

The main advantage of our approach is a flexibility of different data representations in HTML markup with usage of the same code of the crawler and support of invalid HTML.

2.1 Architecture

The parser is implemented in Python and based on Grab Spider framework[4]. This framework allows to build asynchronous site crawlers. Crawler downloads all workshop's pages and papers and then runs the parsing tasks. There is a

---

[4] Grab framework, URL: http://grablib.org/.

collection of specific parsers for each entity. Each parser in collection process a part of some HTML page to build properties and entity relations.

The overall system architecture is shown in Fig. 1.

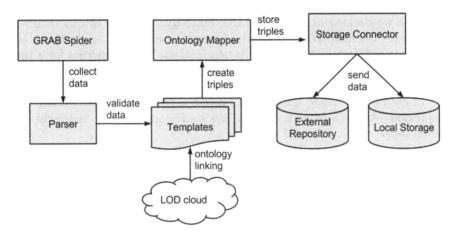

Fig. 1. The overall system architecture

Extensibility. The crawler provides two basic templates with the default implementations: a template for a single entity, in example a workshop page, and a template for a list of entities, in example the index page with the list of workshop names. And to add a new template, one of the basic ones should be extended by implementing the method responsible for the template matching. The rest of the work is done by the default implementations responsible for translating data to triples and writing them to disk.

2.2 Data Representation

To represent crawled data we use several different ontologies such as Semantic Web Conference Ontology (SWC)[5], Semantic Web for Research Communities ontology (SWRC)[6], The Bibliographic Ontology (BIBO)[7], The Timeline Ontology (TIMELINE)[8], Friend of a Friend (FOAF)[9], Dublin Core (DC and

[5] Semantic Web Conference Ontology, URL: http://data.semanticweb.org/ns/swc/ ontology.
[6] Semantic Web for Research Communities, URL: http://ontoware.org/swrc/.
[7] The Bibliographic Ontology, URL: http://purl.org/ontology/bibo/.
[8] The Timeline Ontology, URL: http://purl.org/NET/c4dm/timeline.owl#.
[9] The Friend of a Friend (FOAF), URL: http://www.foaf-project.org/.

DCTERMS)[10] and DBpedia Ontology (DBPEDIA-OWL)[11] and RDF Schema (RDFS)[12].

A part of the data representation schema is shown on Fig. 2. Representation of time and time intervals doesn't use The Event Ontology (EVENT) because it assumes inclusion of blank nodes. Since RDFLib doesn't work well with them we decided to use TIMELINE ontology instead. TIMELINE ontology provides timeline:atDate property for setting a date to an instance and *timeline:beginsAtDateTime* and *timeline:endsAtDateTime* properties for a time interval.

On CEUR Workshop proceedings web site some proceedings volumes has links to each other. These links usually relate a proceedings of a workshop to the previous its editions and we uses *rdfs:seeAlso* property to represent this relationships.

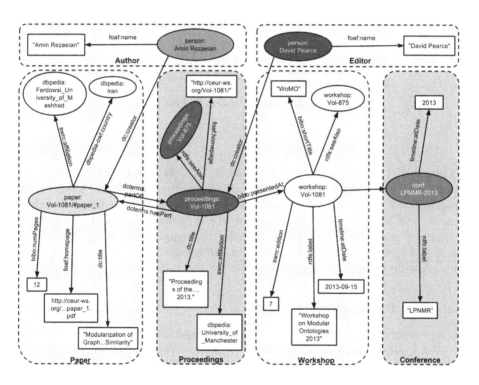

Fig. 2. Schema representing the crawled data

---

[10] Dublin Core, URL: http://purl.org/dc/elements/1.1/.
[11] DBpedia Ontology, URL: http://dbpedia.org/ontology/.
[12] RDF Schema, URL: http://www.w3.org/2000/01/rdf-schema#.

2.3   Specific Solutions

In most cases all problems are solved by an appropriate template, but there are some problems requiring specific solutions.

Extraction of Countries and Affiliations. Identification of countries and affiliations in papers was done with external datasets. In case of extracting countries parser extracts the first page from the PDF document. Country-candidates are extracted using regular expressions with predefined templates. Parser sends request with a list of country-candidates to SPARQL-endpoint of DBpedia [1] resource to get list of unique country's IRIs.

The country extraction query must support different naming conventions of country-candidates. Hence the following SPARQL-query is suggested.

```
SELECT DISTINCT ?country {
    VALUES ?search { "The Netherlands" }
    ?country a dbpedia-owl:Country .
    { ?name_uri dbpedia-owl:wikiPageRedirects ?country ;
                rdfs:label ?label .
    }
    UNION
    { ?country rdfs:label ?label }
    FILTER( STR(?label) = ?search )
}
```

Creation of properties and relations for the current paper entity is based on received list.

Identification of Related Workshops. As mentioned above, in most cases *skos:related* property is used to relate to a previous edition of the corresponding workshops. But sometimes it's not correct. Especially in case of joint proceedings. To identify correct links we implemented the algorithm measuring similarity of two workshops based on its full name and acronym. In case of absence of an acronym we generate one from the full name's upper case characters. For example for "Concept Extraction Challenge at Making Sense of Microposts 2013" workshop the "CECMSM" acronym is generated. String similarity measurement uses the basic Ratcliff-Obershelp algorithm [2]. This algorithm was selected because it is being provided by the Python Standard Library.

3   Conclusion

Task 1 of Semantic Publishing Challenge 2014 is solved with developed parser based on Grab Spider framework. This parser uses SWC, SWRC, BIBO, TIME-LINE ontologies, DBpedia datasets and the basic Ratcliff-Obershelp algorithm for string similarity measurement. Our approach based on templates of web site blocks, the schema representing extracted information and solutions for some specific problems. The main advantages of our approach are flexible representation of different data templates in HTML markup and support of invalid HTML.

3.1 Unsolved Issues

In most cases our solution works well, but there are several "places" where it doesn't work well and therefore may not pass some tests completely:

– extraction of country and university candidates from papers works only for texts consisting only of US-ASCII characters because PDFMiner[13] which we use to extract text from PDF files doesn't work well with Unicode symbols;
– papers written in PostScript or HTML are completely ignored;

3.2 Future Work

This work can be further extended by solving the known issues and implementing additional functionality in the crawler for deeper information extraction to make the dataset more useful for further analysis. To achieve it, the following particular tasks could be done:

– use external repositories such as DBLP[14], Semantic Web Dog Food[15] and other open datasets to extract, link and enrich the information about authors and editors,
– optimise extraction of authors' affiliations from papers and particular connections between the authors and the affiliations,
– extraction of authors' e-mail addresses from papers to improve aligning of ontology instances representing authors and editors.

Acknowledgments. This work has been partially financially supported by the Government of Russian Federation, Grant #074-U01.

References

1. Lehmann, J., Isele, R., Jakob, M., Jentzsch, A., Kontokostas, D., Mendes, P.N., Hellmann, S., Morsey, M., van Kleef, P., Auer, S., Bizer, C.: DBpedia - a large-scale, multilingual knowledge base extracted from wikipedia. Seman. Web J. (2014). http://www.semantic-web-journal.net/content/dbpedia-large-scale-multilingual-knowledge-base-extracted-wikipedia-0
2. Ratcliff, J.W., Metzener, D.E.: Pattern-matching-the gestalt approach. Dr DOBBS J. (DDJ) **13**(7), 1–46 (1988)

---

[13] PDFMiiner, URL: http://www.unixuser.org/~euske/python/pdfminer/.
[14] DBLP, URL: http://www.informatik.uni-trier.de/~ley/db/.
[15] Semantic Web Dog Food, URL: http://data.semanticweb.org/.

Linkitup: Semantic Publishing of Research Data

Rinke Hoekstra[1,2]($\boxtimes$), Paul Groth[1], and Marat Charlaganov[1]

[1] Network Institute, VU University Amsterdam, Amsterdam, The Netherlands
{rinke.hoekstra,p.t.groth,m.charlaganov}@vu.nl
[2] Faculty of Law, University of Amsterdam, Amsterdam, The Netherlands
hoekstra@uva.nl

Abstract. Linkitup is a Web-based dashboard for enrichment of research output published via industry grade data repository services. It takes metadata entered through Figshare.com and tries to find equivalent terms, categories, persons or entities on the Linked Data cloud and several Web 2.0 services. It extracts references from publications, and tries to find the corresponding Digital Object Identifier (DOI). Linkitup feeds the enriched metadata back as links to the original article in the repository, but also builds a RDF representation of the metadata that can be downloaded separately, or published as research output in its own right. In this paper, we compare Linkitup to the standard workflow of publishing linked data, and show that it significantly lowers the threshold for publishing linked research data.

1 Introduction

Researchers are increasingly faced with the requirement to both archive and share their data in a sustainable way. For example, in 2011, the US National Science Foundation began requiring data management plans for all proposals it considers.[1] Neelie Kroes, European Commission Vice-President for the Digital Agenda, has called for open access scientific results and data.[2] However, making data available in a sustainable way is still a difficult hurdle for many researchers [15]. Secondly, even though in some domains sharing research data has been shown to correlate with increased citation rate [13], this increased impact is hampered by a lack of rich, machine interpretable metadata for data publications.

To address the gap in data sharing and archival, a number of *repository services* have been created to help researchers. Examples include Dryad[3], Dataverse[4], and Figshare[5]. These services are adopted as recommended practice by a variety of journals including PLoS and Nature. Good metadata plays an essential role in the proper attribution and discoverability of publications: it explicates

---

[1] See http://www.nsf.gov/bfa/dias/policy/dmp.jsp.
[2] http://europa.eu/rapid/press-release_SPEECH-13-236_en.htm
[3] http://datadryad.org
[4] http://thedata.org
[5] http://figshare.com

© Springer International Publishing Switzerland 2014
V. Presutti et al. (Eds.): SemWebEval 2014, CCIS 475, pp. 95–100, 2014.
DOI: 10.1007/978-3-319-12024-9_12

information that is often hard to glean from the publication itself. It is widely recognized that Linked Data technology is the most likely candidate to offer this functionality.[6] The web-based architecture of Linked Data, combined with the *reuse* of identifiers across descriptions, allows it to form a semantic network that can span across any number of data repositories. Any reuse of an identifier between the description of two datasets forms a bridge that automatically *links* the datasets together.

Unfortunately, existing data repositories do not cater for the generation of Linked Data. And exposing data as Linked Data is even more difficult for individual researchers. Linked Data publication is too *complicated* and too *unreliable*. We address these problems through *Linkitup*, a web-based dashboard that leverages existing repository services (currently Figshare.com) to facilitate the publication of Linked Data. Linkitup helps users find and create links from their data to a variety of existing resources and exposes those links as Linked Data with associated provenance information. We publish the Linked Data produced through Linkitup as a separate data publication within the archive.

Related Work. Data management, archival and sharing has become an increasingly important topic as data sets have grown and many sciences have become more computational in nature [1]. A particular important motivation for scientific data archival and sharing has been the requirement for reproducibility in science [12]. Freire et al. highlight the challenges for reproducibility in computational systems [3]. Systems such as Share [7] and many workflow systems [2] provide mechanisms for reproducing computational science based on shared data [6]. To facilitate data sharing and archival, many data repositories have been created.[7] There is a long history of domain specific data repositories as well as nationally sponsored data repositories. A key aspect of these is that they aim to provide long term hosting and curation of data [11]. Data preparation forms the bulk of work done in scientific workflows [4]. Metadata and semantics is seen as key for leveraging scientific data [8]. A number of disciplines use Semantic Web and Linked Data for sharing data [16].[8] The closest work with respect to ours is the work from Gil et al. on Organic Data Publishing [5]. Like our proposal, this work calls for the use of web environments and semantic standards to ease the scientific data sharing process. A key difference is that our work leverages existing repository services, not semantic wikis, and is focused primarily on link creation rather than data curation.

This paper presents the design and implementation of Linkitup and discusses the benefits with respect to Linked Data publication [10].

2 Linkitup

Linkitup is a Web-based dashboard for interacting with a Figshare "article" and the metadata that is already associated with it. A Figshare "article" can be anything from figures, datasets, media files, papers and posters to sets of files.

---

[6] See http://www.w3.org/DesignIssues/LinkedData.html.
[7] See http://databib.org for a comprehensive listing.
[8] See also, http://www.neuinfo.org/ and http://data.nature.com.

Users can quickly find and select an article to enrich through the article list (top left in Fig. 1). All article details are retrieved directly through the Figshare.com API.[9] Linkitup currently does not support publication and enrichment services independently from Figshare, but the two platforms work together seamlessly.

Fig. 1. The Linkitup dashboard interface

Figure 1 shows a screenshot of the Linkitup dashboard for a paper about a prototype system for clinical decision support. The standard Figshare metadata is shown on the right ("Article Details"), and linking services are accessible on the left ("Plugins"). As mentioned in the introduction, the Figshare metadata is *internal* to that service. Linking services essentially tie Figshare specific identifiers to Linked Data URIs. A verbatim Linked Data version of the Figshare metadata may use the right format, but does not reuse existing URIs, and therefore does not *link* to any other datasets or descriptions thereof. The linking services are separate modules that implement the interaction between an article's metadata, and third party services.

A plugin typically uses a selection of article metadata (tags, categories, authors) to query a remote service, and returns a list of candidate matches. The results are rendered to a dialog using a *standard* UI template. This allows users to select links they deem correct using an interface that is independent of the plugin used. Crucial in this process is that the *user* is in control of which

---

[9] See http://api.figshare.com.

links are added to the dataset. Figure 1 shows candidate links from our paper to DBPedia; selected links lit up in green. The DBPedia plugin retrieves the URIs of resources from DBPedia for which the label matches that of any *tag* or *category* associated with the article through Figshare. At the time of writing, Linkitup is equipped with nine plugins that serve to demonstrate the range of services we can connect to. Four plugins call a REST service, three use a SPARQL endpoint, one uses a custom scraper and one is based on the *content* of the Figshare article (Table 1).

Table 1. Overview of Linkitup plugins

Name	Service	Source	Links to
Elsevier LDR	REST	Tags & Categories	Funding agencies
ORCID	REST	Authors	ORCID Author IDs
NIF Registry	REST	Tags & Categories	Datasets
LinkedLifeData	REST	Tags & Categories	Entities & Concepts
DBPedia	SPARQL	Tags & Categories	Entities & Concepts
DBLP	SPARQL	Authors	Authors
NeuroLex	SPARQL	Tags & Categories	Concepts
DANS EASY	Custom	Tags & Categories	Datasets
Crossref	Custom	Citations	DOIs

Linkitup publishes the results of the enrichment process in two ways: (1) the *links* section of the original article on Figshare is updated with the newly found links to external resources, and (2) it generates a Linked Data representation of all metadata as a *nanopublication* [14] that is made available both as separate article on Figshare, and to a triple store. Since Linkitup nanopublications are essentially *annotations* of other publications, we intermix the nanopublication format with both PROV [9] and the Open Annotation (OA) specification.[10] All PROV and Open Annotation statements are contained in the *provenance* part of the publication. Users can inspect the provenance trace of their enrichment process through a visualization provided by the PROV-O-Viz tool.[11]

Linkitup transforms the process of publishing linked research data by *hiding* the underlying technology. Technology hiding allows researchers to enrich their data without having to go through the steps typically associated with linked data publishing. From the Linked Data Handbook [10, Chap. 4], we identify six

---

[10] The Open Annotation model is defined by the W3C Open Annotation community group, and is subject to change. Linkitup uses the community draft of February 2013, http://www.openannotation.org/spec/core/20130208/index.html.

[11] http://provoviz.org

considerations in the publishing chain: decide how to *mint Cool URIs*, decide on *triples to include* in the description of a resource, *describe the dataset* itself, choose appropriate *vocabularies*, if necessary define additional *terms*, and *make links* to and from external data sources. Linkitup facilitates all six steps: (1) Linkitup uses its own slash-based URI scheme for minting URIs. (2) It hosts Linked Data through an adapted Pubby[12] interface that returns an HTML description of the resource that contains both *incoming* and *outgoing* links. (3) Linkitup describes each dataset in terms of what it *is* about, e.g. using the 'voiD' vocabulary,[13] how it *came* about, using the PROV vocabulary, and how it can be *used* in terms of licensing, waivers and norms. (4 + 5) Linkitup uses a small selection of well known vocabularies for publishing enriched data (DCTerms, FOAF, SKOS, PROV, OA and Nanopub). And (6), every Linkitup plugin tries to put the Figshare article into context by mapping its rudimentary metadata to richer descriptions from (linked) data sets. These plugins – and thus data sets – represent the *external linking targets* described in [10, Sect. 4.3]: Linkitup takes care of identifying and selecting appropriate targets for linking research data.

3   Conclusion

In this paper, we described Linkitup, a dashboard that enables the discovery and publication of linked research data by leveraging an existing repository service. Importantly, Linkitup provides crucial benefits over existing Linked Data publication practices in terms of easy of use (technology hiding) and persistence (i.e. relying on the archives guarantees). Going forward, are working to expand the integration of Linkitup with other commonly used services, e.g. by publishing directly from Dropbox into Figshare via Linkitup, and by supporting other repositories (e.g. DANS EASY).

We already have a prototype implementation to that effect that analyzes, extracts and visualizes information from the data along the way.[14] Additionally, we will expand the number of services that Linkitup supports, in particular, through deeper content analysis. Finally, we aim to provide richer notifications to let users track how their data is being interlinked. While Linkitup is focused on science, it also serves as a model for the integration of user facing Web 2.0 services with Linked Data publication, which potentially help us build a richer Web of Data.

Acknowledgments. This publication was supported by the Dutch national program COMMIT.

---

[12] Pubby is a standard front end for triple stores, see http://github.com/cygri/Pubby.

[13] voiD: vocabulary of interlinked datasets, see http://www.w3.org/TR/void/.

[14] See http://data2semantics.github.io.

References

1. Akil, H., Martone, M.E., Van Essen, D.C.: Challenges and opportunities in mining neuroscience data. Science **331**(6018), 708–712 (2011)
2. Deelman, E., Gannon, D., Shields, M., Taylor, I.: Workflows and e-science: an overview of workflow system features and capabilities. Future Gener. Comput. Syst. **25**(5), 528–540 (2009)
3. Freire, J., Bonnet, P., Shasha, D.: Computational reproducibility: state-of-the-art, challenges, and database research opportunities. In: Proceedings of the 2012 International Conference on Management of Data, pp. 593–596. ACM (2012)
4. Garijo, D., Alper, P., Belhajjame, K., Corcho, O., Gil, Y., Goble, C.: Common motifs in scientific workflows: an empirical analysis. In: 8th IEEE International Conference on eScience, USA. IEEE Computer Society Press (2012)
5. Gil, Y., Ratnakar, V., Hanson, P.C.: Organic data publishing: a novel approach to scientific data sharing. In: Kauppinen, T., Pouchard, L.C., Keßler, C. (eds.) LISC, vol. 783. CEUR Workshop Proceedings. CEUR-WS.org (2012)
6. Goble, C., Stevens, R., Hull, D., Wolstencroft, K., Lopez, R.: Data curation + process curation=data integration + science. Brief. Bioinform. **9**(6), 506–517 (2008)
7. Pieter Van Gorp and Steffen Mazanek. Share: a web portal for creating and sharing executable research papers. Procedia Comput. Sci. **4**, 589–597 (2011). Proceedings of the International Conference on Computational Science, ICCS (2011)
8. Gray, J., Liu, D.T., Nieto-Santisteban, M.A., Szalay, A.S., DeWitt, D.J., Heber, G.: Scientific data management in the coming decade. CoRR, abs/cs/0502008 (2005)
9. Groth, P., Moreau, L.: PROV-Overview: An Overview of the PROV Family of Documents. Working group note, W3C, April 2013. http://www.w3.org/TR/2013/NOTE-prov-overview-20130430/. Latest version available at http://www.w3.org/TR/prov-overview/
10. Heath, T., Bizer, C.: Linked Data: Evolving the Web into a Global Data Space. Synthesis Lectures on the Semantic Web: Theory and Technology. Morgan & Claypool, San Rafael (2011)
11. Marcial, L.H., Hemminger, B.M.: Scientific data repositories on the web: an initial survey. J. Am. Soc. Inf. Sci. Technol. **61**(10), 2029–2048 (2010)
12. Mesirov, J.P.: Accessible reproducible research. Science **327**(5964), 415–416 (2010)
13. Piwowar, H.A., Day, R.S., Fridsma, D.B.: Sharing detailed research data is associated with increased citation rate. PLoS ONE **2**(3), e308 (2007)
14. Schultes, E., Chistester, C., Burger, K., Groth, P., Kotoulas, S., Loizou, A., Tkachenko, V., Waagmeester, A., Askjaer, S., Pettifer, S., Harland, L., Haupt, C., Batchelor, C., Vazquez, M., Fernandez, J.M., Saito, J., Gibson, A., Wich, L.: The Open PHACTS nanopublication guidelines. Technical report, March 2012
15. Tenopir, C., Allard, S., Douglass, K., Aydinoglu, A.U., Wu, L., Read, E., Manoff, M., Frame, M.: Data sharing by scientists: practices and perceptions. PLoS ONE **6**(6), e21101 (2011)
16. Wolstencroft, K., Owen, S., du Preez, F., Krebs, O., Mueller, W., Goble, C., Snoep, J.L.: The seek: a platform for sharing data and models in systems biology. In: Methods in Systems Biology, vol. 500. Methods in Enzymology, pp. 629–655. Academic Press (2011)

Understanding Research Dynamics

Francesco Osborne[(✉)] and Enrico Motta

Knowledge Media Institute, The Open University,
Milton Keynes MK7 6AA, UK
{francesco.osborne, e.motta}@open.ac.uk

Abstract. Rexplore leverages novel solutions in data mining, semantic technologies and visual analytics, and provides an innovative environment for exploring and making sense of scholarly data. Rexplore allows users: (1) to detect and make sense of important trends in research; (2) to identify a variety of interesting relations between researchers, beyond the standard co-authorship relations provided by most other systems; (3) to perform fine-grained expert search with respect to detailed multi-dimensional parameters; (4) to detect and characterize the dynamics of interesting communities of researchers, identified on the basis of shared research interests and scientific trajectories; (5) to analyse research performance at different levels of abstraction, including individual researchers, organizations, countries, and research communities.

Keywords: Scholarly data · Visual analytics · Data exploration · Semantic Web · Semantic technologies · Ontology population · Data mining · Data Integration

1 Introduction

Understanding what goes on in a research area is a complex sensemaking process, which requires exploring information about a variety of entities, such as publications, publication venues, researchers, research communities, events and others, as well as understanding their relationships.

Many currently available tools already provide a variety of functionalities for the exploration of research data. These include bibliographic search engines (e.g., Microsoft Academic Search, Google Scholar), large research databases (e.g., Sciverse Scopus, PubMed), visual analytics tools (e.g., CiteSpace [1]), tools which focus on mining and visualizing relations between researchers (e.g., Arnetminer [2]), and others. These tools however usually miss a number of important functionalities, such as the ability (i) to investigate research trends effectively at different levels of granularity, (ii) to relate authors 'semantically' (e.g., in terms of common interests or shared academic trajectories), (iii) to detect dynamically-characterized research communities (e.g., all researchers working on RDF) and relate them to other entities (e.g., universities, countries, or specific authors), and (iv) to perform fine-grained academic expert search along multiple dimensions. Moreover, while some specific tools may address one or two of the aforementioned functionalities, there is still the need for an integrated solution [3], where the different functionalities and visualizations are provided in a

© Springer International Publishing Switzerland 2014
V. Presutti et al. (Eds.): SemWebEval 2014, CCIS 475, pp. 101–107, 2014.
DOI: 10.1007/978-3-319-12024-9_13

coherent manner, through an environment able to support a seamless navigation between different views, interfaces and entities.

Another important limitation of current tools is their lack of semantic characterization of important entities, such as research areas. Most of the tools use keywords as proxies for research areas [2]; however the keywords associated to academic publications lack structure and are often noisy [4]. Important relations between research areas, such as an area being a sub-area of another one, are neglected: for example, when a user search for papers about "Semantic Web", these systems will ignore the publications tagged only as "Linked Data". Semantic technologies can solve this problem, by allowing for a formal definition of research topics and their relationships.

2   Overview of Rexplore

To address the limitations discussed above, we developed Rexplore [5], a system which leverages novel solutions in data mining, semantic technologies and visual analytics, and provides an innovative environment for exploring and making sense of scholarly data[1]. The back-end of Rexplore is implemented in PHP and Java, while the interface and the visualizations are in HTML5 and JavaScript.

In this short overview we will discuss some of the main features of Rexplore.

Data Integration. Rexplore integrates a variety of data sources in different formats, including: the MAS API[2], DBLP++[3] and DBpedia[4]. The process of generating the populated topic ontology, described in the next subsection, exploits information collected from Google Scholar, EventSeer[5] and Wikipedia.

Rexplore implements also a disambiguation module, which uses a number of features (e.g., co-authorships, topic similarity) to assign each publication to the correct authors. The integration and disambiguation process for the organizations makes use of Linked Open Data and in particular tries to map each organization and location to a DBpedia entity. Rexplore can integrate paper metadata in XML, RDF and SQL, but not yet extract data from PDF. The minimal metadata needed for a paper to be included in Rexplore are the title, the names of the authors and the year. As of June 2014, Rexplore contains 23 million papers and 2.3 million authors.

Topic Ontology and Klink. While most systems use keywords as proxies for research topics, Rexplore relies on an OWL ontology, which characterizes research areas and their relationships. This ontology is automatically populated and periodically updated by Klink [4], an algorithm that uses statistical and machine learning techniques (1) to identify research areas from the given set of keywords, filtering out keywords that do not denote research areas (e.g., "Case Study" or "Large Scale"), (2) to compute three

---

[1] http://technologies.kmi.open.ac.uk/rexplore

[2] http://academic.research.microsoft.com

[3] http://dblp.l3s.de/dblp++.php

[4] http://dbpedia.org

[5] http://eventseer.net

types of semantic relationships between topics and (3) to return a fully populated OWL ontology describing the topic domain.

The three semantic relationships detected by Klink are (1) *skos:broaderGeneric* (topics T_1 is a sub-area of topic T_2; e.g., "Linked Data" is a sub-area of "Semantic Web"), (2) *contributesTo* (research in topic T_1 is an important contribution to research in topic T_2, however T_1 is not a sub-topic of T_2; e.g., "Ontology Engineering" contributes to "Semantic Web"), and (3) *relatedEquivalent* (T_1 is equivalent to topic T_2; e.g., "Ontology Matching" is equivalent to "Ontology Alignment"). Klink has been tested mainly on Computer Science, but we plan to evaluate it soon on other fields. The returned topic ontology is used in a variety of ways, e.g., for rewriting queries by taking in consideration topic relationships, for analysing authors' trends at different levels of granularity, and for enhancing the community detection algorithm.

Semantic Topic Analysis. A simple but effective method to take advantage of the OWL knowledge base is to consider every publication tagged with topic T_1 to be also about topic T_2, if T_2 is *broaderGeneric* than T_1, or *relatedEquivalent* to T_1 (it should be noted that *broaderGeneric* is transitive). This has a dramatic effect on the quality and size of data available for each topic: for example, our knowledge base includes 11,998 publications tagged with the *string* "Semantic Web", while the publications regarding the *topic* "Semantic Web" (including sub-topics, such as "Linked Data") are almost twice as many (22,143).

For analysing a topic, Rexplore provides an interface that includes: (i) general information about the topic, e.g., the relevant authors and publications, (ii) the *topic navigator,* an interface to browse topics via their semantic connections, (iii) visual analytics on *broaderGeneric* and *contributesTo* topics, (iv) visual analytics on authors' migration patterns, (v) a graph view to explore the research communities active in the topic and their relationships with authors, countries and organizations. For a given topic, Rexplore allows users to visualize on a timeline three kinds of trends: publication trends, author trends and migration trends. The first two provide a concise view of the number of publications and the number of researchers working on the topic over time. The latter illustrate the number of estimated migrations between two topics and it is computed by analysing the degree of shifting in authors' interest. More information on how Rexplore handles topic trends can be found in [6].

Multi-criteria Search. Rexplore offers a fine-grained search functionality for authors, publications and organizations with respect to detailed multi-dimensional parameters. For example, authors can be filtered by (i) name or part of it, (ii) career age (i.e., the time from the first published work), (iii) topics of interest, (iv) venues in which they have published and (v) country/organization. Both venue and topic fields accept multiple values, which can be combined using logical connectives. Moreover, the search interface is enhanced by the *graph view*, which shows the connections of query results with other entities. Hence, the search results can be further refined, explored or filtered by considering their connections. This solution allows building with a few clicks complex queries such as "the career young co-authors (with expertise in Machine Learning) of the prominent researchers in Semantic Web and Data Mining who work for a UK institution". Rexplore also supports the subsequent data exploration by remembering the initial queries and highlighting the related concepts in the following pages. For example, if the user searches for "authors with expertise in Semantic Web who published in ESWC", the system will highlight the research area and the venue in the following views.

The Graph View. The *graph view* is a highly interactive tool to explore the space of research entities and their relationships using faceted filters. It takes as input authors, organizations, countries or research communities and generates their relationship graph, allowing the user to choose among a variety of connections, ranking criteria, views and filters. Entities, represented by nodes, and connections, represented by links, can be clicked on to obtain additional information. The dimensions of the nodes are proportional to the metric chosen by the user, e.g. if the user chooses "citations in Artificial Intelligence" the entities with more citations in this topic will be the biggest.

Users can choose from four types of relations: co-publication, co-citation, topic similarity and temporal topic similarity. The topic similarity reflects how similar two authors are with respect to their research areas and takes advantage of the topic ontology generated by Klink. The temporal topic similarity (TTS) (see [4, 7]) builds on the topic similarity and makes possible the identification of researchers who worked on similar semantic topics at the same time. Both the nodes and the relationships can be filtered by a variety of parameters. For example, the user can visualize only the collaboration in the field of "Ontology Matching" with career young researchers who published in ESWC.

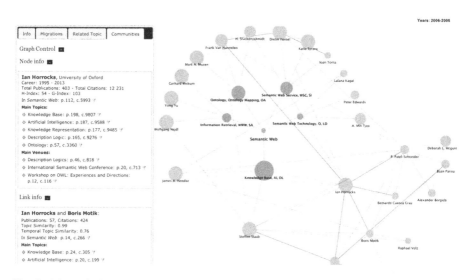

Fig. 1. The main Semantic Web communities in 2006–2008 and some of their most significant authors.

Community Detection. Rexplore integrates a novel algorithm called *TST* [7] (*Temporal Semantic Topic-Based Clustering*), which exploits the TTS to identify communities of researchers who appear to follow a similar *research trajectory*. Technically this is achieved by running a Fuzzy C-Mean algorithm, which uses as norm a variation of the *temporal topic similarity* metric, applied to distributions of semantic topics over time, associated with each researcher.

The communities produced by the TST algorithm have some very interesting features. First, they are not snapshots of static collaborations, but rather they are diachronic entities, with topic distributions and interests evolving over time, mirroring trends, technological breakthroughs and new visions. Hence, they allow users to make sense of the dynamics of the research world – e.g., migrations of researchers from one topic to another, new communities being spawn by older ones, shifts of interests, communities splitting, merging, ceasing to exist, etc. Secondly, in contrast with methods that rely on co-authorship or citation networks, their computation does not require a complete graph of relations between community members. Finally, since they are fuzzy clusters, they can address the common situation in which a researcher is active in more than one community. For a full description of TST see [7].

Rexplore relies on TST to detect the communities within a certain *broad topic* (e.g., Semantic Web) and offers a graph view in the topic page to explore their most significant authors and organizations. Hence, it makes it easy to gain an immediate knowledge about the main dynamics of a research area. For example, Fig. 1 shows the top 5 sub-communities in the Semantic Web area in the interval 2006-2008 (shown as first level nodes in the graph view): Knowledge Base/AI/Description Logic, Ontology/Ontology Matching, Information Retrieval/WWW, Semantic Web Service/ Semantic Interoperability and Semantic Web Technology/Linked Data. Here the user has chosen to visualize some of the most significant researchers of each community and is exploring the co-authors of Ian Horrocks, which is one of protagonists of the "Knowledge Base/AI/Description Logic" community. Links in the graph view can also be inspected and Fig. 1 also shows additional details about the academic connections between Ian Horrocks and Boris Motik.

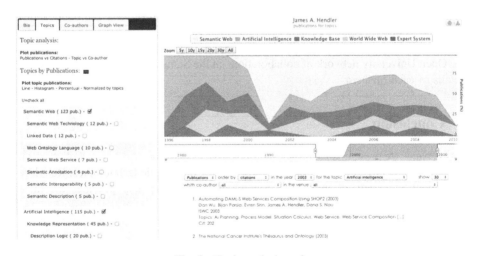

Fig. 2. Topic analysis tool.

Author and Group Analysis. Every author in Rexplore has a personal page which offers a variety of metrics and visualizations to analyse the authors' performance, trends and collaborations. One of the most useful features is the topic analysis tool, which allows users to plot on a timeline the performance of an author in different research areas. Figure 2 shows a view of this tool displaying the main topics of the publications by James Hendler, one of the originators of Semantic Web. On the left the user can select the kind of chart and the topics to be shown. The chart is interactive and the user can click on it to visualize the list of publications relative to a year and a topic. For example, Fig. 2 shows the publications of James Hendler on "Artificial Intelligence" in 2003. The publication list can be further refined by selecting additional filters, such as the co-author and the venue.

By default, Rexplore selects the more general topics (e.g., "Semantic Web" rather than "Linked Data") to show the big picture of the author's interests and how they evolved in time. However the topics and sub-topics are displayed in a multilevel list and the user can choose to adopt different granularity levels. For example a user can conduct a high level analysis by focusing on the main topics (e.g., "Artificial Intelligence" or "Ontology") or otherwise zoom in on one of them (e.g., "Ontology") and further analyse its sub-topics (e.g., "Ontology Engineering", "Ontology Mapping", "Ontology Learning"). Citations and publications can also be normalized according to the average citation numbers of the considered topics, allowing users to easily compare researchers from different disciplines (e.g., Biology and Mathematics). The topic analysis tool can also compare a researcher with those working in the same field or having similar seniority or coming from a specific country/organisation. For example, it can be used to check how a career young researcher from UK working in "Machine Learning" ranks in term of a certain metric (e.g., H-Index) among the researchers with the same characteristics.

Authors' groups, which can be organizations, countries or research communities, have a simpler interface at the moment. It is possible to study the trends of a group in terms of publications and citations and to browse the main researchers and publications by years. Moreover, the user can rely on the graph view to explore the connections of a group with significant authors or with other groups. For example, it is possible to plot the Open University network of collaborations in the Semantic Web and to explore the details of each of them.

3   Conclusion

In this paper we presented Rexplore, an innovative system for exploring scholarly data, which relies on advanced data mining algorithms and semantic technologies. Rexplore implements a variety of innovative functionalities and arguably provides the most advanced solution currently available.

References

1. Chen, C.: CiteSpace II: detecting and visualizing emerging trends and transient patterns in scientific literature. J. Am. Soc. Inf. Sci. Technol. **57**(3), 359–377 (2006)
2. Tang, J., Zhang, J., Yao, L., Li, J., Zhang, L., Su, Z.: ArnetMiner: extraction and mining of academic social networks. In: Proceeding of the 14th International Conference on Knowledge Discovery and Data Mining, pp. 990–998 (2008)
3. Dunne, C., Shneiderman, B., Gove, R., Klavans, J., Dorr, B.: Rapid understanding of scientific paper collections: integrating statistics, text analytics, and visualization. J. Am. Soc. Inf. Sci. Technol. **63**(12), 2351–2369 (2012)
4. Osborne, F., Motta, E.: Mining semantic relations between research areas. In: Cudré-Mauroux, P., et al. (eds.) ISWC 2012, Part I. LNCS, vol. 7649, pp. 410–426. Springer, Heidelberg (2012)
5. Osborne, F., Motta, E., Mulholland, P.: Exploring scholarly data with rexplore. In: Alani, H., et al. (eds.) ISWC 2013, Part I. LNCS, vol. 8218, pp. 460–477. Springer, Heidelberg (2013)
6. Osborne, F., Motta, E.: Exploring research trends with Rexplore. D-Lib Mag. **19**(9/10), 4 (2013)
7. Osborne, F., Scavo, G., Motta, E.: Identifying diachronic topic-based research communities by clustering shared research trajectories. In: Presutti, V., d'Amato, C., Gandon, F., d'Aquin, M., Staab, S., Tordai, A. (eds.) ESWC 2014. LNCS, vol. 8465, pp. 114–129. Springer, Heidelberg (2014)

Semantic Facets for Scientific Information Retrieval

Iana Atanassova$^{(\boxtimes)}$ and Marc Bertin

CIRST, Université du Québec à Montréal, Succ. Centre-ville, B.P. 8888, Montreal,
QC H3C 3P8, Canada
`iana.atanassova@nlp-labs.org, bertin.marc@courrier.uqam.ca`

Abstract. We present an Information Retrieval System for scientific publications that provides the possibility to filter results according to semantic facets. We use sentence-level semantic annotations that identify specific semantic relations in texts, such as methods, definitions, hypotheses, that correspond to common information needs related to scientific literature. The semantic annotations are obtained using a rule-based method that identifies linguistic clues organized into a linguistic ontology. The system is implemented using Solr Search Server and offers efficient search and navigation in scientific papers.

Keywords: Semantic annotation · Information retrieval · Faceted search · Semantic facets · Solr

1 Introduction

Today, the emergence of open science leads to the greater availability of scientific papers in full text. The ever larger volume of textual data provided fosters the development of new tools to explore the content of research papers. This problem has been studied from the point of view of the development of annotation frameworks for scientific papers [6,10]. Furthermore, the exploitation of this kind of annotations for information retrieval has been the object of many papers (e.g. [4,8]) and the extraction of key-phrases from scientific articles (see [11]) is a closely related subject.

In this paper, we describe a search engine that uses annotations related to a set of semantic categories as semantic facets in order to filter relevant information in scientific papers. The idea is to automatically identify specific discourse categories in the publications' content and make them directly accessible for the user to enhance text navigation and search. The goal of the development of semantic facets for information retrieval is to reduce the mental workload of users in the production of mental representations of documents in order to identify relevant information. This point of view has been discussed by Bertin and Atanassova [1].

© Springer International Publishing Switzerland 2014
V. Presutti et al. (Eds.): SemWebEval 2014, CCIS 475, pp. 108–113, 2014.
DOI: 10.1007/978-3-319-12024-9_14

Table 1. Dataset - PLOS journals

Journal	Number of articles	Number of sentences
PLOS Biology	2,965	426,522
PLOS Computational Biology	2,107	518,289
PLOS Genetics	2,560	566,323
PLOS Medicine	2,228	218,459
PLOS Neglected Tropical Diseases	1,366	217,861
PLOS Pathogens	2,354	514,751
PLOS ONE	33,782	6,080,566
Total	*47,362*	*8,542,771*

2   Semantic Annotation

For this study, we have processed research articles from seven journals, published by the Public Library of Science (PLOS) and available in Open Access. The articles are in the XML format, structured using the Journal Article Tag Suite (JATS), which provides the complete metadata and the full-text body of the articles. The sections and paragraphs in the text are represented as separate elements. We have processed the entire set of research articles of these journals up to September/October 2012. Table 1 presents the number of articles and sentences processed for each journal.

Metadata fields, such as titles, authors, abstract, journal and subject, are extracted from the XML documents. Additionally, we extract all the bibliographic data, i.e. the list of references in the bibliography, and locate the text segments where these references are cited in the text. Thus we are able to provide in the user interface counters for the number of references and in-text citations for each article, as well as pointers to the in-text citations of each reference.

We consider sentences as the basic textual unit in our processing. Our goal is to provide semantic annotations of some of the sentences and to do this we have identified a set of categories corresponding to common information needs in the context of scientific information retrieval. The semantic categories assigned to the annotated sentences can be then used to implement faceted semantic search functionalities combined with classical key-word information retrieval. Faceted search allows the user to visualize multiple categories and to filter the results according to these categories.

We segment all the paragraphs in the dataset into sentences. The segmentation process, based on the analysis of the punctuation and capitalization of the text, has already been discussed in several publications and the detailed results of the segmentation of this dataset has been given in Bertin et al. [3], using a method proposed by Mourad [7].

Our linguistic resources are based on the Contextual Exploration (CE) method described in Descles [5]. This method carries out the automatic semantic annotation of text segments for a given annotation task, such as the identification and classification of citations, the extraction of segments for summarization and the identification of specific semantic categories such as definitions, hypotheses, etc. The CE method is a decision-making procedure, presented in the form of a set of rules and linguistic clues that trigger the application of the rules. The semantic categories and the linguistic clues are organized in linguistic ontologies that correspond to the annotation tasks.

We have annotated the sentences in our corpus with a set of categories that correspond to common semantic relations expressed in scientific articles:

result: sentences that express a result obtained by the paper or by cited papers.

summarize: sentences that summarize a method, a paper, etc. typically found in the results and discussion sections.

scientific monitoring: sentences that express facts and speculations that are important for the monitoring of innovation and new results.

definition: sentences that express definitions given by the paper or by cited papers.

conclusion: sentences that express the conclusion of a paper.

controversy: sentences that express controversies, diverging opinions, etc.

agreement: sentences that express agreement in the methods, results, etc. of a paper and of cited papers.

opinion: sentences that express opinions of the authors of a paper.

The eight semantic categories are not equally represented in the corpus. Figure 1 presents the relative percentage of sentences annotated by each semantic category. The majority of annotated sentences were categorized as *result, summarize* and *scientific monitoring*, and these three categories account for more than 75 % of the annotations. The categories expressing opinions and subjective

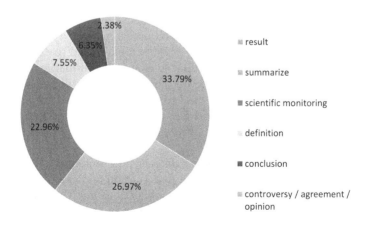

Fig. 1. Annotations by semantic category

Table 2. Semantic annotations

Journal	Articles with annotations	Annotated sentences
PLOS Biology	1,157	1,654
PLOS Computational Biology	1,440	2,782
PLOS Genetics	1,644	2,428
PLOS Medicine	635	778
PLOS Neglected Tropical Diseases	590	752
PLOS Pathogens	1,459	2,408
PLOS ONE	18,419	26,855
Total	*25,344*	*37,657*

evaluations of previous research, *controversy*, *agreement* and *opinion*, are less frequent in the corpus (about 2.4 % of the annotated sentences), as could be expected for scientific writing.

Table 2 presents the number of articles containing annotations and the number of annotated sentences. We have not evaluated the annotations for this dataset. Previous works [2] have provided evaluations of the annotation methodology working on other datasets and have obtained rather high precision values. The annotations can be converted into Linked Data using machine-readable RDF for interoperability with other tools. Our results can be used to provide an annotated corpus for the development of other approaches, for example using name-spaces and already existing vocabularies such as SPAR and DoCO [9].

3   Semantic Search Engine

We have implemented a semantic search engine using Apache Solr Search Server. The annotated XML documents were indexed using XSLT import handles. Solr uses the Lucene Java search library for full-text indexing and search. We have indexed both the articles and the sentences as two different document types that are linked in Solr's index. All annotated sentences were indexed together with their annotation categories and with their immediate context (previous and next sentence).

The search interface provides search on two levels, documents and sentences. On each level, the semantic annotations are visible and can be used as facets in order to filter the results. The initial result list is obtained by keyword search. Classical query syntax (use of *, AND, OR, etc.) is supported by Solr's query parser.

On the document level, the user has access to the list of relevant papers. Each paper is presented by its metadata. Two new types of information are given compared to classical document search: the annotations in the paper (categories

Fig. 2. Semantic search interface - sentence level search

and sentences extracted from the document) and some statistics about the article (numbers of references, number of in-text citations, etc.).

On the sentence level, as shown on Fig. 2, the search results are given as a list of annotated sentences in their contexts (previous and next sentence in the same paragraph). A sentence is considered as relevant if it contains the keywords and is annotated with one of the semantic categories that the used has selected as filters. For each sentence, the interface provides additional information for its position in the paper (the first number that appears in a red bullet), its position in the section and the bibliographic information of the paper.

The interface is available on http://sempub2014.nlp-labs.org/task3/.

4   Discussion and Conclusion

The semantic facets that we propose enable the user to filter the results according to a set of semantic categories. The annotations that generate the semantic facets are obtained using resources, such as linguistic clues and rules, and can be viewed as complex query patterns that, combined with keyword search, allow the user to access specific types of information in scientific papers. Thus, the semantic facets provide the possibility to identify highly relevant sentences among the results of keyword search. Furthermore, the automatic semantic annotation approach also allows the generation of Linked Open Data in order to propose semantic resources that can be used by different systems for the purpose of scientific knowledge extraction.

Our demonstrator presents a first implementation of an information retrieval system using semantic facets on the sentence level. This approach provides a new way to navigate in scientific papers and access relevant information. Further improvements can be made in the segmentation and annotation processing. This online version is an early prototype and our goal is to develop other semantic categories and facets related to scientific articles.

Acknowledgments. We thank Benoît Macaluso of the Observatoire des Sciences et des Technologies (OST), Montreal, Canada, for harvesting and providing the PLOS dataset.

References

1. Bertin, M., Atanassova, I.: Semantic enrichment of scientific publications and metadata : citation analysis through contextual and cognitive analysis. In: Proceedings of the 1st International Workshop on Mining Scientific Publications, in Conjunction with Joint Conference on Digital Libraries JCDL-2012. ACM/IEEE (2012)
2. Bertin, M., Atanassova, I., Desclés, J.P.: Automatic analysis of author judgment in scientific articles based on semantic annotation. In: Proceedings of the 22nd International Florida Artificial Intelligence, Research Society Conference, Sanibel Island, Florida. pp. 19–21 (2009)
3. Bertin, M., Atanassova, I., Lariviere, V., Gingras, Y.: The distribution of references in scientific papers: an analysis of the IMRaD structure. In: 14th International Society of Scientometrics and Informetrics Conference, pp. 591–603. International Society for Informetrics and Sciento (2013)
4. Buscaldi, D., Zargayouna, H.: Yasemir: yet another semantic information retrieval system. In: Proceedings of the Sixth International Workshop on Exploiting Semantic Annotations in Information Retrieval, pp. 13–16. ACM (2013)
5. Desclés, J.P.: Contextual exploration processing for discourse and automatic annotations of texts. In: FLAIRS Conference, pp. 281–284 (2006)
6. Liakata, M., Thompson, P., de Waard, A., Nawaz, R., Maat, H.P., Ananiadou, S.: A three-way perspective on scientific discourse annotation for knowledge extraction. In: Proceedings of the Workshop on Detecting Structure in Scholarly Discourse, pp. 37–46. Association for Computational Linguistics (2012)
7. Mourad, G.: La segmentation de textes par exploration contextuelle automatique, présentation du module segatex. ISLsp, Inscription Spatiale du Langage : structure et processus IRIT, Université Paul Sabatier, Toulouse (2002)
8. Novacek, V., Groza, T., Handschuh, S., Decker, S.: Coraal - dive into publications, bathe in the knowledge. Web Semant. Sci. Serv. Agents World Wide Web **8**(2–3), 1–10 (2010)
9. Shotton, D., Peroni, S.: DoCO, the document components ontology (2011)
10. Teufel, S., Siddharthan, A., Tidhar, D.: Automatic classification of citation function. In: Proceedings of the 2006 Conference on Empirical Methods in Natural Language Processing, EMNLP '06, pp. 103–110. Association for Computational Linguistics, Stroudsburg, PA, USA (2006)
11. You, W., Fontaine, D., Barthès, J.P.: An automatic keyphrase extraction system for scientific documents. Knowl. Inf. Syst. **34**(3), 691–724 (2013)

Extraction and Semantic Annotation of Workshop Proceedings in HTML Using RML

Anastasia Dimou$^{(\boxtimes)}$, Miel Vander Sande, Pieter Colpaert, Laurens De Vocht, Ruben Verborgh, Erik Mannens, and Rik Van de Walle

Ghent University, iMinds, Multimedia Lab, Gent, Belgium
{anastasia.dimou,miel.vandersande,pieter.colpaert,
laurens.devocht,ruben.verborgh,erik.mannens,rik.vandewalle}@ugent.be

Abstract. Despite the significant number of existing tools, incorporating data into the Linked Open Data cloud remains complicated; hence discouraging data owners to publish their data as Linked Data. Unlocking the semantics of published data, even if they are not provided by the data owners, can contribute to surpass the barriers posed by the low availability of Linked Data and come closer to the realisation of the envisaged Semantic Web. RML, a generic mapping language based on an extension over R2RML, the W3C standard for mapping relational databases into RDF, offers a uniform way of defining the mapping rules for data in heterogeneous formats. In this paper, we present how we adjusted our prototype RML Processor, taking advantage of RML's scalability, to extract and map data of workshop proceedings published in HTML to the RDF data model for the Semantic Publishing Challenge needs.

1 Introduction

Data owners lack of incentives to publish their data in a format processable by Semantic Web clients, partly because incorporating data into the Linked Open Data still remains complicated. *Generic solutions* fail to efficiently support them, as it is impossible to predict every potential input, while *case-specific solutions*, in their turn, need individual investment and they are not reused at the end. Furthermore, most of the existing solutions are *source-specific*. Only few tools provide mappings from different source formats to RDF; but even those tools actually employ separate *source-centric approaches* for each of the supported formats. Thus, whenever a new need to map data from a source in an arbitrary format emerges, the whole implementation is developed from scratch.

The low availability of Linked Data, mainly caused by data owners who do not publish their data as Linked Data for different reasons, remains a barrier to the realisation of the Semantic Web. There are a lot of data published as Open Data but even more data are published on Web pages and only a few of them have any semantic annotations. Unlocking the semantics of this data is of high importance if we want to be able to query their content. Therefore, we need solutions that allow us easily to get the published data in RDF, even if the data providers do not publish them as such.

© Springer International Publishing Switzerland 2014
V. Presutti et al. (Eds.): SemWebEval 2014, CCIS 475, pp. 114–119, 2014.
DOI: 10.1007/978-3-319-12024-9_15

In an effort to address, among others, the aforementioned issues, we defined RML [3] in our previous works. In the frame of the Semantic Publishing challenge[1], selected computer science workshop proceedings published with the CEUR-WS.org open access service were mapped in RDF in order to answer more complicated queries related to the quality of the workshops. To address the challenge of semantically annotating the content of HTML pages, we exploited and proved RML's extensibility and flexibility. Our RML Processor implementation[2], which was configured so far to map data in CSV, XML and JSON formats, was extended further to support mapping of data in HTML to the RDF data model.

2   Related Work

Most of the proposed solutions for publishing data in HTML Web pages, rely on the page's DOM or on processing the HTML source as XML documents. A variety of solutions map data in valid XHTML[3] pages to RDF using Gleaning Resource Descriptions from Dialects of Languages (GRDDL) [2], such as Triplr[4]. GRDDL essentially provides the links, identified by URIs, to the transformations, typically represented in XS, that map the data to RDF. Other approaches chose alternative solutions, such as executing XQuery statements against the DOM of HTML pages [5].

Approaching (X)HTML pages as XML documents implies that they should be well-formed documents, as wrong syntax, misused labels, or any type of inconsistencies cause the entire mapping to fail. To deal with invalid HTML documents, Coetzee [1], for instance, balances the tags and validates the model before performing the mappings. However prior cleansing and *re-formatting* is not always possible, especially when performing mappings *on-the-fly*.

3   HTML to RDF Mappings with RML

The *RDF Mapping language* (RML)[5] is a generic language defined to express customized mapping rules from data in heterogeneous formats to the RDF data model [3]. RML is defined as a superset of the W3C-standardized mapping language R2RML, extending its applicability and broadening its scope. RML keeps the mapping definitions as in R2RML and follows the same syntax, providing a generic way of defining the mappings that is easily transferable to cover references to other data structures, combined with case-specific extensions. RML considers that sets of sources that all together describe a certain domain, can be mapped to RDF in a combined and uniform way, while the mapping definitions may be re-used across different sources that describe the same domain.

---

[1] http://2014.eswc-conferences.org/semantic-publishing-challenge

[2] https://github.com/mmlab/RMLProcessor

[3] http://www.w3.org/TR/xhtml11/

[4] http://triplr.org/

[5] http://rml.io

Structure of an RML Mapping

In RML, the mapping to the RDF data model is based on one or more Triples Maps. A Triples Map consists of three main parts: the Logical Source (rr:LogicalSource), the Subject Map and zero or more Predicate-Object Maps. The Subject Map (rr:SubjectMap) defines the rule that generates unique identifiers (URIs) for the resources which are mapped and is used as the subject of all the RDF triples that are generated from this Triples Map. A Predicate-Object Map consists of Predicate Maps, which define the rule that generates the triple's predicate and Object Maps or Referencing Object Maps, which defines the rule that generates the triple's object. The Subject Map, the Predicate Map and the Object Map are Term Maps, namely rules that generate an RDF term (an IRI, a blank node or a literal).

Leveraging HTML with RML

A Logical Source (rml:LogicalSource) is used to determine the input source with the data to be mapped. RML deals with different data serializations which use different ways to refer to their content. Thus RML considers that any reference to the Logical Source should be defined in a form relevant to the input data, e.g. XPATH for XML files or JSONPATH for JSON files. The Reference Formulation (rml:referenceFormulation) indicates the formulation (for instance, a standard or a query language) to refer to its data. Any reference to the data of the input source must be valid expressions according to the Reference Formulation defined at the Logical Source. This makes RML highly extensible towards new source formats.

At the current version of RML, the ql:CSV, ql:XPath and ql:JSONPath Reference Formulations are predefined while the ql:css3 was introduced for the challenge's needs as we chose the Selectors Level 3 expressions (CSS3)[6] to access the elements within the document. CSS3 selectors are standardized by W3C, they are easily used and broadly-known as they are used for selecting the HTML elements both for cascading styles and for jQuery[7]. CSS3 selectors can be used not only to refer to data in HTML documents but they could also be used for XML documents.

Defining RML Documents for CEUR Proceedings

The vocabularies used to describe the domain were selected to be aligned with the annotations provided in the case of volumes that already included RDFa annotations and considering vocabularies relevant to the domain as listed at http://linkeduniversities.org/lu/index.php/vocabularies/. The RML document for the *challenge* can be found at http://rml.io/spc/spc.html.

4   Performing Mappings to RDF with RML

Defining and executing a mapping with RML requires the user to provide an *input source* to be mapped and the *mapping document* according to which the

---

[6] http://www.w3.org/TR/selectors/

[7] http://jquery.com

mapping will be executed to generate the corresponding RDF *output dataset*. Data cleansing is out of RML's scope and should be performed in advance. Baring in mind that such data cleansing is not always possible, e.g. mapping live HTML documents *on-the-fly*, regular expressions were preferred to be used whenever it is required to be more selective over the returned values. For instance, a reference to h3 span.CEURLOCTIME returns Montpellier, France, May 26, 2013 for the aforementioned example and, as there is no further HTML annotation, regular expressions are required to select parts of the returned value to be mapped separately(e.g. city).

```
<a href="http://salad2013.linkedservices.org/">
  <span class="CEURVOLACRONYM'>SALAD 2013</span></a>
<h3><span class="CEURVOLEDITOR">Ruben Verborgh</span><br>
    <span class="CEURVOLEDITOR">Maria Maleshkova</span><br>
    ....</h3>

<#VolumeMapping>
  rr:subjectMap
  [ rr:template "http://ceur-ws.org/{span.CEURVOLNR}/";
    rr:class bibo:Volume ];
  rr:predicateObjectMap
  [ rr:predicate bibo:shortTitle;
    rr:objectMap [ rml:reference "span.CEURVOLACRONYM"; ] ];
  rr:predicateObjectMap
  [ rr:predicate bibo:editor;
    rr:objectMap [ rr:template "http://ceur-ws.org/person/{span.CEURVOLEDITOR}"; ] ].

<http://ceur-ws.org/Vol-1056/> a bibo:Volume ;
  bibo:shortTitle "SALAD 2013" ;
  bibo:editor <http://ceur-ws.org/person/Ruben
  bibo:editor <http://ceur-ws.org/person/Maria
  ....
```

Listing 1.1. An extract of Vol-996 of CEUR proceedings, following by an extract of the RML document that generates the triples specified.

Performing HTML to RDF Mappings with the RML Processor

Our prototype RML processor[8], implemented in Java, was used but, for the challenge needs, we extended it to leverage also HTML documents. We used CSSelly[9], a Java implementation of the W3C CSS3 specification. The HTML documents were stored locally and mapped as the RML processor was implemented so far with the scope of mapping files owned by data publishers and existing locally to the system. The definition of RML though allows to refer to resources even if they are published on the web and be retrieved as Web resources instead of local files.

The core functionality of the processor is used as such, we only added the CSS3 selectors to access the HTML input. Each defined Triples Maps is processed in a consecutive order and the defined Subject Map and Predicate-Object Maps are applied. For each reference to the input HTML, the HTML extractor returns an extract of the data. If a regular expression is specified, it is applied over the returned value and the corresponding triples are generated. The output dataset for the challenge can be found at http://rml.io/spc/spc.html.

---

[8] https://github.com/mmlab/RMLProcessor
[9] http://jodd.org/doc/csselly/

5   Discussion and Conclusions

It is beneficial that CSS3 selectors become part of a formalisation that performs mappings of data in HTML. Considering that the RML processor takes care of executing the mappings while the CSS3 extractor parses the document, the data publishers' contribution is limited in providing only the mapping document. As RML enables the re-use of the same mappings over different files, the effort they put is even less. In the case of the challenge, the same mapping documents were used to define the mappings for different HTML input sources.

This happens because most of the websites use templates thus the content of their pages is structured in a similar way, which is defined using CSS3 selectors, the same point of reference as the one used by RML. This allows us to use RML mapping documents as a "translation layer" over the published content and extract the content. Furthermore, as the mappings are partitioned in independent Triples Maps, data owners can select the Triples Maps they want to execute at any time. This provides them with the flexibility to execute only a part of the mappings at any time. For instance, if they identify a faulty mapping to their RDF output, they can isolate the Triples Map that generated those triples, correct it and re-execute it without affecting the rest of the dataset.

This becomes even more valuable considering that the mappings in RML are defined as triples themselves. The triples' provenance can be tracked and used to identify the mappings and data that cause the "faulty" RDF result [4]. Last, the mapping rules are interoperable; any tool that supports RML can process them either to execute them, as our RML Processor does or to refine them, e.g. by importing them to an application, such as Karma[10] or OpenRefine[11].

Beyond re-using the same mapping documents, data publishers can combine data from different input sources either they are in the same format or not. This leads to enhanced results as integration of data from different sources occurs during the mapping and relations between data appearing in different resources can be defined instead of interlinking them afterwards. For instance, the proceedings appearing in HTML can be mapped in an integrated fashion with the XML versions of the papers published at the workshops, enriching the resulting dataset with properties defined considering the combination of the two documents.

To sum up, this solution proves the scalability of the RML, as it was successfully extended to define mappings from data in HTML to the RDF data model.

Acknowledgments. The described research activities were funded by Ghent University, the Institute for the Promotion of Innovation by Science and Technology in Flanders (IWT), the Fund for Scientific Research Flanders (FWO Flanders), and the European Union.

---

[10] http://www.isi.edu/integration/karma/
[11] http://openrefine.org/

References

1. Coetzee, P., Heath, T., Motta, E.: Sparqplug: generating linked data from legacy HTML, SPARQL and the DOM (2008)
2. Connolly, D.: Gleaning resource descriptions from dialects of languages (GRDDL). W3C recommendation, September 2007
3. Dimou, A., Vander Sande, M., Colpaert, P., Verborgh, R., Mannens, E., Van de Walle, R.: RML: a generic language for integrated RDF mappings of heterogeneous data. In: Workshop on Linked Data on the Web (2013)
4. Dimou, A., Vander Sande, M., De Nies, T., Verborgh, R., Mannens, E., Van de Walle, R.: RDF mapping rules refinements according to data consumers feedback. In: 2nd International World Wide Web Conference, Poster Track Proceedings (2014)
5. Droop, M., et al.: Translating XPath queries into SPARQL queries. In: Meersman, R., Tari, Z. (eds.) OTM 2007 Workshops, Part I. LNCS, vol. 4805, pp. 9–10. Springer, Heidelberg (2007)

Extraction and Characterization of Citations in Scientific Papers

Marc Bertin$^{(\boxtimes)}$ and Iana Atanassova

CIRST, Université du Québec à Montréal, B.P. 8888, Succ. Centre-ville, Montreal,
QC H3C 3P8, Canada
`bertin.marc@courrier.uqam.ca, iana.atanassova@nlp-labs.org`

Abstract. We propose a hybrid method for the extraction and characterization of citations in scientific papers using machine learning combined with rule-based approaches. Our protocol consists of the extraction of metadata, bibliography parsing, section titles processing, and fine-grained semantic annotation on the sentence level of texts. This allows us to generate Linked Open Data from a set of research papers in XML.

Keywords: Semantic annotation · Citation acts · CRF · RDF graphs · Linked Open Data · Bibliography parsing

1 Introduction

With Open Science and the free access to standardized scientific articles, it becomes possible to explore and process massive amounts of textual data. Many studies deal with the text mining and semantic annotation of scientific papers. The Task 2 of ESWC-14 Semantic Publishing Challenge focuses on the extraction of information about in-text citations and bibliographic references in scientific articles and their relevance. Several different types of processing are necessary: citation extraction and characterization, analysis of author names, identification of grants and funding agencies, identification of literary review sections. Table 1 presents the set of queries for the task.

2 Method

Our implementation uses a hybrid approach combining rule-based and machine learning methods. The quality and consistency of the input data, especially the correct identification of citations and reference metadata in the papers, is crucial to the quality of the output. For this reason, the most important steps is our processing are the initial parsing and citation identification. The choice to work on the sentence level rather than on the paragraph level of texts allows us to develop more fine-grained annotation and in some cases limit the noise. It also opens the possibility for other applications such as sentence extraction and automatic production of document of syntheses.

© Springer International Publishing Switzerland 2014
V. Presutti et al. (Eds.): SemWebEval 2014, CCIS 475, pp. 120–126, 2014.
DOI: 10.1007/978-3-319-12024-9_16

Table 1. Queries for Task2

Q2.1	Identify all papers cited by the paper X
Q2.2	Identify all journal papers cited by the paper X
Q2.3	Identify all authors cited by the author whose surname is X
Q2.4	Identify all papers cited by the paper X and written by the same authors
Q2.5	Identify all papers cited multiple times by the paper X
Q2.6	Identify all papers cited multiple times in the same paragraph by the paper X
Q2.7	Identify the grant that supported the research presented in the paper X, along with the funding agency that funded it
Q2.8	Identify the 'literature review' section of the paper X
Q2.9	Identify all papers of which paper X declares to use methodologies or theories
Q2.10	Identify all papers of which paper X declares to provide an extension of the results

The protocol described below is based on the XML parsing, segmentation and semantic annotation of texts. We have developed a stand-alone application in Java for the processing of scientific papers that uses several other software libraries available in open source. Figure 1 gives an overview of the processing stages that will be detailed below.

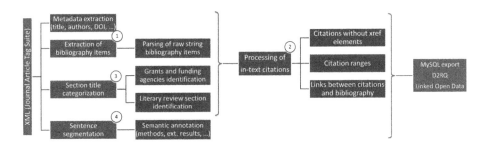

Fig. 1. Processing stages

Two datasets were provided for the task: a Training Dataset of 150 papers from 15 different journals and an Evaluation Dataset which is a superset of 400 papers from 71 journals. The documents are in XML JATS (Journal Article Tag Suite) and TaxPub, an official extension of JATS customized for taxonomic treatments.

Our processing relies on the full segmentation into sentences of all paragraphs. Thus we use sentences as the basic unit for the further processing stages. The segmentation method consists of an analysis of the punctuation and capitalization patterns in texts. This approach has already been used to process the PLOS journals (see [1]). Table 2 presents the number of articles processed for Task 2, as well as the average number of sentences, citations and references in the bibliography per article.

Table 2. Datasets

Dataset	Articles	Avg sentences	Avg in-text citations	Avg references
Training	150	202.64	69.39	36.13
Evaluation	400	170.23	63.12	41.56

Each article's metadata are extracted from the `front` element in the XML document. Paper identifiers, namely DOI and PubMedId are also extracted. If an identifier is missing, we try to recover it using the PubMed ID Converter API[1].

2.1 Bibliography Parsing and Processing of In-Text Citations

The processing of the bibliography items is more complex. In some journals, references are given as raw text strings in the bibliography. In such cases, in order to identify the metadata for each bibliography item, we use ParsCit (see [2,3]), which is an open source CRF reference parser. We have also designed another algorithm based on rules for the analysis of the punctuation in the strings. We first identify the year in the reference string and then analyze the substrings to the left and to the right of the year. Our algorithm identifies author names, years and titles successfully for more than 60 % of the references, including some references that were not correctly parsed by ParsCit. However, the rule-based approach fails for some of the references processed by ParsCit, which means that the combination of the two approaches gives better results than any of the two algorithms separately. Table 3 presents the results of this processing.

Table 3. Parsed raw string references using ParsCit and rule-based algorithm

Dataset	Total references	Raw string references	Rule-based algorithm	ParsCit + rule-based	Not parsed
Training	10,408	104	85 (81.73 %)	95 (91.34 %)	9 (8.65 %)
Evaluation	25,246	471	292 (62.00 %)	337 (71.54 %)	134 (28.45 %)

The XML schema provides `xref` elements for in-text citations. Each `xref` element contains an attribute that points to an item in the bibliography allowing to link in-text-citation with the corresponding reference. However, two different problems can occur. Firstly, some in-text citations are not identified as `xref` elements in the corpus. To resolve this, we have used regular expressions in order to identify strings that are likely to be citations. For further disambiguation, the obtained strings were then matched against reference labels, first author names

---

[1] PubMed ID Converter API: http://www.ncbi.nlm.nih.gov/pmc/tools/id-converter-api/

and years in the bibliography. Thus we were able to establish the links between the new in-text citations and the reference.

Secondly, multiple in-text citations can be grouped in a range (e.g. *"[10–13]"*) and in such cases, depending on the journal, pointers to all cited papers may or may not be present in the `xref` elements. We have analyzed the punctuation patterns between each two `xref` elements in the text, and identified possible citation ranges. All citations in the ranges candidates were then matched against reference labels in the bibliography to establish the new links.

2.2 Literary Review Section, Grants and Funding Agencies

The categorization of section titles is useful for identifying the literary review sections and also for retrieving the grants and funding agencies that are given either in the acknowledgments or in a separate funding section. We have categorized the section titles into 18 categories such as *introduction, method, analysis, funding.*

Bertin et al. [1] have shown that the distribution of in-text citations in scientific papers is closely related to the cognitive structure. Their results point out that the introductory sections, where we could expect to find the literary review, tend to have significantly higher concentration of citations than the rest of the papers. However, not every article contains a literary review section and in general the section with the highest density of citations is not guaranteed to be the literary review section. For this reason, to identify literary review sections we consider two criteria. Firstly, the average number of citations per sentence in the section must be 1 or higher. Secondly, the section title must be categorized as *introduction/background* or *related literature*. About 22 % of the sections could not be categorized and for those we rely only on the first criterion. If more than one sections correspond to these criteria, we take the section with the highest density of citations.

We suppose that information about grants and funding agencies is found in the acknowledgments or in the *Funding* section. To extract grant identifiers, we first filter the sentences that are likely to contain grants. We use linguistic clues, implemented by regular expressions, such as *"(was/is/were) (supported/funded)by"*. In this way, we limit the processing to only a small part of the sentences and reduce the noise. They next steps are identifying the grants and the organizations in the sentences. Grant identifiers are literals containing numbers, letters and dashes. They are recognized using a set of regular expressions. Then, to identify funding agencies we used Stanford Named Entity Recognizer [4,5].

2.3 Semantic Annotation of Methods and Extended Results

In order to characterize the function of citations, we need to take into consideration the semantic relations in their contexts. To do this, we use a rule-based semantic annotation approach [6] which relies on linguistic ontology of citation acts. Using the previous work of Bertin et al. [7], who characterizes citations related to methods, we have extended this approach to process the extending results of a paper.

3   Results and Evaluation

The data obtained by our processing is exported to a MySQL relational database and as RDF graph [8,9] using D2RQ[2]. The ten natural language queries for the task (see Table 1) were modeled with SPARQL. The web interface that shows the SPARQL queries and their output is accessible on: http://sempub2014.nlp-labs. org/task2/, optimized for Mozilla Firefox.

The evaluation was carried out by the challenge organizers. The result of a set of queries on the submitted LOD is compared with a gold standard, and precision and recall are measured. For each query only some properties are considered. For instance, the articles are compared by DOI, PMID and (normalized) titles only. Unexpected duplicates are considered errors.

Table 4. SemPub challenge evaluation

Task 2	Strict evaluation			Loose evaluation		
	Precision	Recall	F-measure	Precision	Recall	F-measure
Q2.1	0.675	0.750	0.710	0.867	0.956	0.909
Q2.2	0.034	0.035	0.035	0.914	0.931	0.922
Q2.3	0.777	0.777	0.777	0.800	0.800	0.800
Q2.4	0.533	0.411	0.464	0.533	0.411	0.464
Q2.5	0.743	1.000	0.853	0.743	1.000	0.853
Q2.6	0.783	0.798	0.790	0.833	0.831	0.832
Q2.7	0.150	0.400	0.218	0.325	0.600	0.422
Q2.8	0.400	0.267	0.320	0.400	0.267	0.320
Q2.9	0.267	0.333	0.296	0.300	0.400	0.343
Q2.10	0.200	0.200	0.200	0.200	0.200	0.200
Total	0.461	0.502	0.481	0.596	0.644	0.619

Two evaluation modes are supported: strict (only complete matches are considered correct) and loose (partial matches are considered correct too; some missing information is not taken into account).

Table 4 presents the results of the evaluation on 50 queries (5 queries for each query type). The overall F-measure is 0.619, but the performance of the system varies considerably according to the query. The evaluation shows that the system performs well for some of the questions (Q2.1–Q2.3, Q2.5 and Q2.6). For the last

---

[2] The D2RQ Platform is a system for accessing relational databases as RDF graphs: http://d2rq.org/

three queries types (Q2.8–Q2.10) that require heavy semantic processing, the F-measure is quite low (about 0.3) which shows that the system is not yet well adapted for these queries.

4 Conclusions and Perspectives

In producing our RDF data we use our proper ontology that is specifically designed to cover all of the task requirements. However, a mapping to already existing ontologies could be done for better interoperability with other tools. For example, we could consider CiTO [4] for the characterization of citations, DoCO [10] for document components and BiRO[3] for the description of bibliographic references.

Some of the processing steps that we describe can be improved by machine learning from datasets specifically designed for these tasks. For example, given the similarity in the bibliographic patterns throughout the corpus, the parser of raw string references could be improved by using the set of references that are already parsed in the corpus as training dataset.

Acknowledgments. We thank Angelo Di Iorio at the Department of Computer Science and Engineering (DISI) of the University of Bologna for providing the gold standard and the evaluation.

References

1. Bertin, M., Atanassova, I., Lariviere, V., Gingras, Y.: The distribution of references in scientific papers: an analysis of the IMRaD structure. In: Proceedings of the 14th ISSI Conference, pp. 591–603 (2013)
2. Councill, I.G., Giles, C.L., Kan, M.Y.: ParsCit: an open-source CRF reference string parsing package. In: LREC (2008)
3. Do, H.H.N., Chandrasekaran, M.K., Cho, P.S., Kan, M.Y.: Extracting and matching authors and affiliations in scholarly documents. In: Proceedings of the 13th ACM/IEEE-CS Joint Conference on Digital Libraries, pp. 219–228. ACM (2013)
4. Shotton, D.: Cito, the citation typing ontology. J. Biomed. Semant. **1**(Suppl 1), S6 (2010)
5. Finkel, J.R., Grenager, T., Manning, C.: Incorporating non-local information into information extraction systems by gibbs sampling. In: Proceedings of the 43rd Annual Meeting on Association for Computational Linguistics, Association for Computational Linguistics, pp. 363–370 (2005)
6. Desclés, J.P.: Contextual exploration processing for discourse and automatic annotations of texts. In: FLAIRS Conference, pp. 281–284 (2006)
7. Bertin, M., Atanassova, I., Descles, J.P.: Automatic analysis of author judgment in scientific articles based on semantic annotation. In: 22nd International Florida Artificial Intelligence, Research Society Conference, Sanibel Island, Florida. AAAI Press (2009)

---

[3] http://purl.org/spar/biro

8. Bizer, C., Seaborne, A.: D2RQ-treating non-RDF databases as virtual RDF graphs. In: Proceedings of the 3rd International Semantic Web Conference (ISWC 2004), vol. 2004 (2004)
9. Cyganiak, R., Bizer, C.: D2R server: a semantic web front-end to existing relational databases. In: XML Tage, 2006, pp. 171–173 (2006)
10. Shotton, D., Peroni, S.: DoCo, the document components ontology (2011)

Linked-Data Enabled
Recommender Systems

Linked Open Data-Enabled Recommender Systems: ESWC 2014 Challenge on Book Recommendation

Tommaso Di Noia[1(✉)], Iván Cantador[2], and Vito Claudio Ostuni[1]

[1] Department of Electrical and Electronic Engineering,
Politecnico di Bari, Bari, Italy
{tommaso.dinoia,vitoclaudio.ostuni}@poliba.it
[2] Department of Computer Science, Universidad Autónoma de Madrid,
Madrid, Spain
ivan.cantador@uam.es

Abstract. In this chapter we present a report of the ESWC 2014 Challenge on Linked Open Data-enabled Recommender Systems, which consisted of three tasks in the context of book recommendation: rating prediction in cold-start situations, top N recommendations from binary user feedback, and diversity in content-based recommendations. Participants were requested to address the tasks by means of recommendation approaches that made use of Linked Open Data and semantic technologies. In the chapter we describe the challenge motivation, goals and tasks, summarize and compare the nine final participant recommendation approaches, and discuss their experimental results and lessons learned. Finally, we end with some conclusions and potential lines of future research.

1 Introduction

People generally need more and more advanced tools that go beyond those implementing the canonical search paradigm for seeking relevant information. A new search paradigm is emerging, where the user perspective is completely reversed: from finding to being found. Recommender systems may help to support this new perspective, because they have the effect of pushing relevant items (movies, videos, music albums, books, job offers, etc.), selected from a large space of possible options, to potentially interested users [12]. To achieve this objective, recommendation methods generally rely on data referring to three types of entities: users, items, and their relations.

Recent developments in the Semantic Web community offer novel strategies to represent data that may improve the current state of the art on recommender systems, in order to move towards a new generation of systems that fully understand the user preferences (tastes, interests, and goals), item features (e.g., domain attributes, categories, and related concepts), and contextual signals (e.g., time, location, mood, and social company) they deal with.

© Springer International Publishing Switzerland 2014
V. Presutti et al. (Eds.): SemWebEval 2014, CCIS 475, pp. 129–143, 2014.
DOI: 10.1007/978-3-319-12024-9_17

More and more semantic data are published following the Linked Open Data principles[1,2] (LOD), which enable to set up links between entities in different knowledge sources, by connecting information in a single global data space: the Web of Data [4]. Today, the Web of Data includes different types of knowledge represented in a homogeneous form, both sedimentary (encyclopedic, cultural, linguistic, commonsense) and real-time (news, data streams, etc.) types.

This knowledge might be useful to interlink diverse information about users, items, and their relations, and implement reasoning mechanisms that can support and improve the recommendation process. Hence, the primary goal of the ESWC 2014 Challenge on Linked Open Data-enabled Recommender Systems[3] was twofold. On the one hand, we wanted to create a link between the Semantic Web and the Recommender Systems communities. On the other hand, we aimed to show how Linked Open Data and semantic technologies can boost the creation of a new breed of knowledge-enabled and content-based recommender systems. In particular, we focused on the particular scenario of book recommendation, and stated three tasks, namely rating prediction in cold-start situations, top N recommendations from binary user feedback, and diversity in content-based recommendations. Participants were requested to address the tasks by means of recommendation approaches that made use of Linked Data and semantic technologies.

In the remainder of the chapter, we describe the challenge dataset (Sect. 2), tasks (Sect. 3), and evaluation protocol (Sect. 4), summarize and compare the nine final participant recommendation approaches (Sect. 5), and present the obtained experimental results (Sect. 6) and derived conclusions (Sect. 7) in the challenge.

2 Challenge Dataset

The challenge tasks were conducted on the DBbook dataset, which was built upon the LibraryThing dataset[4], and relies on user preferences (ratings in the [0, 5] integer interval) for books retrieved from the Web. As explained in [6], the books available in the original rating dataset were mapped to their corresponding DBpedia URIs, allowing participants extract semantic features from DBpedia [1] and other Linked Open Data repositories, which could be exploited by their recommendation approaches in the challenge tasks.

The final mapping contained 8170 DBpedia URIs. For each task, the dataset was split into a training set and a test set. In the former, user ratings were provided to build the recommender systems, while in the latter ratings were removed, since they were used in an eventual evaluation stage.

---

[1] Linking Open Data, http://www.w3.org/wiki/SweoIG/TaskForces/CommunityProjects/LinkingOpen Data.

[2] Linked Data, http://linkeddata.org.

[3] ESWC 2014 Challenge on Linked Open Data-enabled Recommender Systems, http://challenges. 2014.eswc-conferences.org/index.php/RecSys.

[4] LibraryThing dataset, http://www.macle.nl/tud/LT.

For Task 1 – rating prediction in cold-start situations –, the training dataset contained the numeric values of the user ratings. A total of 75559 ratings from 6181 users for 6166 distinct books were provided as training data.

For Task 2 – top N recommendations from binary user feedback – and Task 3 – diversity in content-based recommendations –, in contrast, the ratings were given in a binary scale, where 1 meant that a book was relevant for a user, and 0 otherwise. In this case, a total of 72372 ratings from 6181 users for 6733 distinct books were provided as training data.

3   Challenge Tasks

3.1   Rating Prediction in Cold-Start Situations

This task dealt with the rating prediction problem, in which a system is requested to estimate the value of unknown numeric ratings that a target user would assign to available items, indicating whether she likes or dislikes them.

In order to favor the proposal of content-based, LOD-enabled recommendation approaches, and limit the use of collaborative filtering strategies, this task aimed to predict ratings in cold-start situations, that is, predicting ratings for users with a few past ratings, and predicting ratings of items rated by a few users.

Participants were asked to exploit the ratings provided as training data, in addition to semantic features freely chosen and extracted from Linked Data repositories, in order to estimate missing ratings of a test set. Estimated ratings were submitted in the format userID \t itemID \t rating.

Recommendation approaches were evaluated on the test set Te by means of the well known Root Mean Square Error (RMSE), which measures the differences between actual ratings $r_{u,i}$ and predicted ratings $p_{u,i}$ of users u and items i:

$$RMSE = \sqrt{\frac{1}{|Te|} \sum_{(u,i,r_{u,i}) \in Te} \left(p_{u,i} - r_{u,i}\right)^2}$$

3.2   Top N Recommendations from Binary User Feedback

This task dealt with the top N recommendations problem, in which a system is requested to find and recommend a limited set of N items that best match a user profile, instead of correctly predicting the ratings for all available items.

Similarly to Task 1, in order to favor the proposal of content-based, LOD-enabled recommendation approaches, and limit the use of collaborative filtering strategies, this task aimed to generate ranked lists of items, in cold-start situations, for which no graded ratings were available, but binary ones.

Participants were asked to complete the user-item pairs in the test set by adding the correspondent relevance score according to the format userID \t itemID \t score. These relevance scores were used by an evaluation service to form a Top 5 item recommendation list for each user. This means that for each user, only items in the test set were considered to form the top 5 recommendation list. The evaluation metric for this task was the F-measure@5:

$$F\text{-}measure@5 = Precisions@5 \cdot Recall@5$$

where

$$Precision@5 = \frac{1}{|U|}Precision_u@5 \qquad Precision_u@5 = \frac{1}{5}\sum_{i=1}^{5} rel_{i,u}$$

$$Recall@5 = \frac{1}{|U|}Recall_u@5 \qquad Recall_u@5 = \frac{1}{R_u}\sum_{i=1}^{5} rel_{i,u}$$

being U the set of users, $rel_{i,u}$ the binary relevance value of the item with the i-th highest predicted rating for user u, and R_u the set of u's relevant items.

3.3   Diversity in Content-Based Recommendations

A very interesting aspect of content-based recommender systems, and then of LOD-enabled ones, is giving the possibility to evaluate the diversity of recommended items in a straight way. This is a very popular topic in content-based recommendations, which usually suffer from over-specialization.

In this task, the evaluation was made by considering a combination of both accuracy of the recommendation list, and the diversity of items belonging to it. Given the domain of books and the challenge focus on Linked Data, we considered diversity with respect to two properties: http://dbpedia.org/ontology/author and http://www.w3.org/2004/02/skos/core#subject.

Participants were asked to submit a top 20 recommendations list for each user. The submitted lists had to be computed considering all unrated items of each user, and selecting the 20 items with highest predicted ratings. Similarly to Task 2, in this case, the line format of the submission file was userID \t itemID \t score.

In this task, the evaluation metric was a combination of accuracy and diversity. In particular, F-measure@20 was used for measuring accuracy, and Intra-List Diversity ILD@20 [15] for diversity. ILD@20 was defined based on ILS@20:

$$ILS@20 = \frac{1}{|U|}ILS_u@20 \qquad ILS_u@20 = \frac{1}{2}\sum_{i\in L_u^{20}}\sum_{j\in L_u^{20}} sim(i,j)$$

where L_u^{20} is the list of 20 items recommended to user u with highest predicted ratings, and $sim(i,j) \in [-1,+1]$ is a content-based similarity between items i and j. The final ranking is computed as follows. First, F-measure@20 and ILD@20 alone were used to form two initial rankings. Then, a final ranking was produced by considering each participant's score as the mean of her rank positions in the two initial rankings.

4   Evaluation Protocol

For Task 1, the training and test sets were available at the following URLs:

- `root_url/DBbook_train_ratings.zip`
- `root_url/task1_useritem_evaluation_data.tsv.zip`

where `root_url` has to be replaced by
http://sisinflab.poliba.it/semanticweb/lod/recsys/2014challenge.
For Task 2 and 3, the training and test sets were available at the following URLs:

- `root_url/DBbook_train_binary.zip`
- `root_url/task2_useritem_evaluation_data.tsv.zip`

The training sets were provided as tab-separated value files, in which each line had the format `userID \t itemID \t rating`, and the test sets were also provided as tab-separated value files, but having the line format `userID \t itemID`.

To evaluate their approaches, participants were asked to submit a file containing the rating predictions or recommendations to an evaluation system using the web form available at http://193.204.59.20:8181/eswc2014lodrecsys/.

Alternatively, participants could also submit their results using a Java client available at `root_url/lodrecsys2014challenge_evaluation.jar`, by launching the following command:

```
Java -jar lodrecsys2014challenge_evaluation.jar
TaskNumber GroupID filePath
```

5   Participant Approaches

During the challenge, 14 approaches participated in Task 1, 24 approaches participated in Task 2, and 12 approaches participated in Task 3. Finally, 9 distinct approaches completed the challenge, by taking part in one or more of the challenge tasks, and being described in a paper accepted by three program committee members in a blind review process. In the following, we describe and compare the final participant approaches, and highlight their lessons learned.

SemWex1. Hybrid Recommending Exploiting Multiple DBpedia Language Editions [11]

By Ladislav Peska, and Peter Vojtas (Charles University in Prague, Czech Republic)

This is a hybrid recommendation approach that is based on a content-based extension of the matrix factorization method for collaborative filtering. The approach incorporates item features into the matrix to factorize, and generates item latent factor vectors from the latent factors of the items features.

A total of 100 features and 35 K feature-value pairs were obtained from RDF data associated to books and writers in DBpedia. The final features were generated from different transformations of the original ones:

- Discretizing numeric feature values;
- Grouping equivalent features, e.g., the `precededBy` and `notableWork` properties were unified into a `similarWork` property;
- Manually annotating authors and genres with metadata, such as serious or fun literature, male or female target audience, and literary genre clusters;
- Extending the items categories by 3 levels of super categories (obtained through the `skos:broader` property);
- Filtering low informative features.

To increase the diversity of generated recommendations, the approach applies a heuristic that selects the book (item) with the highest rating of each author from the top N recommendations list.

One of the lessons learned with this approach is that super categories were often too general to provide valuable information.

The approach took the 4th position in Task 1, the 4th position in Task 2, and the 4th position in Task 3.

helloWorld. **A Hybrid Multi-strategy Recommender System Using Linked Open Data** [13]

By Petar Ristoski, Eneldo Loza Mencía, and Heiko Paulheim (University of Mannheim, Germany)

This is a hybrid recommendation approach that uses stack regression and rank aggregation techniques to combine recommendations from several methods:

- Content-based recommendation methods that use different sets of item features;
- User- and item-based heuristic collaborative filtering methods using the cosine similarity function;
- Popularity-based recommendation method that returns global item popularity scores, which are independent of the target user, and are computed with the books average scores in Amazon and the number of ingoing/outgoing links with Wikipedia and other datasets.

For each book, the considered features were:

- the direct (YAGO) types of the book,
- the direct categories of the book,
- the super categories of the book categories,
- all books written by the book author,
- the genres of the book and author's books,
- the writers who influenced or were influenced by the book author, and
- a bag of keywords extracted from the Wikipedia abstract of the book.

These features were extracted from DBpedia, the RDF Book Mashup dataset (http://datahub.io/dataset/rdf-book-mashup), the British Library Bibliography (http://bnb.data.bl.uk), and the DBTropes catalogue (http://dbtropes.org).

To increase the diversity of generated recommendations, the approach applies a heuristic that filters out books whose authors and categories already appear as metadata of books in the top N recommendations list.

The main lessons learned with this approach are that item popularity allowed increasing accuracy, and hybridization allowed increasing diversity.

The approach took the 1st position in Task 1, the 2nd position in Task 2, and the 1st position in Task 3.

IDEAL. Exploring Semantic Features for Producing Top N Recommendation Lists from Binary User Feedback [2]

By Nicholas Ampazis, and Theodoros Emmanouilidis (University of the Aegean, Greece)

This is a content-based recommendation approach that uses a feature vector representation for users and items. The approach computes similarities between the items liked by the user in the past and the reminder items, to suggest those with highest similarities. Several similarities were tested, namely the cosine, Euclidean distance, and Tanimoto similarities. The best performing was Tanimoto similarity, which is computed as the ratio between the size of the intersection of two vectors by the size of their union.

The features used for testing the approach were the book authors and categories, extracted from DBpedia.

In order to account for recommendation diversity, the approach generates an initial list with the top 50 recommended items. Next, it measures the pair-wise similarities of the 50 items. Finally, it selects for the top 20 recommendation list, those items that more frequently exhibit the lowest similarities with the other items.

A lesson learned with this approach is that even simple content-based similarities and diversification strategies may obtain good recommendation results.

The approach took the 5th position in Task 3.

UNIBA. Aggregation Strategies for Linked Open Data-Enabled Recommender Systems [3]

By Pierpaolo Basile, Cataldo Musto, Marco De Gemmis, Pasquale Lops, Fedelucio Narducci, and Giovanni Semeraro (University of Bari, Italy).

This is a hybrid recommendation approach that consists of a linear combination of recommendations from some (depending on the challenge task) of the following methods:

- Popularity-based recommendation method, in which item popularity is computed as the ratio between the number of positive ratings perceived by the item and the total number of ratings (positive and negative) of the item;
- Enhanced Vector Space Model (eSVM) with negation, which is a content-based method based on an incremental dimensionality reduction technique;
- Page Rank with priors (PR), in which a personalization vector may be used for assigning different initial weighs to certain nodes liked/disliked by the user;

- Random Forest (RF), which is an ensemble classification method that consists of several decision trees built with different training items and features;
- Logistic Regression (LR), which is a classification method that builds a linear model based on a transformed target variable.

The above methods used a combination of the following features:

- Keywords extracted from Wikipedia descriptions and DBpedia abstracts of the books;
- DBpedia concepts appearing in the book description and abstract;
- DBpedia properties of the books, in particular, the 10 most frequent properties (http://dbpedia.org/ removed for brevity); `ontology/wikiPageWikiLink`, http://purl.org/dc/terms/subject, `property/genre`, `property/publisher`, `ontology/author`, `property/followedBy`, `property/precededBy`, `property/series`, `property/dewey`, `ontology/nonFiction Subject`.

To account for recommendation diversity, the approach applies the PageRank algorithm with different priors:

- 80 % of the initial weight evenly distributed to those nodes that correspond to books liked by the user (0 for those disliked by the user);
- 10 % of the initial weight evenly distributed to those nodes that do not correspond to books;
- 10 % of the initial weights proportionally distributed to those nodes that correspond to books not rated by the user; the weight distribution is done according to a diversity score, which is an average of similarity and novelty metrics.

The main lessons learn with this approach were:

- Very simple methods based on SVM and probabilistic models are capable of obtain accurate recommendation;
- The usefulness of semantic data was evident in recommendation methods based on classifiers;
- The application of a graph-based ranking algorithm on a semantic network built with DBpedia concepts and properties allowed diversifying recommendation lists.

The approach took the 2nd position in Task 1, the 1st position in Task 2, and shared the 2nd position with UIMR-NUIGalway in Task 3.

UIMR-NUIGalway. SemStim at the LOD-RecSys 2014 Challenge [7]

By Benjamin Heitmann, and Conor Hayes (National University of Ireland - Galway, Ireland)

This is a graph-based recommendation algorithm based on Constrained Spreading Activation (CSA), which uses generic constraint functions for the activation, restart, and termination of the weight propagation process. The approach is executed on a semantic graph where source nodes are associated to concepts (books) liked by the user, and target nodes are associated to books not rated by the user. The reminder nodes are associated to concepts associated to book categories, properties, and Wikipedia disambiguation and redirect links.

The approach was only tested in the diversity task. In the cases in which the approach generated recommendation lists with less than 20 items, randomly selected items were aggregated to the lists.

Similarly to other approaches that made use of graph-based algorithms, this approach performed well when providing diversity in recommendation lists.

The approach shared the 2nd position with UNIBA in Task 3.

UniMannheim. Popular Books and Linked Data: Some Results for the ESWC'14 RecSys Challenge [14]

By Michael Schuhmacher, and Christian Meilicke (University of Mannheim, Germany)

This team tested two approaches. The first approach was a naive, non personalized recommendation approach based on the items popularity computed on the training dataset according to the top rated items, and without making use of any external knowledge. The second approach was a hybrid method composed of a Naive Bayes classifier that was built with item features on user neighbor clusters. In this approach, other classifiers (Support Vector Machines, Linear Regression, and Decision Trees) were also tested.

The used features were:

- DBpedia properties: genre (dbo:literaryGenre), Wikipedia subjects (dcterms:subject), YAGO types (rdf:type), authors (dbo:author, dbo:writer), book series (dbo:series), publisher (dbo:publisher).
- DBpedia categories: the Wikipedia categories of each book plus their immediate (1 level) super categories, obtained via the skos:broader and the dbo:wikiPageWikiLink (Wikipedia links) properties.
- 30 manually defined categories (e.g., *science fiction*, *fantasy*, *horror*, and *philosophy*), each of them assigned to a book if certain pattern (usually the category name) was found in the book abstract (dbo:abstract), genre (dbo:literaryGenre, dbp:genre), or subject (dcterms:subject).
- Expanded categories, selected based on the highest Dice similarity between the values of dcterms:subject, dbo:literaryGenre, and dbp:genre properties, e.g., Literary_history and History_of_literature.

The approach was only tested on the top N recommendations for binary user feedback task. Since it did not perform well isolated, their results were combined with a user-based collaborative filtering method, which generated user neighbor clusters on which the classifier was executed.

The main lessons learn with this approach were:

- The popularity-based baseline achieved competitive recommendation results;
- The user aggregation methods showed a significant influence on the overall performance;
- There was a marginal contribution from each feature to the overall performance, especially from the expanded categories.

The approach took the 3rd position in Task 2.

VUAgroup. Semantic Pattern-based Recommender [9]

By Valentina Maccatrozzo, Davide Ceolin, Lora Aroyo, and Paul Groth (VU University Amsterdam, The Netherlands)

This approach extracts semantic patterns from DBpedia, and exploits such patterns for user modeling and recommendation purposes. For instance, a user who liked books written by Jack Kerouac, may be interested in a book written by Ernest Hemming, since the former *influenced* the latter.

The approach uses the patterns to automatically (via SPARQL queries) build semantic paths between the user's rated books and other books. The user's ratings for the unrated items are computed by means of personalized positive/negative scores assigned to patterns and books.

The approach was only tested in the top N recommendations for binary user feedback task, achieving reasonable performance results without any setup and exploration of alternative configurations or adaptations.

The approach took the 5th position in Task 2.

LDOS. Increasing Top 20 Diversity Through Recommendation Post-processing [8]

By Matevz Kunaver, Tomaz Pozrl, Stefan Dobravec, Andrej Kosir, and Uros Droftina (University of Ljubljana, Slovenia)

This approach is a rule-based recommendation method that represent each book with some of 17 DBpedia features (author, year of publishing, type, etc.), and Dublin Core categories; each item having on average 5 different categories.

The approach applies a post-processing method to generated recommendations in order to increase diversity. Specifically, it applies a *leave one out* technique measuring the ILD@19 metric on the 40 top ranked items. The approach sorts the recommendation list in ascending order by the ILD@19 value, and excludes the item whose absence has the smallest impact on the diversity of the recommendation list. This process is iteratively done until discarding 20 items.

The main lesson learned with this approach is that the followed diversification strategy, which aims to optimize ILD (the evaluation metric), indeed increases diversity, but entails a high loss of precision and recall.

The approach shared the 5th position with IDEAL in Task 3.

UniAndes1. Hybrid Model Rating Prediction with Linked Open Data for Recommender Systems [10]

By Andrés Moreno, Christian Ariza-Porras, Paula Lago, Claudia Lucía Jiménez-Guarín, Harold Castro, and Michel Riveill (Universidad de los Andes, Colombia)

This approach is a switched hybrid recommendation method that maintains different models in parallel, and reports to the user the rating predictions and recommendations of the model with highest confidence. Specifically, it uses a collaborative filtering strategy (the SVD++ matrix factorization algorithm) when enough ratings are present, and uses a content-based recommendation strategy otherwise.

Additionally, the approach clusters the feature values to reduce the dimensionality of the user and item profiles. For the content-based recommendation method, the used features were the book authors, categories, literary genres, and the subject property.

The approach took the 3rd position in Task 1.

Table 1 depicts a comparison of the challenge final participant approaches. For each approach, we show:

- The type of **hybridization technique** used (if any), based on Burke's hybrid recommender system taxonomy [5]: *feature combination* (putting features from different recommendation data sources into a single method), *feature augmentation* (using output from a recommendation method as input to another), *mixed hybridization* (jointly presenting recommendations from several methods), *weighting hybridization* (combining the recommendation scores from several methods), and *switching hybridization* (using some criterion to switch between recommendation methods).
- The type of the underlying **recommendation method(s)**, e.g., *content-based, collaborative filtering*, and *popularity-based*.
- The nature of the content- and semantic-based **features** exploited by the recommendation methods, such as *book attributes (title, author, genres, etc.)*, *Wikipedia categories*, and *text keywords*.
- The type of **diversification strategy** applied (if any), namely *pre-processing* if the approach itself is modeled to provide diversity in generated recommendations, and *post-processing* if the approach makes use of a strategy to diversify generated recommendations.

It can be seen that 5 out of the 9 approaches used some type of hybridization technique, without a predominant one existing among the participants. It seems that those techniques that combine recommendations from different methods (*mixed* and *weighting*) performed better than the others. Regarding the recommendation methods, we note that exploiting item popularity information helped to increase accuracy in cold-start situations (Task 1), and graph-based approaches achieved both high accuracy and diversity (Task 3). Moreover, as stated by some of the authors, the use of the books Wikipedia categories and super-categories was not a relevant feature to improve recommendations. In contrast, extending user and item profiles by means of keywords extracted from the book abstracts and descriptions may help dealing with binary user feedback (Task 2). Finally, we note that all except one approach applied a post-processing diversification strategy. In this context, those strategies aimed to avoid repetitions of book authors and genres within the recommendation lists achieved the best results in Task 3; optimizing ILD of recommendation lists alone was not a good solution to the task, since it did not account for the loss of accuracy.

6   Results of the Participant Approaches

Overall, 14 teams participated in Task 1, 24 in Task 2 and 12 in Task 3. Among them, 15 submitted a paper describing the approach they adopted for competing in the challenge, and 9 of them were selected by the program committee and chairs as final

Table 1. Comparison of the challenge final participant approaches. The superscript * indicates that the participant shares rank position with other participant(s).

Approach	Hybridization technique	Recommendation methods	Features	Diversification strategy	Ranking		
					T1	T2	T3
SemWex1 [11]	Feature combination	Content-based extension of matrix factorization	Attributes Extended categories Manual metadata	Post-processing (non repeated authors)	4	4	4
helloWorld [13]	Mixed	Content-based User-based collaborative filtering Item-based collaborative filtering Popularity-based	Attributes Extended categories Abstract keywords Popularity	Post-processing (non repeated authors and genres)	1	2	1
IDEAL [2]	–	Content-based	Authors Categories	Post-processing (non similar books)			5*
UNIBA [3]	Weighting	Content-based Graph-based (PageRank) Machine learning (RF, LR) Popularity-based	Most popular attributes Description keywords Description concepts	Pre-processing (diversity scores on graph nodes)	2	1	2*
UIMR-NUIGalway [7]	–	Graph-based (CSA)	Attributes Categories Disambiguation links Redirect links	–			2*
UniMannheim [14]	Feature augmentation	User-based collaborative filtering Machine learning (Naive Bayes) Popularity-based	Attributes Extended categories	–		3	
VUAgroup [9]	–	Semantic pattern-based	Attributes	–		5	
LDOS [8]	–	Rule-based	Attributes Categories	Post-processing (filtering books via relative ILD values)			5*
UniAndes1 [10]	Switching	Content-based Matrix factorization	Authors Literary genres Categories	–	3		

participants. Those final participants are the ones just presented in Sect. 5, and were the ones who were considered in computing the final rankings to determine the winner for each task. In the following, we discuss the results achieved by those final participants in the three tasks. Such results are shown in Table 2.

Table 2. Participant results. The superscript * indicates that the participant shares rank position with other participants.

Approach	Task 1		Task 2		Task 3		
	Ranking	RMSE	Ranking	F-measure@5	Ranking	F-measure@20	ILD@20
SemWex1 [11]	4	0.93686	4	0.55396	4	0.01989	0.48025
helloWorld [13]	1	**0.86322**	2	0.57148	1	**0.04816**	**0.48460**
IDEAL [2]	–	–	–	0.53312	5*	0.03479	0.44471
UNIBA [3]	2	0.87422	1	**0.57151**	2*	0.04813	0.47169
UIMR-NUIGalway [7]	–	–	–	–	2*	0.04129	0.47603
UniMannheim [14]	–		3	0.56070	–	–	–
VUAgroup [9]	–	–	5	0.51622	–	–	–
LDOS [8]	–	–	–	–	5*	0.03085	0.45489
UniAndes1 [10]	3	0.87871	–	–	–	–	–

6.1 Results of the Rating Prediction in Cold-Start Situations Task

The best performing participant in this task was *helloWorld* who achieved the lowest RMSE score. *UNIBA* and *UniAndes1* ranked second and third, respectively. As we can note, the difference between *UNIBA* and *UniAndes1* is limited, while the gap between those groups and *SemWex1*, who ranked fourth, is quite marked. Looking at Table 1 we can see that both the two best performing approaches used hybridization strategies based on recommendation combinations.

6.2 Results of the Top N Recommendations from Binary User Feedback Task

In this task, instead, the best performing approach was the one adopted by *UNIBA* which achieved a F-measure of 0.57151. *helloWorld* ranked at the second position with a score only 3×10^{-5} lower than the highest one. Then, *UniMannheim* ranked third and the other participants to follow. Also in this case, the two best performing approaches were the ones based on an ensemble of several different recommendation methods.

6.3 Results of the Diversity in Content-Based Recommendations Task

In this task, the best performing participant was again *helloWorld*, which obtained the best ILD and F-measure values of 0.04816 and 0.4846, respectively. At the second position there were two participants: *UNIBA* and *UIMR-NUIGalway*. The first got a F-measure value of 0.04813, and ranked fourth in the ILD ranking with a ILD score of 0.47169. While the second ranked third in the F-measure ranking with a score of 0.04129 and third in the ILD ranking with a score of 0.47603.

Looking at the individual metrics alone, the best approaches in terms of accuracy were the ones proposed by *helloWorld* and *UNIBA* in accordance also with their results in Task 2. The differences in scale between the F-measure scores in Task 2 and Task 3 are due to the different evaluation protocols. Particularly, in Task 2, each user recommendation list had to be generated considering only test items, while in Task 3, considering all items except the ones in the user training data.

Regarding diversity, the highest scores were achieved by *helloWorld* and *SemWex1* who both adopted a post-processing diversification strategy aimed to avoid repetitions of book authors and genres within the recommendation lists.

7   Conclusions from the Challenge

The Linked Open Data-enabled Recommender Systems Challenge at ESWC 2014 was among the first attempts to bring together the two communities of Recommender Systems and Semantic Web. The high number of participants and the quality of results obtained by the different teams show that there is an increasing interest in the topic, as well as that recommender systems have been recognized as a potential killer application for the exploitation of Linked Open Data.

What emerges by looking at the different approaches proposed by the participants is that the best performing techniques, with respect to the provided dataset, for rating prediction and top-N recommendations use an ensemble of several different recommendation methods, while post-processing results are very effective in increasing the diversity of the recommendation list.

We think that there is still room to better exploit both the semantics encoded in LOD datasets and the connections among items to improve the quality of recommendation results both in terms of accuracy and in terms of diversity, in the future, novelty and serendipity. We also believe that contextual semantic data, e.g., coming from data streams, can be easily integrated with the information currently available in LOD datasets to build a new wave of context-aware recommender systems.

Acknowledgements. We thank all participants for their interest in the challenge, their submissions, and presentations and discussion during the conference. We also thank the program committee members for their valuable reviews of submissions, and Valentina Presutti and Milan Stankovic for their help with the organization of the challenge.

References

1. Auer, S., Bizer, C., Kobilarov, G., Lehmann, J., Cyganiak, R., Ives, Z.G.: DBpedia: a nucleus for a Web of open data. In: Aberer, K., Choi, K.-S., Noy, N., Allemang, D., Lee, K.-I., Nixon, L.J.B., Golbeck, J., Mika, P., Maynard, D., Mizoguchi, R., Schreiber, G., Cudré-Mauroux, P. (eds.) ASWC 2007 and ISWC 2007. LNCS, vol. 4825, pp. 722–735. Springer, Heidelberg (2007)
2. Ampazis, N., Emmanouilidis, T.: Exploring semantic features for producing top-N recommendation lists from binary user feedback. In: Presutti, V., et al. (eds.) SemWebEval 2014, CCIS, vol. 475, pp. 157–162. Springer, Heidelberg (2014)

3. Basile, P., Musto, C., De Gemmis, M., Lops, P., Narducci, F., Semeraro, G.: Aggregation strategies for linked open data-enabled recommender systems. In: Presutti, V., et al. (eds.) European Semantic Web Conference (Satellite Events) (2014), CCIS, vol. 475, Springer, Heidelberg (2014)
4. Bizer, C., Heath, T., Berners-Lee, T.: Linked data - the story so far. Int. J. Semant. Web Inf. Syst. **5**(3), 1–22 (2009)
5. Burke, R.D.: Hybrid recommender systems: survey and experiments. User Model. User-Adap. Inter. **12**(4), 331–370 (2002)
6. Di Noia, T., Mirizzi, R., Ostuni, V.C., Romito, D., Zanker, M.: Linked open data to support content-based recommender systems. In: Proceedings of the 8th International Conference on Semantic Systems, pp. 1–8 (2012)
7. Heitmann, B., Hayes, C.: SemStim at the LOD-RecSys 2014 Challenge. In: Presutti, V., et al. (eds.) SemWebEval 2014, CCIS, vol. 475, pp. 170–175. Springer, Heidelberg (2014)
8. Kunaver, M., Pozrl, T., Dobravec, S., Kosir, A., Droftina, U.: Increasing top 20 diversity through recommendation post-processing. In: Presutti, V., et al. (eds.) SemWebEval 2014, CCIS, vol. 475, pp. 188–192. Springer, Heidelberg (2014)
9. Maccatrozzo, V., Ceolin, D., Aroyo, L., Groth, P.: A semantic pattern-based recommender. In: Presutti, V., et al. (eds.) SemWebEval 2014, CCIS, vol. 475, pp. 182–187. Springer, Heidelberg (2014)
10. Moreno, A., Ariza-Porras, C., Lago, P., Jiménez-Guarín, C.L., Castro, H., Riveill, M.: Hybrid model rating prediction with linked open data for recommender systems. In: Presutti, V., et al. (eds.) SemWebEval 2014, CCIS, vol. 475, pp. 193–198. Springer, Heidelberg (2014)
11. Peska, L., Vojtas, P.: Hybrid recommending exploiting multiple DBpedia language editions. In: Presutti, V., et al. (eds.) SemWebEval 2014, CCIS, vol. 475, pp. 144–149. Springer, Heidelberg (2014)
12. Ricci, F., Rokach, L., Shapira, B., Kantor, P.B.: Recommender Systems Handbook. Springer, Heidelberg (2011)
13. Ristoski, P., Mencía, E.L., Paulheim, H.: A hybrid multi-strategy recommender system using linked open data. In: Presutti, V., et al. (eds.) SemWebEval 2014, CCIS, vol. 475, pp. 150–156. Springer, Heidelberg (2014)
14. Schuhmacher, M., Meilicke, C.: Popular books and linked data: some results for the ESWC'14 RecSys challenge. In: Presutti, V., et al. (eds.) SemWebEval 2014, CCIS, vol. 475, pp. 176–181. Springer, Heidelberg (2014)
15. Ziegler, C.-N., McNee, S.M., Konstan, J.A., Lausen, G.: Improving recommendation lists through topic diversification. In: Proceedings of the 14th International Conference on World Wide Web, pp. 22–32 (2005)

Hybrid Recommending Exploiting Multiple DBPedia Language Editions

Ladislav Peska[(⊠)] and Peter Vojtas

Faculty of Mathematics and Physics, Charles University in Prague,
Malostranske namesti 25, Prague, Czech Republic
{peska,vojtas}@ksi.mff.cuni.cz

Abstract. In this paper we describe approach of our SemWex1 group to the
ESWC 2014 RecSys Challenge. Our method is based on using an adaptation of
Content Boosted Matrix factorization [1], where objects are defined through
their content-based features. Features were comprised of both direct DBPedia
RDF triples and derived semantic information (with some WIE and NLP features). Total of seven DBPedia language editions were used to form the dataset.
In the paper we will further describe our methods for semantic information
creation, data filtration, algorithm details and settings as well as decisions made
during the challenge and dead ends we explored.

Keywords: Hybrid recommender systems · Linked open data · DBPedia ·
Matrix factorization · Content boosting

1 Introduction

The amount of data on the web grows continuously and it is impossible to process it
directly by a human. Many solutions were adopted ranging from keyword search
engines to information aggregators, semantic web or recommender systems. Although
the majority of the research effort in recommender systems was initially spent on the
collaborative filtering based on the explicit user rating, collaborative systems might
highly suffer from *cold start* problem.

Using attributes of the objects (and hence content-based or hybrid recommenders)
can speed up learning curve and reduce *cold start* (and also *new object*) problems.
Various domains and systems however differ greatly in amount and usefulness of its
content-based attributes. This is where Linked Open Data and DBPedia come into play.
With its vast amount of machine-readable data it can be used to populate object
attributes and features and thus improve content-based recommending.

Related Work: Unfortunately it is out of scope of this paper to provide more elaborated overview, so we stick only to the closest work. Our preference learning method is
based on third-party algorithm Content-boosted matrix factorization (CBMF) originally
presented by Forbes and Zhu [1]. This method extends common matrix factorization
[2] by adding object attributes and stating that each object's latent factors vector is a
function of its attributes latent factors. Our previous experiments with this method are
described in paper [4]. Some decisions made during dataset preparation and evaluation

© Springer International Publishing Switzerland 2014
V. Presutti et al. (Eds.): SemWebEval 2014, CCIS 475, pp. 144–149, 2014.
DOI: 10.1007/978-3-319-12024-9_18

are based on observations from this work. CBMF laid some constraints on usage of RDF triples. The RDF records are mapped directly as attributes of the object. Although some graph based features can be employed manually, it is not natural for CBMF. As an alternative, we suggest Ostuni et al. [3] leveraging graph nature of LOD.

Main Contributions: Semantic adaptation of CBMF, usage of multiple DBPedia language editions and novel re-ranking algorithm addressing diversity problem.

2   Recommending Method

Matrix factorization techniques are currently leading methods for learning user preferences. Given the list of users $U = \{u_1, \ldots, u_n\}$ and objects $O = \{o_1, \ldots, o_m\}$, we can form the user-object rating matrix $\mathbf{R} = [r_{uo}]_{n \times m}$. For a given number of latent factors f, matrix factorization aims to decompose original $\mathbf{R}$ matrix into $\mathbf{UO}^T$ (1), where $\mathbf{U}$ is $n \times f$ matrix of user latent factors (μ_i^T stands for latent factors vector for particular user u_i) and $\mathbf{O}^T$ is $f \times m$ matrix of object latent factors (σ_i is vector for particular object o_i). Unknown rating for user i and object j is predicted as $\hat{r}_{ij} = \mu_i^T \sigma_j$. Our target is to learn matrixes $\mathbf{U}$ and $\mathbf{O}$ minimizing errors on known ratings (usually with some regularization penalty to prevent overfitting). Such equation can be solved e.g. by Stochastic Gradient Descent (SGD) iteratively updating user and object latent factors. See e.g. Koren et al. [2] for more elaborated overview.

Content boosted matrix factorization method (CBMF) is based on the assumption that each object's latent factors is a function of its attributes latent factors. Having $\mathbf{O}_{m \times f}$ matrix of object latent factors, $\mathbf{A}_{m \times a}$ matrix of object attributes and $\mathbf{B}_{a \times f}$ matrix of latent factors for each attribute, the constraint can be formulated as $\mathbf{O} = \mathbf{AB}$. Under this constraint, we can reformulate both matrix factorization problem (1), its optimization equation and gradient descend Eq. (2):

$$\mathbf{R} \approx \mathbf{UO}^T = \mathbf{UB}^T\mathbf{A}^T = \underbrace{\begin{bmatrix} \mu_1^T \\ \mu_2^T \\ \vdots \end{bmatrix}}_{n \times f} \times \underbrace{\mathbf{B}^T}_{f \times a} \times \underbrace{\begin{bmatrix} a_1 & a_2 & \cdots \end{bmatrix}}_{a \times m} \tag{1}$$

$$\begin{aligned} \mu_i &= \mu_i + \eta \left(\sum_{j \in K_{ui}} (r_{ij} - \mu_i^T \mathbf{B}^T a_j) \mathbf{B}^T a_j - \lambda \mu_i \right) \\ \sigma_j &= \sigma_j + \eta \left(\sum_{(i,j) \in K} (r_{ij} - \mu_i^T \mathbf{B}^T a_j) a_j \mu_i^T - \lambda \mathbf{B} \right) \end{aligned} \tag{2}$$

CBMF method has also some drawbacks. One of the most important is time complexity, rising with both number of latent factors f and number of attributes a. This prevents us from using all crawled attributes and forced us to choose a sample of them. We have implemented our adaptation of CBMF with varying $\mathbf{A}$ matrix using NoSQL approach to decrease time complexity problems. Maximal running time and number of iteration parameters were also employed.

The ratings were normalized by simple ANOVA model (3) consisting of average rating for user b_u, object b_i and global average μ. We have tested also additional normalizers based on dataset features, but they did not improve evaluation metrics.

$$r_{u,i} = \mu + b_u + b_i + \varepsilon_{u,i} \tag{3}$$

Post-processing (see Algorithm 1) was applied for Task 3 (recommending top-20 objects for each user) in order to increase diversity of the resulting set. During Task 3 evaluation, we have observed high fluctuation of recommended objects, so we have employed bagging over several CBMF runs (object rating was summed over all runs, then applied Algorithm 1), which highly improved F-measure.

Algorithm 1: For producing top-k list of recommending objects, we first produce list of $top\text{-}k_1$, $k_1 > k$ best rated objects for each user (k_1=100 performed best). Then iteratively algorithm takes the best rated object and eliminates all objects with the same author (or any other restricted features listed in *feat* array). If no more objects are available, then the $top\text{-}k_1$ is reset to all objects except the already selected ones.

```
function PostProc(List top-k₁, k, List feat){
    while(selectObj < k){
        reset top-k₁;
        while(sizeof(top-k₁)>0 && selectObj < k){
            get best object from top-k₁; selecObj++;
            delete O ∈ top-k₁: feat[O] ∩ feat[bestO] != ∅; }}}
```

3   Dataset and Semantics

The dataset used in evaluation consisted of both direct DBPedia triples and added semantic information based on original RDF. As for original RDF, we first downloaded all direct attributes of books and its authors. The *core dataset* consisted of RDF triples with patterns: *(<book_uri>, ?p, ?o), (?o, ?p, <book_uri>), (<author_uri>, ?p, ?o) or (?o, ?p,<author_uri>)*. For each triple, the corresponding *DBbook_itemID* is also stored forming new triples *(DBbook_itemID, ?p, ?o)* – we do not distinguish whether book or author is in the role of subject or object. Data were then transformed to fill feature matrix **A** in a following way: Rows consist of *DBbook_itemIDs*, columns – object attributes – consists of all known (seen in the data) combinations of ?o, and ?p and value of each cell is binary information whether *(DBbook_itemID, ?p, ?o)* exists.

Enrichment and Alteration of the *Core Dataset*: Generally the main disadvantage of using CBMF for RDF data is flat nature of the object attributes. We can either stick only to the direct attributes or automatically traverse attributes up to a certain depth. We choose the third option to explore only some parts of RDF graph as using sole direct attributes would result in large loss of information and uniform traversing would on the other hand produce too much useless data. Some data alternations were performed when necessary; we mention only the more interesting data enrichment and transformations.

Transformation of RDF into **A** matrix is particularly unfriendly to the numeric values, so several features with numeric values (e.g. number of pages or release date) were mapped into equipotent intervals and further used in that way.

All notions of similar books (e.g. *preceededBy, notableWork* etc.) and similar persons (e.g. *influences, author* etc.) were grouped together and published as *similarWork* and *similarPerson* features. In some cases the value (RDF object) of a predicate might not be so important as the sole existence of the feature carries enough information. So, for each *?p*, attribute *has_predicate+?p* was added with binary value whether current book has feature *?p*. The information whether the book has wiki page also in other Wikipedia language editions was added to exploit multilingual nature of users. Also if DBPedia language edition exists, we can add language specific data to the core dataset (e.g. gender of an author can be easily extracted from German Wikipedia). Nevertheless the data analysis showed that language editions contain mostly the same information except for *wikiPageWikiLink* property, which was added to the dataset. Further manually annotated semantic information was added for *authors* and *genres* exploiting axes like serious or fun literature, male or female target audience or clustering genres (in future this can be done automatically using WIE/NLP, our annotations will serve as training data). To reflect possible similarity on super categories of books, 3 levels of super-categories through *skos:broader* property was crawled and added to the dataset.

Dataset Filtration: The above described raw dataset contained about 2.5 M triples, 2800 distinct features and over 400 K distinct feature × value pairs. Algorithm running on such dataset would get far beyond reasonable computation time. The algorithm time complexity is dependent on #attributes i.e. feature × value pairs, so we focused on decreasing its number without severe damage to information richness of the dataset. Three basic filters were designed:

- **Feature name filter:** Keep only features not present on the list of useless features. The list was formed manually containing features with no or too little meaning e.g. *dbpedia-owl:wikiPageId, rdfs:label, rdfs:comment* etc.
- **Feature filter:** Keep only features with at least k_s support among objects and at least k_{vc} distinct values, with k_s set to 5 % and k_{vc} to 2.
- **Feature values support filter:** Keep only feature values, where its support is between k_{v1} and $k_{v2,}$ with $k_{v1} = 5$ books and $k_{v2,} = 90$ %.

Setting right boundaries is a bit tricky: basically we need features and values which will reasonably distinguish books into not too small or big groups. The exact setting was tuned experimentally. After applying filters, approx. 100 features and 35 K distinct feature × value pairs remained. Although this is already reasonable amount of data for some initial experiments, the running time was still slow and only a few iterations could be done. More speculative heuristics were applied thereafter mostly in form of not using/using only certain features or using only top-k features (feature values) according to its support. After series of preliminary evaluations, the resulting dataset was formed after applying:

- Not using super-categories and *has_predicate* features.
- Use only top-k most supported *similarWork, similarPersons* and other feature values (evaluated separately, k = 300).

After applying these heuristics, the resulting dataset contains approx. 285 K triples, and 60 different features.

4   Results, Discussion, Conclusions

Table 1 contains results of the on-line evaluation. Methods with less latent factors or based on smaller datasets were generally more successful. This might be caused by constraint on maximal CBMF running time, or perhaps caused by noise in larger datasets. Our *future work* should definitely include experiments and metrics defining data purity and usefulness specially if comes from third party resources.

Table 1.   Results of an online evaluation. Table shows only a small sample focusing on different aspects of our recommending methods.

Task	Method	Score
Task 1	CBMF (5 lat. factors) + ANOVA	0.9369 RMSE
Task 1	Sole baseline predictors	0.9421 RMSE
Task 2	CBMF (5 lat. factors) + ANOVA	0.5550 F-measure
Task 2	CBMF (5 lat. factors)	0.5207 F-measure
Task 3	CBMF (5 lat. factors)	0.0138 F-measure, 0.4556 ILD
Task 3	Bagging + post-proc. (various CBMF)	0.0199 F-measure, 0.4803 ILD

During work on the challenge we have discovered several dead ends and problems, namely super-categories are often too general to provide any reasonable information, hypothesis about importance of feature occurrence itself (*has_predicate* feature) was also not confirmed. The effect of using multiple DBPedia language editions is questionable, however we do not abandon this idea yet as the challenge dataset seems to be comprised mostly from English-speaking users.

On the other hand ANOVA normalization was very useful in both Tasks 1 and 2 (note that for Task 2 it means simple object popularity). Other variants of rating normalization should be examined. The post-processing effectively increased diversity and bagging improved F-measure with minimal decrease of diversity for task 3, so we encourage others to use it as well.

Acknowledgments.   This work was supported by grants SVV-2014-260100, P46 and GAUK-126313.

References

1. Forbes, P., Zhu, M.: Content-boosted matrix factorization for recommender systems: experiments with recipe recommendation. In: RecSys 2011, pp. 261–264. ACM (2011)
2. Koren, Y., Bell, R., Volinsky, C.: Matrix factorization techniques for recommender systems. Comput. IEEE **42**, 30–37 (2009)
3. Ostuni, V.C., Di Noia, T., Di Sciascio, E., Mirizzi, R.: Top-N recommendations from implicit feedback leveraging linked open data. In: RecSys 2013, pp. 85–92. ACM (2013)
4. Peska, L., Vojtas, P.: Using LOD to improve recommending on e-commerce. In: SerSy'13 (2013). http://www.ksi.mff.cuni.cz/ ~ peska/sersy13.pdf

A Hybrid Multi-strategy Recommender System Using Linked Open Data

Petar Ristoski[1]([⊠]), Eneldo Loza Mencía[2], and Heiko Paulheim[1]

[1] Research Group Data and Web Science, University of Mannheim,
Mannheim, Germany
{petar.ristoski,heiko}@informatik.uni-mannheim.de
[2] Knowledge Engineering Group, Technische Universität Darmstadt,
Darmstadt, Germany
eneldo@ke.tu-darmstadt.de

Abstract. In this paper, we discuss the development of a hybrid multi-strategy book recommendation system using Linked Open Data. Our approach builds on training individual base recommenders and using global popularity scores as generic recommenders. The results of the individual recommenders are combined using stacking regression and rank aggregation. We show that this approach delivers very good results in different recommendation settings and also allows for incorporating diversity of recommendations.

Keywords: Linked Open Data · Hybrid recommender systems · Stacking

1   Overall Approach

We propose a hybrid, multi-strategy approach that combines the results of different base recommenders and generic recommenders into a final recommendation. A *base recommender* is an individual collaborative or content based recommender system, whereas a *generic recommender* makes a recommendation solely on some global popularity score, which is the same for all users. The approach has been evaluated on the three tasks of the *LOD-enabled Recommender Systems Challenge 2014* from the domain of book recommendations.[1] For base recommenders, we use two collaborative filtering strategies (item and user based), as well as different content-based strategies exploiting various feature sets created from DBpedia[2].

Generic Recommenders. We use different generic recommenders in our approach. First, the RDF Book Mashup dataset[3] provides the average score assigned

---

[1] 75,559 numeric ratings on 6,166 books (from 0–5, Task 1) and 72,372 binary ratings on 6733 books (Tasks 2 and 3), resp., from 6,181 users for training, and evaluation on 65,560 and 67,990 unknown ratings, resp. See http://challenges.2014.eswc-conferences.org/index.php/RecSys for details.

[2] http://dbpedia.org

[3] http://wifo5-03.informatik.uni-mannheim.de/bizer/bookmashup/

© Springer International Publishing Switzerland 2014
V. Presutti et al. (Eds.): SemWebEval 2014, CCIS 475, pp. 150–156, 2014.
DOI: 10.1007/978-3-319-12024-9_19

to a book on Amazon. Furthermore, DBpedia provides the number of ingoing links to the Wikipedia article corresponding to a DBpedia instance, and the number of links to other datasets (e.g., other language editions of DBpedia), which we also use as global popularity measures. Finally, SubjectiveEye3D delivers a subjective importance score computed from Wikipedia usage information.[4]

Features for Content-Based Recommendation. The features for content-based recommendation were extracted from DBpedia using the RapidMiner Linked Open Data extension [8]. We use the following feature sets for describing a book:

- All *direct types*, i.e., `rdf:type`, of a book[5]
- All *categories of a book*
- All *categories of a book including broader categories*[6]
- All *categories of a book's author(s)*
- All *categories of a book's author(s) and of all other books* by the book's authors
- All *genres of a book* and of all other books by the book's authors
- All *authors that influenced or were influenced* by the book's authors
- A bag of words created from the *abstract* of the book in DBpedia. That bag of words is preprocessed by tokenization, stemming, removing tokens with less than three characters, and removing all tokens less frequent than 3 % or more frequent than 80 %.

Furthermore, we created a *combined book's feature set*, comprising direct types, qualified relations, genres and categories of the book itself, its previous and subsequent work and the author's notable work, the language and publisher, and the bag of words from the abstract. Table 1 depicts the number of features in each set.

Besides DBpedia, we made an effort to retrieve additional features from two additional LOD sources: British Library Bibliography and DBTropes[7]. Using the RapidMiner LOD extension, we were able to link more than 90 % of the books to BLB entities, but only 15 % to DBTropes entities. However, the generated features from BLB were redundant with the features retrieved from DBpedia, and the coverage of DBTropes was too low to derive meaningful features. Hence, we did not pursue those sources further.

Recommender Strategies. For implementing the collaborative and content-based recommendation systems, we used the RapidMiner Recommendation Extension [5], which uses k-NN classification. We use $k = 80$ and cosine similarity for the base recommenders. The rationale of using cosine similarity is that,

---

[4] https://github.com/paulhoule/telepath/wiki/SubjectiveEye3D
[5] This includes types in the YAGO ontology, which can be quite specific (e.g., *American Thriller Novels*).
[6] The reason for not including broader categories by default is that the category graph is not a cycle-free tree, with some subsumptions being rather questionable.
[7] http://bnb.data.bl.uk/ and http://skipforward.opendfki.de/wiki/DBTropes

unlike, e.g., Euclidean distance, only common features influence the similarity, but not common absence of features (e.g., two books *not* being American Thriller Novels).

Furthermore, we train an additional recommender on the joint feature set, using Random Decision Trees (RDTs) [11].[8] RDTs generate k_1 decision trees with maximal depth k_2 and random attribute tests at the inner nodes. Each tree collects a distribution over the target variables at each of its leaf nodes by seeing the training data. E.g. for multilabel data, RDT's leaves collect the label distribution so that each RDT predicts for each test instance a distribution over the labels. These predictions are subsequently averaged over all trees in order to produce one single prediction. The predictions of several of such trees are then combined into a final prediction. RDTs provide a good tradeoff between scalability for large example sets and prediction accuracy (often outperforming SVMs).

For applying RDTs to the collaborative filtering data, we transformed the problem into a multilabel task: For each user we generated n different labels indicating each of the possible user ratings, i.e. $n = 5$ for task 1 and $n = 2$ for task 2. During training RDTs learn – for each known book/user combination – the mapping between the feature set of each book and the generated labels. Given an unknown book/user combination x, y, we are now able to estimate a distribution $P(i|\ x, y)$ over the different ratings i. The final predicted rating r is obtained by weighting the ratings $r = \sum_{i=0}^{5} i \cdot P(i|\ x, y)$ (task 1) or by computing the probability difference $P(1|\ x, y) - P(0|\ x, y)$ (task 2).

RDTs do not suffer from high dimensionality and sparseness as much as k-NN does, thus we have built $k_1 = 10$ trees with depth $k_2 = 10$ on the combined book's properties feature set, instead of individual RDTs on each feature set.[9]

2   Predicting Ratings and Top K Lists

For predicting ratings (task 1 in the challenge), we use all the recommendation algorithms discussed above for training a regression model in the range of $[0; 5]$. The results for the base and generic recommenders are shown in Fig. 1.

In order to create a more sophisticated combination of those recommenders, we trained a *stacking* model as described in [10]: We trained the base recommenders in 10 rounds in a cross validation like setting, collected their predictions, and learned a stacking model on the predictions. The results in Table 1 show that the stacked prediction outperforms the base and generic recommenders, with the RDT based stacking (with $k_1 = 500$ and $k_2 = 20$) slightly ahead of linear

---

[8] We used the implementation available at http://www.dice4dm.com/.

[9] In general, it holds that the higher k_1 and k_2 the better, since this increases the number of covered feature dimensions and the diversity of the ensemble. However, comparably small values of k_1 and k_2, around 10 or 20 and maximally 100, are sufficient according to experiments by Zhang et al. [11] and Kong and Yu [4]. In our experiments, we tried to find a good balance between computational costs and predictive quality, and we report the combination which we used for our final recommendations.

Table 1. Performances of the base and generic recommenders, the number of features used for each base recommender, and the performance of the combined recommenders

Recommender	#Features	Task 1		Task 2
		RMSE	LR β	F-Score
Item-based collaborative filtering	–	0.8843	+0.269	0.5621
User-based collaborative filtering	–	0.9475	+0.145	0.5483
Book's direct types	534	0.8895	-0.230	0.5583
Author's categories	2,270	0.9183	+0.098	0.5576
Book's (and author's other books') genres	582	0.9198	+0.082	0.5567
Combined book's properties	4,372	0.9421	+0.0196	0.5557
Author and influenced/influencedBy authors	1,878	0.9294	+0.122	0.5534
Books' categories and broader categories	1,987	0.939	+0.012	0.5509
Abstract bag of words	227	0.8893	+0.124	0.5609
RDT recommender on combined book's properties	4,372	0.9223	+0.128	0.5119
Amazon rating	–	1.037	+0.155	0.5442
Ingoing Wikipedia links	–	3.9629	+0.001	0.5377
SubjectiveEye3D score	–	3.7088	+0.001	0.5369
Links to other datasets	–	3.3211	+0.001	0.5321
Average of all individual recommenders	14	0.8824	–	–
Stacking with linear regression	14	0.8636	–	0.4645
Stacking with RDT	14	**0.8632**	–	0.4966
Borda rank aggregation	14	–	–	**0.5715**

regression, and both stacking approaches outperforming the baseline approach of averaging all recommenders' ratings.

To further analyze the contribution of each feature, we also report the β parameters found by linear regression. It can be observed that apart from the direct types, all base and generic recommenders contribute to the linear regression. A possible reason for that anomaly is that direct types and categories are rather redundant. Furthermore, we can see the benefit of using stacking approaches as the three generic recommenders with high RMSE are filtered out by the LR model.

For creating top k lists from binary ratings (task 2 in the challenge), we again trained regression models like for rating prediction, using a range of $[0; 1]$. The top k lists were then obtained by ranking by the predicted rating. As shown in Table 1, the base recommenders worked quite well, but the combination with linear regression delivered non-satisfying results. The reason is that the outcome of the base recommenders is not scaled equally for each user, but strongly depends on the user's total number of positive and negative ratings. This made it impossible to learn a suitable regression function.

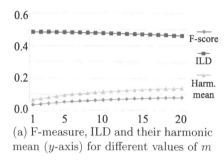
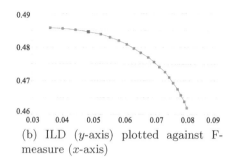

(a) F-measure, ILD and their harmonic mean (y-axis) for different values of m

(b) ILD (y-axis) plotted against F-measure (x-axis)

Fig. 1. Trade-off between F-measure and diversity

However, we observed that despite being incompatible in scale, the base and generic recommenders delivered good *rankings* for each user. Thus, we performed an aggregation of the rankings produced by the different recommenders, using Borda's rank aggregation algorithm, which outperforms all the individual recommenders, as well as the stacking regression.

3   Creating Diverse Predictions

The final task in the challenge was to address *diversity* of predictions, i.e., trade off the accuracy of predictions, measured in F1 score, and their diversity, measured in intra-list diversity (ILD), both on a top k list. To address that trade-off, we followed a greedy top down approach which creates a ranking as for top k lists. First, we select the top m items from that list. Then, we process the list from position $m + 1$ on, adding each book that does not share author and categories with any of the books already on the list, until the list has k items.

The results are depicted in Fig. 1 for k = 20, selecting items from a list of the top 100 predictions. It can be observed that the F1 score gradually rises when using higher values of m, while the ILD drops. Although the harmonic mean is optimal for using simply the top 20 predictions (given the different orders of magnitude of F1 and ILD), we decided to submit the solution with $m = 4$ to the challenge.[10]

4   Related Work

The area of recommender systems has been extensively studied in the literature, resulting in a variety of techniques for performing recommendation, including content-based, collaborative, and hybrid techniques. However, only a handful of approaches exploit Linked Open Data to provide recommendations. Among the

---

[10] The reason is that the challenge uses the average rank w.r.t. F1 and ILD as a scoring function, which makes the selection of an optimal parameter strongly depend on the other participants' solutions. It turned out that $m = 4$ optimized our scoring.

earliest such efforts is *dbrec* [7], which is using DBpedia as a knowledge base to build a music content-based recommender system. Heitmann et al. [3] propose an open recommender system which utilize Linked Data to mitigate the new-user, new-item and sparsity problems of collaborative recommender systems.

More recent approaches [1,2,6,9] have shown that using data from the LOD cloud can improve the performances for both content-based and collaborative recommender systems, in various domains.

5   Conclusion and Outlook

In this paper, we have layed out a hybrid multi-strategy approach for linked data enabled recommender systems. We have shown that combining the predictions of different base recommenders is a feasible strategy, and that generic (i.e., non user specific) recommenders can be a useful ingredient.

In particular, our approach allows for the addition of new feature groups without interaction effects, and for the combination of different recommender strategies. By exploiting stacking regression, an optimal combination of different recommenders can be found automatically, however, for ranking-based problems, rank aggregation turned out to be the more promising strategy.

Acknowledgements. The work presented in this paper has been partly funded by the German Research Foundation (DFG) under grant number PA 2373/1-1 (Mine@LOD).

References

1. Di Noia, T., Mirizzi, R., Ostuni, V.C., Romito, D.: Exploiting the web of data in model-based recommender systems. In: Proceedings of the Sixth ACM Conference on Recommender Systems, RecSys '12, pp. 253–256, ACM. New York (2012)
2. Di Noia, T., Mirizzi, R., Ostuni, V.C., Romito, D., Zanker, M.: Linked open data to support content-based recommender systems. In: Proceedings of the 8th International Conference on Semantic Systems, I-SEMANTICS '12, pp. 1–8. ACM, New York (2012)
3. Heitmann, B., Hayes, C.: Using linked data to build open, collaborative recommender systems. In: AAAI Spring Symposium: Linked Data Meets Artificial Intelligence (2010)
4. Kong, X., Yu, P.S.: An ensemble-based approach to fast classification of multi-label data streams. In: CollaborateCom, pp. 95–104 (2011)
5. Mihelčić, M., Antulov-Fantulin, N., Bošnjak, M., Šmuc, T.: Extending rapidminer with recommender systems algorithms. In: RapidMiner Community Meeting and Conference (RCOMM 2012) (2012)
6. Ostuni, V.C., Di Noia, T., Mirizzi, R., Di Sciascio, E.: Top-n recommendations from implicit feedback leveraging linked open data. In: IIR, pp. 20–27 (2014)
7. Passant, A.: dbrec — music recommendations using DBpedia. In: Patel-Schneider, P.F., Pan, Y., Hitzler, P., Mika, P., Zhang, L., Pan, J.Z., Horrocks, I., Glimm, B. (eds.) ISWC 2010, Part II. LNCS, vol. 6497, pp. 209–224. Springer, Heidelberg (2010)

8. Paulheim, H., Ristoski, P., Mitichkin, E., Christian, B.: Data mining with background knowledge from the web. In: RapidMiner World (2014)
9. Schmachtenberg, M., Strufe, T., Paulheim, H.: Enhancing a location-based recommendation system by enrichment with structured data from the web. In: Web Intelligence, Mining and Semantics (2014)
10. Ting, K.M., Witten, I.H.: Issues in stacked generalization. J. Artif. Intell. Res. **10**(1), 271–289 (1999)
11. Zhang, X., Yuan, Q., Zhao, S., Fan, W., Zheng, W., Wang, Z.: Multi-label classification without the multi-label cost. In: Proceedings of the 2010 SDM (2010)

Exploring Semantic Features for Producing Top-N Recommendation Lists from Binary User Feedback

Nicholas Ampazis[✉] and Theodoros Emmanouilidis

Intelligent Data Exploration and Analysis Laboratory (IDEAL),
Department of Financial and Management Engineering,
University of the Aegean, 82100 Chios, Greece
{n.ampazis,emman}@fme.aegean.gr
http://labs.fme.aegean.gr/ideal

Abstract. In this paper, we report the experiments that we conducted for two of the tasks of the ESWC'14 Challenge on Linked Open Data (LOD)-enabled Recommender Systems. Task 2 and Task 3 dealt with the top-N recommendation problem from a binary user feedback dataset and results were evaluated on the accuracy and diversity respectively of the recommendations produced in a Top-N recommendation list for each user. The DBbook dataset was used in both tracks in which the books had been mapped to their corresponding DBpedia URIs. Since the mappings could be used to extract semantic features from DBpedia, in all our experiments, we avoided the use of any collaborative filtering methods (e.g. user/item K-nearest neighbors and matrix factorization approaches) and instead focused exclusively on the semantic features of the items. Even though the performance of our methods did not beat the best performing approaches of other teams, our results indicate that it is indeed feasible to create effective recommender systems which fully utilize the content of the items they deal with by utilizing information from the Semantic Web.

Keywords: Top-N recommendations · Content-based recommender systems · Semantic Web

1 Introduction

The literature review of studies on recommender systems (see for example, the Netflix prize solutions summarizing paper of "Bellkor's Pragmatic Chaos" team [1,2]), readily makes apparent that latent factor models (matrix factorization, singular value decomposition, etc), and K-nearest neighbors approaches are among the ones most suited to the problem. However, besides the knowledge of explicit user-item ratings, additional information (if available) can be exploited to define or improve similarities between users and/or items.

Recent developments in the Semantic Web community now enable us to set up links between items in different data sources, and allow us to automatically extract content and meta information for the available items. Item similarity can

© Springer International Publishing Switzerland 2014
V. Presutti et al. (Eds.): SemWebEval 2014, CCIS 475, pp. 157–162, 2014.
DOI: 10.1007/978-3-319-12024-9_20

hence be calculated based on the content comparison of the given items. In the literature this approach is known as content-based recommendation [3]. Unlike Collaborative Filtering (CF) approaches, in a content-based recommender system, recommendations are based solely on the profile built up by analyzing the content of items that the target user has interacted with in the past. The recommendation problem hence becomes a search for items, the content of which is most similar to the content of items already preferred by the target user. In addition, users can be modeled on the basis of the items that they have collected and thus we can define content-based similarity metrics between the users and the different items.

In this work, we explored a content-based recommendation approach for both Tasks 2 and 3 of the ESWC'14 Challenge on LOD-enabled Recommender Systems and we report on the obtained results. By using LOD and semantic technologies alone, in favour of adopting any of the well known collaborative filtering approaches, we developed a knowledge-enabled content-based recommendation methodology which performed sufficiently well on both tasks. This indicates that content-based approaches that rely entirely on the utilization of semantic features can perform reasonably well on a variety of recommendation metrics.

2   Methodology

Both tracks utilized the Dbook dataset which contains user preferences on items retrieved from the Web. The common training set provided for Task 2 and Task 3 contained tab-separated triplets of the form userID/itemID/rating. The ratings were binary, with 1 indicating that the item was relevant for the user, and 0 meaning irrelevant. The training set contained 72372 ratings that 6181 users gave to 6733 items. Overall 8170 book titles were available in the Dbook dataset which were mapped to their corresponding DBpedia URIs. Those DBpedia URIs were used to extract semantic features from DBpedia by issuing SPARQL queries at the endpoint http://dbpedia.org/sparql. For each $DBpedia_uri we extracted the subjects and author(s) using the following queries respectively:

SELECT ?o WHERE { < "$DBpedia_uri" > <http://purl.org/dc/terms/subject> ?o.}

SELECT ?o WHERE { < "$DBpedia_uri" > <http://dbpedia.org/ontology/author> ?o.}

We extracted 7079 distinct subjects and 3046 different authors which were used to represent documents as binary semantic feature vectors in $\mathbb{R}^N$ with $N = 7079 + 3046 = 10125$.

For running our experiments we utilized a PostgreSQL[1] database schema which is shown in Fig. 1. The "ratings" table contains the binary ratings training set and the table "features_documents" contains the binary document feature vectors described above. For representing the document vectors in the database we employed MADlib[2] which is an open-source library for scalable in-database analytics with support for PostgreSQL. Madlib implements a sparse vector data type, named "svec", which provides compressed storage of vectors

[1] http://www.postgresql.org

[2] http://madlib.net

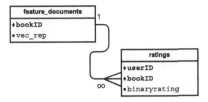

Fig. 1. Database schema

that have many duplicate elements (in our case zeros). The svec type employs a simple Run Length Encoding (RLE) scheme to represent sparse vectors as pairs of count-value arrays. For example, the svec array representation:

'{1085,1,3777,1,532,1,1682}:{0.0,1.0,0.0,1.0,0.0,1.0,0.0}'::madlib.svec

says that 1085 occurrences of 0 are followed by 1 occurence of 1, followed by 3777 occurrences of 0, etc. This example uses just 7 integers and 7 floating point numbers to store the array. Further, it is easy to implement vector operations that can take advantage of the RLE representation to make computations faster. The SVEC module provides a library of such functions like adding svec vectors and calculating distances between them. The field "vec_rep" in the "features_documents" contains the svec vector representation of each bookID.

Our approach for providing Top-N recommendation is that users can be modeled on the basis of the items for which they've expressed a preference. Thus users can be also represented as vectors in $\mathbb{R}^N$ ($N = 10125$), where their feature vectors can be calculated iteratively by adding or subtracting the document semantic feature vectors for which they've expressed a positive or negative signal respectively. This allows us to embed the users onto the document semantic feature space and define content-based similarity metrics between the users and the different items. Consequently we are able to populate the Top-N recommendation list for each user with the items that exhibit the highest similarities with the user's feature vector.

The first listing in Algorithm 1 depicts the MADLib SQL methodology for constructing the feature vector "uvec" for each $DBbook_userID in the training set. For each user we loop over the items for which this user has expressed a binary rating and add or subtract the correspond item feature vector according to the rating being 1 or 0 respectively. At the end of looping process each user has been assigned a semantic feature vector which can then be used to provide Top-N recommendations for Tasks 2 and 3 as explained below.

3   Task 2 Experiments

Task 2 participants were asked to add a corresponding relevance score for specific user-item pairs in the evaluation dataset. The relevance scores were used by the evaluation service to form a Top-5 item recommendation list for each user. Thus for each user only items in the evaluation set were considered to

Algorithm 1. Methodology in SQL

```
1: for r,p in (SELECT ratings.bookID, ratings.binaryrating from ratings,feature_documents
       WHERE  ratings.bookID=feature_documents.bookID  AND  ratings.userID=$DBbook_userID)
       loop
           –CONSTRUCT THE USER FEATURE VECTOR
           if p=1 then
           uvec:= (SELECT MADlib.svec_plus(uvec, (SELECT vec_rep FROM feature_documents
       WHERE bookID = r)));
           else
           uvec:= (SELECT MADlib.svec_minus(uvec, (SELECT vec_rep FROM feature_documents
       WHERE bookID = r)));
           end if;
           end loop;
2: Task2: for r in SELECT bookID, 1- MADlib.tanimoto_distance(vec_rep, uvec)
           FROM feature_documents
           WHERE bookID=$DBbook_itemID loop
           return next r;
           end loop;
3: Task3: for r in SELECT bookID, 1- MADlib.tanimoto_distance(vec_rep, uvec)
           FROM feature_documents
           ORDER BY 2 DESC LIMIT 50 loop
           return next r;
           end loop;
```

form the Top-5 recommendation list. The evaluation metric for the task was the F-measure@5[3].

Listing 2 in Algorithm 1 shows how the relevance score for each "$DBbook_userID / $DBbook_itemID" pair in the evaluation can be calculated within the database, provided that the semantic feature vector for the user in question has been calculated as in listing 1. We tried a variety of similarity/distance metrics (cosine, euclidean distance, etc), but the best results were obtained by calculating the Tanimoto distance which is based on the ratio between the size of the intersection of two vectors by the size of the union. Table 1(a) shows the summary of the submission results as reported by the evaluation service.

Table 1. Results on the evaluation set for Task 2 (a) and Task 3 (b)

Task 2	Submitted		Task 3	Submitted	Corrected
P@5	0.6225		P@20	0.0228	0.0134
R@5	0.4662		R@20	0.0738	0.0447
F1@5	0.5331		F1@20	0.0348	0.0206
			ILD@20	0.4447	0.4635
(a)				(b)	

4   Task 3 Experiments

Task 3 dealt with the diversity of the items produced in a Top-20 recommendation list for each user with respect to the author and subject properties of

---

[3] http://sisinflab.poliba.it/semanticweb/lod/recsys/2014challenge/
   eswc2014-lodrecsys-metrics_evaluationservice.pdf

the items. The recommendations lists were computed by considering all unrated items by each user and selecting the Top-20.

Even though the required format of the submission was of the form "$DBbook_userID/$DBbook_itemID/score", the ranking of the items by their score within the Top-20 list was not taken into account by the evaluation system. Instead the evaluation metric considered the participants' positions in the respective F-measure@20 and ILD@20 (as defined in Footnote 3) rankings. More specifically, first a ranking with all participants was generated according to their ILD@20 values. A second ranking with all participants was then generated according to their F-measure@20 values. For each participant the score was finally computed as the mean of the positions in the first two rankings.

Listing 3 in Algorithm 1 shows how we calculated within the database the Top-N recommendations for unseen items for each distinct "$DBbook_userID" in the evaluation set. Again the semantic feature vector for each user is calculated as in listing 1. As in Task 2, we tried a variety of similarity/distance metrics and the best results were still obtained by utilizing the Tanimoto distance. In order to account for the diversity of the items in the list we initially produced a larger Top-50 list of items and we then measured all the pairwise similarities between those 50 items in the 10125-dimensional feature space. The items that appeared more frequently to exhibit zero similarities with their peers finally made it to the Top-20 list. That list was then ordered by the similarity of the items to the user's feature vector (even though that was unnecessary since item ranking within the list was not taken into account, as explained above). Unfortunately due to a bug in the driver script, all the initial items in the Top-50 list were take into account during sorting (not just the Top-20 more diverse items), which resulted in just keeping the first 20 items from the initial Top-50 list, and therefore neglecting the diversity calculations. The bug was discovered just a few hours after the Challenge's deadline, but since the evaluation service was still accepting solutions we report it here for completeness[4]. It is interesting to note the increase in the ILD@20 value of the corrected submission which comes of course at the price of a drop in the F1@20 score. Table 1(b) shows the summary of the submission results as reported by the evaluation service both for the last result submitted within the deadline, and the bug-corrected result.

5   Discussion and Conclusions

In this paper, we investigated the exclusive use of semantic technologies for Tasks 2 and 3 of the ESWC'14 Challenge on LOD-enabled Recommender Systems, combined with an efficient in-database analytics approach for efficiently producing the recommendations. Our approach was based on the computation of aggregated user profiles from the semantic feature vectors of the items that the target user has interacted with. The semantic features of the items where extracted from specific DBpedia item properties (subject and author) which were

---

[4] Final reported ranking for the teams is based on results submitted up to the deadline.

used to represent documents as binary semantic feature vectors. Eventually recommendation lists were formed by taking the most similar items with respect to the user profile. Even though our recommendation strategy may seem simple it showed promising results on both tasks which indicates that the sole utilization of semantic technologies can perform well on a variety of recommendation metrics.

When compared to the few previously attempts to use LOD to build recommender systems, the novelty of our approach relies mainly on a particularly interesting aspect, which is the adoption and discussion of an in-database analytics library for representing the item content descriptions and for computing recommendations. We have also provided detailed SQL listings that depict the approach and which hopefully can be useful for those practitioners interested in developing a fast and efficient recommender system using LOD.

Additionally, since typical content-based systems explicitly incorporate similarities across different items but not across different users, a further novelty of our approach is that the aggregated user profiles from the semantic feature vectors of the items can also allow for explicitly calculating user similarities. Thus, one of the most attractive aspects of our approach is its potential for suggesting interesting directions for further exploitation. For example, the user profiles similarity information can be further utilized within the framework of a typical CF approach such a user K-nearest neighbors setting. This will result in a hybrid algorithm between CF and the semantic approach that would effectively complement each other, for example by alleviating the sparsity and cold-start problems of CF. It is thus within our intension, in a future work, to exploit the potential of such a hybrid algorithm so as to take full advantage of the merits of each approach, which will allow us to propose an improved and efficient hybrid CF/LOD recommender system.

References

1. Koren, Y.: The BellKor Solution to the Netflix Grand Prize, August 2009. http://www.netflixprize.com/assets/GrandPrize2009_BPC_BellKor.pdf
2. Toscher, A., Jahrer, M., Bell, R.: The Big Chaos Solution to the Netflix Grand Prize, August 2009. http://www.netflixprize.com/assets/GrandPrize2009_BPC_BigChaos.pdf
3. Pazzani, M.J., Billsus, D.: Content-based recommendation systems. In: Brusilovsky, P., Kobsa, A., Nejdl, W. (eds.) The Adaptive Web. LNCS, vol. 4321, pp. 325–341. Springer, Heidelberg (2007)

Content-Based Recommender Systems + DBpedia Knowledge = Semantics-Aware Recommender Systems

Pierpaolo Basile[✉], Cataldo Musto, Marco de Gemmis, Pasquale Lops,
Fedelucio Narducci, and Giovanni Semeraro

Department of Computer Science, University of Bari Aldo Moro,
Via E. Orabona 4, 70125 Bari, Italy
{pierpaolo.basile,cataldo.musto,marco.degemmis,pasquale.lops,
fedelucio.narducci,giovanni.semeraro}@uniba.it

Abstract. This paper provides an overview of the work done in the ESWC
Linked Open Data-enabled Recommender Systems challenge, in which we
proposed an ensemble of algorithms based on popularity, Vector Space
Model, Random Forests, Logistic Regression, and PageRank, running on
a diverse set of semantic features. We ranked 1st in the top-N recommendation task, and 3rd in the tasks of rating prediction and diversity.

1 Introduction and Description of the Challenge

Over the last years, more and more semantic data are published following the
Linked Data principles. These datasets, interlinked with each other, form a global
graph, called Linked Open Data (LOD) cloud. In the context of recommender
systems, this data might be useful to interlink information about users, items,
and their relations. The challenge is to investigate whether and how this large
amount of linked knowledge may help to mitigate the cold-start and the data
sparsity problems. This was the primary goal of the LOD-enabled Recommender
Systems challenge, aiming to show how LOD can boost the creation of a new
breed of knowledge-enabled and content-based recommender systems. The con-
test consisted of 3 tasks: *Task 1: Rating Prediction in Cold-start Situations*, i.e.
when users have a few past ratings, and when items have been rated by a few
users; *Task 2: Top-N Recommendation from Binary User Feedback*, i.e. generating ranked lists of items for which only binary ratings are available; *Task 3:
Diversity*, i.e. evaluation of both accuracy of the recommendation list, and diversity of items in the list (in terms of Intra-List Diversity - ILD). Given the domain
of books, diversity is measured with respect to the properties: http://dbpedia.
org/ontology/author and http://purl.org/dc/terms/subject.

The dataset used is DBbook, which contains user data and preferences
retrieved from the Web in the book domain. Each book is mapped to the corresponding DBpedia URI. The mapping contains 8,170 DBpedia URIs, which can
be used to extract features from datasets in the LOD cloud. The training set

© Springer International Publishing Switzerland 2014
V. Presutti et al. (Eds.): SemWebEval 2014, CCIS 475, pp. 163–169, 2014.
DOI: 10.1007/978-3-319-12024-9_21

for Task 1 contains 75,559 ratings (scale 0–5) provided by 6,181 users on 6,166 items which have been rated by at least one user. The training set for Task 2 and Task 3 contains 72,372 binary ratings provided by 6,181 users on 6,733 items.

2   Description of the UNIBA Approach

2.1   Methods

The methodology adopted by UNIBA is based on a blend of the following methods/algorithms to face the three different tasks of the challenge:

(1) **Popularity:** item-based popularity recommender, where the popularity of an item is computed as the ratio between the number of positive ratings and the total number of ratings (positive and negative) it received by all users.

(2) **enhanced Vector Space Model (eVSM) with negation:** content-based recommender based on an incremental dimensionality reduction technique called Random Indexing. Details about the approach are in [4], in which a negation operator [6] is adopted to represent negative preferences, besides positive ones.

(3) **PageRank with Priors:** widely used method to obtain an authority score for a node based on the network connectivity, in which a non-uniform personalization vector may be used for assigning different weights to different nodes [3].

(4) **Random Forests (RF)** [1]: ensemble learning method used for classification or regression, which combines different tree predictors constructed using different samples of the training data and random subsets of the data features.

(5) **Logistic Regression (LR):** supervised learning method for classification which builds a linear model based on a transformed target variable.

2.2   Data Model

The above mentioned methods used a combination of the following features:

(1) **Keywords:** we processed the book descriptions extracted from Wikipedia. Stopwords were removed, and keywords were stemmed. For books not existing in Wikipedia, we processed the DBpedia abstracts.

(2) **Tagme concepts:** Tagme [2] implements an anchor disambiguation algorithm to produce a Wikipedia-based representation of text fragments, where the most relevant concepts occurring in the text are mapped to the Wikipedia articles (i.e. DBpedia nodes) they refer to. Tagme performs a sort of feature selection by filtering out the noise in text fragments, and its main advantage is the ability to annotate very short texts. As an example, the resulting representation obtained for the book *The Great and Secret Show* is: *Dead letter office, Nebraska, New Mexico, Quiddity, Ephemeris, Narcissistic personality disorder, Nuncio, California, Rape.* Interestingly, the technique is able to associate several concepts which are somehow related to the book, and which could be useful to provide accurate and diverse recommendations, as well.

(3) **DBpedia properties:** for each book, we selected the following 10 most frequent properties in DBpedia (http://dbpedia.org/ prefix removed for brevity): (1) `ontology/wikiPageWikiLink`, providing the link from a Wikipedia page to another Wikipedia page. This property allows to take into account other Wikipedia pages which are somehow related; (2) http://purl.org/dc/terms/ subject, providing the topic of a book; (3) `property/genre`, providing the genre of a book; (4) `property/publisher`, providing the publisher of a book; (5) ontology/author, providing the author of a book; (6) `property/followed By`, providing the book followed by a specific book; (7) `property/precededBy`, providing the book preceded by a specific book; (8) property/series, providing the series of a book; (9) `property/dewey`, providing the Dewey Decimal library Classification code; and (10) `ontology/nonFictionSubject` providing the subject of a non-fiction book (e.g.: history, biography, cookbook, ...). PageRank with Priors is performed (for each single user) using graphs with different sets of nodes. Initially, only users, items and links represented by the positive feedback are included; next, we enriched the graph with the 10 properties extracted from DBpedia. Then, we ran a second level expansion stage of the graph to retrieve the following additional resources: (1) internal wiki links of the new added nodes; (2) more generic categories according to the hierarchy in DBpedia; (3) resources of the same category; (4) resources of the same genre; (5) genres pertaining to the author of the book; (6) resources written by the author; and (7) genres of the series the book belongs to.

The graph is pruned by removing nodes which are neither users nor books having a total number of inlinks and outlinks less than 5, and eventually consisted of 340,000 nodes and about 6 millions links.

3   Experimental Evaluation

3.1   Task 1: Rating Prediction in Cold-Start Situations

We ranked 3rd in Task 1 using a *linear combination* of the following algorithms, by obtaining a RMSE equal to 0.8742:

Random Forests, using 2,500 trees, and *Tagme concepts* as features, along with *DBpedia properties* described in Sect. 2.2. We adopted the implementation provided by the Weka library (www.cs.waikato.ac.nz/ml/weka/).

Logistic Regression, using the following features: number of positive, negative and total feedbacks provided by the users (items), ratio between positive (negative) and total number of feedbacks provided by the users (items), stems extracted by the item descriptions, *DBpedia properties* (Sect. 2.2), and *Tagme concepts*. As regards the last three sets of features, their value is the number of occurrences of that feature. Each example, represented using more than 220,000 features, is labelled with the rating provided by that specific user for that specific item. All the features were normalized in the [0,1] interval. We adopted the implementation provided by Liblinear[1]. RF and LR ranked items according to the class probability.

---

[1] http://www.csie.ntu.edu.tw/~cjlin/liblinear/

Combination of baseline predictors, i.e. user/item average rating.

Since 520 out of 6,181 users did not have positive ratings in the training set, we assigned as positive feedback the 5 most popular items (5 is the average number of users' positive ratings in the dataset). Results for Task 1 are reported in Table 1. The weights used in the linear combination (0.2 to RF, 0.2 to the baseline predictors and 0.6 to LR) are selected to maximize performance on testing data, without the use of a validation set.

Table 1. Results for Task 1.

	RF	LR	Baseline predictors	Linear combination
RMSE	0.9285	0.8915	0.8945	**0.8742**

3.2   Task 2: Top-N Recommendation from Binary User Feedback

We ranked 1st in Task 2 by blending together the following five different algorithms, using the Borda count aggregation method:

eVSM: we implemented a content-based recommender as described in [4]. The best result was obtained using *Tagme concepts* as features, 500 as the context vectors dimension, and the negation operator for negative users' preferences.

Popularity: simple baseline as described in Sect. 2.1, which recommends items by ranking them according to their popularity (in decreasing order).

Random Forests: we used 5,000 trees and the same features as in Task 1.

PageRank with Priors: a different configuration of weights is assigned to the nodes. Generally, the prior probability assigned to each node is evenly distributed ($\frac{1}{N}$, where N is the number of nodes). We assigned a higher weight to some nodes according to the user profile. More specifically, 80 % of the weight is evenly distributed among books liked by the users (0 assigned to books disliked by the users), and 20 % of the weight is evenly distributed among the remaining nodes. The damping factor of PageRank was set to 0.85. Both weights and damping factor are chosen after a tuning step on a subset of the training data. The PageRank computed for each node is used to rank the items in the test set. We adopted the implementation of PageRank provided by the Jung library[2].

Logistic Regression: the configuration is as in Task 1. The only difference is that each example is labelled with the binary feedback provided by that specific user for that specific item.

Similarly to Task 1, RF and LR ranked items according to the probability of the class, and the 5 most popular items are used for users with no positive ratings in the training set. Table 2 reports the performance of the single methods, eventually aggregated using the linear combination and Borda count. As regards the linear

---

[2] jung.sourceforge.net

Table 2. Results for Task 2.

	eVSM	Popularity	RF	PageRank	LR	Linear Comb.	Borda
Pr@5	0.6195	0.6431	0.6260	0.6433	0.6445	0.6568	**0.6586**
Re@5	0.4688	0.4875	0.4751	0.4871	0.4888	0.5009	**0.5048**
F1@5	0.5337	0.5546	0.5402	0.5544	0.5560	0.5684	**0.5715**

combination, we assigned 0.1 to eVSM, 0.2 to the popularity baseline and to LR, and finally 0.25 to RF and Page Rank. As for Task 1, the weights were set after a rough tuning.

In Borda count, each item in a ranked list produced by each single method is awarded with a score given according to its position in that list. The lower the item position in the list, the smaller the score. The final score of each item is obtained by summing all the single scores, and this allows to produce the aggregated ranking (in decreasing score value). The single scores in the sum were weighed in order to boost some single methods (weights are reported in parenthesis). As for Task 1, weights are chosen to maximize performance on testing data.

3.3   Task 3: Diversity

We ranked 3rd in the Task 3 by using the PageRank with Priors algorithm, running on the graph described in Sect. 2.2. We assigned a higher weight to some nodes according to the user profile, and to a heuristic of diversity. More specifically, 80 % of the weight is evenly distributed among books liked by the users (0 for books disliked by the users), 10 % of the weight is evenly distributed between all the nodes which are not books, and 10 % of the weight is proportionally distributed among the remaining books (not rated as positive or negative) according to a *diversity score* computed for each item. The diversity score of each item it_j with respect to the profile u_i of the user i is computed in order to take into account both the *similarity* of, and the *novelty* between the user profile and the item. Let U_i the set of *DBpedia properties* of items liked by the user i, and I_j the set of *DBpedia properties* of it_j. The similarity is computed as the Jaccard index between U_i and I_j, while the novelty is the ratio between the cardinality of $I_j \backslash U_i$ (i.e. the set of features of I_j different from those of items liked by the user), and the cardinality of I_j. If the item has features not overlapping with those occurring in the user profile, the similarity is equal to 0, and the novelty is equal to 1. The diversity score is an average between similarity and novelty. Weighing more those items with a higher diversity score allows to impose a bias to the PageRank towards items different from the user profile. The final score computed by the PageRank for each node is used to rank the nodes. Then, the top-20 (book) nodes are selected, as requested by the task. The results obtained by our algorithm are: F@20 = 0.0481 (Pr@20 = 0.0319, Re@20 = 0.0977), and ILD@20 = 0.4717.

4 Discussion

An important outcome of our participation to the challenge is that it was not possible to face all the different tasks using just a single method. We ran hundreds of experiments using different algorithms and features. Results are not reported in the paper due to space limitation, but allow to draw important conclusions. Very simple algorithms based on Vector Space Model and probabilistic models (BM25 and Divergence from Randomness) have performance comparable to more complex algorithms, when fed with semantic features coming from the LOD cloud. The usefulness of the semantic features is also evident when using recommendation algorithms based on classifiers, such as RF or LR, in which the best results were obtained using features based on *DBpedia properties* and *Tagme concepts*. The use of LOD also helps to diversify the results, due to the wealth of relations taken into account in the recommendation process. To sum up, there is an empirical evidence of the potential of the LOD to define advanced semantic recommender systems, even though it is necessary to investigate innovative ways to leverage this huge amount of knowledge. When compared to (few) previous attempts to use LOD to build recommender systems, the novelty of our methods relies on 1) the use of entity linking approaches, such as *Tagme*, which represents an innovative way to access DBpedia knowledge, and on 2) the use of domain-specific DBpedia properties/paths to build the graph model. As to the former aspect, the typical way to define an entry point to DBpedia is to identify the URIs corresponding to items (books for example) and extract the corresponding properties. This complex process of mapping may hinder the use of DBpedia; indeed, the organizers of the challenge explicitly provided a mapping of books to DBpedia URIs. The use of entity linking algorithms represents a novel way to access the DBpedia knowledge through the analysis of the item descriptions, without exploiting any explicit mapping of items to URIs. As regards the exploitation of domain-specific properties/paths in DBpedia, this could allow to fully exploit the semantics of DBpedia relations, differently from previous approaches based just on link-based measures built on DBpedia [5].

References

1. Breiman, L.: Random forests. Mach. Learn. **45**(1), 5–32 (2001)
2. Ferragina, P., Scaiella, U.: Fast and accurate annotation of short texts with wikipedia pages. IEEE Softw. **29**(1), 70–75 (2012)
3. Haveliwala, T.H.: Topic-sensitive pagerank: a context-sensitive ranking algorithm for web search. IEEE Trans. Knowl. Data Eng. **15**(4), 784–796 (2003)
4. Musto, C., Semeraro, G., Lops, P., de Gemmis, M.: Random indexing and negative user preferences for enhancing content-based recommender systems. In: Huemer, C., Setzer, T. (eds.) EC-Web 2011. LNBIP, vol. 85, pp. 270–281. Springer, Heidelberg (2011)

5. Passant, A.: dbrec — music recommendations using DBpedia. In: Patel-Schneider, P.F., Pan, Y., Hitzler, P., Mika, P., Zhang, L., Pan, J.Z., Horrocks, I., Glimm, B. (eds.) ISWC 2010, Part II. LNCS, vol. 6497, pp. 209–224. Springer, Heidelberg (2010)
6. Widdows, D.: Orthogonal negation in vector spaces for modelling word-meanings and document retrieval. In: Proceedings of the 41st Annual Meeting of the Association for Computational Linguistics, pp. 136–143 (2003)

SemStim at the LOD-RecSys 2014 Challenge

Benjamin Heitmann[✉] and Conor Hayes

INSIGHT @ NUI Galway, National University of Ireland, Galway,
Galway, Ireland
{benjamin.heitmann,conor.hayes}@insight-centre.org

Abstract. SemStim is a graph-based recommendation algorithm which is based on Spreading Activation and adds targeted activation and duration constraints. SemStim is not affected by data sparsity, the cold-start problem or data quality issues beyond the linking of items to DBpedia. The overall results show that the performance of SemStim for the diversity task of the challenge is comparable to the other participants, as it took 3rd place out of 12 participants with 0.0413 F1@20 and 0.476 ILD@20. In addition, as SemStim has been designed for the requirements of cross-domain recommendations with different target and source domains, this shows that SemStim can also provide competitive single-domain recommendations.

1 Introduction

In this paper we describe our contribution to the "Linked Open Data-enabled Recommender Systems" challenge at the Extended Semantic Web Conference (ESWC) 2014. The recommender system which we built in order to participate at the challenge employs our SemStim algorithm.

SemStim is a graph-based recommendation algorithm which uses Linked Data from DBpedia in order to provide recommendations. Our approach is innovative due to the three main **design choices** of our algorithm: (1) It is not affected by the *sparsity of rating data* or by the *cold-start problem* (cf. Schein et al. [1]), as it only requires user preferences of the user for whom recommendations are being generated. In other words, it will even work when there is only a single user in the system. (2) It is not dependent on *availability or quality of meta-data* about recommendable items, beyond the quality of linking items to DBpedia. It only makes use of DBpedia as a graph. Other features of Linked Data such as reasoning or the content of literals are not used. (3) Our algorithm has been designed to generate recommendations in a target domain based on user interests in a different source domain, by using indirect connections from DBpedia between items of the two domains. This enables us to provide *cross-domain recommendations* as defined by Fernandez-Tobias et al. [2], even in the worst-case scenario, when there is no overlap between users and items of the two domains.

All three evaluation tasks of the challenge are single-domain recommendation tasks, as both the user preferences and the recommendable items are taken from the provided DBbook dataset. Therefore, the *goal* of our participation

© Springer International Publishing Switzerland 2014
V. Presutti et al. (Eds.): SemWebEval 2014, CCIS 475, pp. 170–175, 2014.
DOI: 10.1007/978-3-319-12024-9_22

in the challenge, is to show that SemStim has a competitive performance for single-domain recommendation, despite the disadvantage of being designed for the requirements of cross-domain recommendation.

The goal of our participation in the challenge, is to show that SemStim has a competitive performance for single-domain recommendation, despite the disadvantage of being designed for the requirements of cross-domain recommendation.

2   High-Level Overview of the SemStim Algorithm

Our SemStim algorithm is an enhanced version of spreading activation (SA) as described by Crestani in [3]. SA enables finding related entities in a semantic network in a fuzzy way without using reasoning, while still being deterministic and taking the semantics of the network into account. SemStim extends basic SA, by adding (1) *targeted activation*, which allows us to describe the target domain of the personalisation, and (2) *constraints* to control the algorithm *duration*. Due to the space constraints of this paper, we will only provide a high-level overview of the algorithm. However, the publication of a detailed, formal description is forthcoming.

SemStim spreads activation on a graph using the RDF data model, so we define the graph $G = (V, E)$, with V as the set of nodes $V = \{v_1, \ldots, v_n\}$ used as vertices in the graph, and $E = \{e_1, \ldots, e_m\}$ as the set of predicates used as edges in the graph.

We denote each iteration of the algorithm as *wave* $w \in \mathbb{N}_0$, and each restart of the algorithm as a *phase* $p \in \mathbb{N}_0$. The *activation state* of the graph G in wave w is denoted by $\mathbf{a}^{(w)} \in \mathbb{R}^n$, with $\mathbf{a}_v^{(w)}$ as the activation of node $v \in V$. The *source domain* $S = \{s_1, \ldots, s_f | s_i \in V\}$ is the subset of V from which items in the user profiles are taken, e.g. all URIs from DBbooks on DBpedia. The *target domain* $D = \{d_1, \ldots, d_e | d_i \in V\}$ is the set of nodes which represent the recommendable items among all of the nodes in V.

Each *user profile* P is a set of nodes $P = \{p_1, \ldots, p_k | p_i \in S\}$. τ is the activation threshold of a node, which determines how much activation a node needs to accumulate before it can fire. Then the *initial activation state* $\mathbf{a}^{(0)}$ is defined by setting the initial activation of all nodes in the user profile P to τ, so that nodes in the user profile can immediately fire and contribute to the activation state $\mathbf{a}^{(1)}$ in wave 1.

For each iteration w of the algorithm, and all nodes $v \in V$, the activation state $\mathbf{a}_v^{(w)}$ with $w > 0$, is obtained from the previous state $\mathbf{a}_v^{(w-1)}$ by first applying the input function $I(v, w)$ to v. Then the activation function $A(v, w)$ is applied to the result of $I(v, w)$. As the last step, the output function $O(v, w)$ is applied to the result of $A(v, w)$.

The *input function* $I(v, w)$ aggregates the weighted output of the direct neighbors of node v in wave w. The direction of an edge in the graph is not taken into account, resulting in an undirected view on the graph. The *activation function* $A(v, w)$ determines the amount of activation which a node can spread to its neighbors when it reaches its activation threshold. The *output function* $O(v, w)$

determines if a node can fire in wave w. This is dependent not just on the activation function $A(v, w)$, but also on binary functions which determine if the node can fire, or if the algorithm has reached the termination condition.

The $Restart(\mathbf{a}^{(w)})$ function determines if a restart is necessary. Whenever the number of activated nodes stays the same between wave $w - 1$ and wave w, then no further activation is possible without restarting by firing all activated nodes again. Each restart marks the start of a new *phase* of the algorithm.

The $Fire(v, w)$ function determines if a specific node v in wave w can spread the result of its activation function to its neighbours. There are 2 conditions for firing: (1) The accumulated activation of the node was below the activation threshold τ in the previous wave $w - 1$, and has reached τ in the current wave w. (2) If the $Restart(\mathbf{a}^{(w)})$ function signals a restart, and if the total number of restarts is below the maximum number of phases ρ_{max}. Note that each node can only cross the activation threshold once, while it can be restarted up to ρ_{max} times.

The $Terminate(\mathbf{a}^{(w)})$ function determines if the algorithm as a whole can terminate. There are two termination conditions: (1) the number of activated nodes from the target domain D is higher then the required number of targets, which is given as θ. Or (2) if the algorithm has reached the maximum number of waves, which is specified by w_{max}.

The *top-k recommendations* for target domain D are determined after the termination by sorting the set $\{\mathbf{a}_v^{(w)} > \tau \mid v \in D\}$ of all activated nodes from the target domain by their activation values, and returning the first k items.

Please note that SemStim uses a non-linear activation model. This differentiates it from other variations of SA, such as the linear activation model, which is described in Berthold et al. [4]. The linear activation model introduces the problem of making SA "query independent", as the SA algorithm then converges on the principal eigenvector of the weighted adjacency matrix [4] independent of the user preferences. In order to avoid this problem and allow making personalised recommendations for each individual user, SemStim uses input, activation and output functions which constrain the activation and which implement a non-linear activation model.

3   System Description

3.1   Selection of Evaluation Tasks

The challenge provides data for 3 evaluation tasks, which are (1) the rating prediction task, (2) the top-N recommendation task and (3) the diversity recommendation task. As we now explain, SemStim is only applicable to the diversity recommendation task.

SemStim is not applicable to the *rating prediction task*, as our algorithm does not make use of rating data. In addition, SemStim could not perform the *top-N recommendation task*, given the properties of the evaluation data set. We analysed the test data set, and we found that the median number of items in the test profiles is 12. In order to perform the given top-N recommendation task, the items in the test profile need to be ranked and the top-5 items need to be recommended. SemStim would need to start with the train profile of a user and then find at least 5 books from the 12 books in the test profile in a graph with 11 million vertices. Initial testing showed that this exceeds reasonable limits for runtime and memory, so we were not able to participate in the top-N recommendation task.

However, we were able to apply SemStim to the given *diversity recommendation task*. In order to perform the diversity recommendation task, a list of top-20 recommendations needs to be made, using the unrated books of a user. As the DBbook data set contains 6733 books, this amounts to using SemStim to find 20 of 6733 books on the DBpedia graph for 6181 users. Testing showed that using the available data, SemStim can perform the diversity recommendation task for all 6181 users.

3.2   Applying SemStim to the Diversity Recommendation Task

We use SemStim to generate 20 recommendations for each user profile in the training data of the diversity recommendation task in 6 steps, as follows:

1. We determine the set P of start nodes for the active user. The train data contains binary ratings, where 1 indicates relevance for the user and 0 indicates irrelevance. If the user has any positive preferences, then their corresponding DBpedia URIs are added to P, while ignoring all negative preferences. However, if the user has no positive preferences at all, then the DBpedia URIs of all his negative preferences are added to P. 1463 users have only negative preferences in their user profiles.
2. We set the target domain T to be the set of DBpedia URIs for all unrated books of the active user.
3. We set the constants of SemStim. We experimentally determined that we achieve the best results for the following configuration: activation threshold: $\tau = 0.7$; maximum number of waves: $w_{max} = 1$; maximum number of phases: $\rho_{max} = 5$; required number of activated nodes from T: $\theta = 20$; default weight of predicates: $\beta = 1.0$; initial node output before applying modifiers: $\alpha = 4.0$.
4. Then we run the algorithm. When the algorithm terminates, we rank the activated nodes by their activation value in descending order, and return the corresponding DBbook IDs of the first 20 nodes.
5. If the number of activated nodes is less than 20, we add random, unrated items to reach the target size of 20, as the evaluation system requires all users to have 20 recommendations.

3.3   Usage of Linked Data

We use a subset of DBpedia 3.8 with 67 million edges and 11 million vertices, which includes all article categories, disambiguation links, instance types, mapping-based properties, transitive redirects, categories, and entity types. We choose this subset, because SemStim as a graph algorithm requires as much available data about edges between vertices on DBpedia as possible, and this subset contains all the available edge data. Conversely we did not use any literals from DBpedia, as they are not used by SemStim. The linkage data which connects the books in the DBbook data of the challenge to DBpedia, has been provided by the challenge organisers.

In order to store this subset of DBpedia, we used the Header-Dictionary-Triple (HDT) store [5], which provides a compact data structure and binary serialisation format for RDF. HDT keeps big datasets compressed in memory while allowing read-only access to the graph without prior decompression. The HDT serialisation of our DBpedia subset takes up 559 MB. The average duration of a simple subject or object query using HDT on this data set is 0.2 ms.

3.4 Hardware Infrastructure

To run the diversity evaluation task, we used a server with 24 Intel Xeon cores at 2.40 GHz and with 96 GB RAM. We ran 12 threads concurrently, the remaining capacity was used for e.g. garbage collection, and by other users of the server. The duration of executing the diversity evaluation task is around 4 hours.

4   Lessons Learned

The overall results show that SemStim has a competitive performance which is comparable to that of the other participants in the diversity task. This is supported by SemStim taking the 3rd place out of 12 participants in the leader board of the diversity recommendation task. This is based on the average of the rankings on F1-score and intra-list diversity (ILD). The F1-score of SemStim was ranked in 4th place with 0.0413, and the ILD of SemStim was ranked in 7th place with 0.476.

Further, we found out that our algorithm is not over-optimised for either F1-score or diversity, as the parameters of the algorithm can be tuned towards either of these metrics. Independent of the algorithm parameters, the baseline of the ILD diversity is 0.4570. By setting the activation threshold very low at 0.1, and setting a maximum of 4 phases and 3 waves, SemStim can achieve an F1-score of 0.0593, which comes at the cost of a comparatively low ILD of 0.4591. On the other hand, SemStim can achieve a high ILD of 0.4858, by setting a higher threshold of 0.6 and using only a maximum of 1 phase and 1 wave. However this is at the expense of a low F1 score of 0.0019.

5   Conclusions

In this paper we described our contribution to the "Linked Open Data-enabled Recommender Systems" challenge at the Extended Semantic Web Conference (ESWC) 2014. By participating in the challenge we showed that SemStim has a competitive performance which is comparable to that of the other participants in the diversity task, as SemStim took the 3rd place out of 12 participants.

This shows that SemStim can provide competitive recommendations for the single domain recommendation task, although the algorithm was designed for the requirements of cross-domain recommendations.

Acknowledgements. This publication has emanated from research supported in part by a research grant from Science Foundation Ireland (SFI) under Grant Number SFI/12/RC/2289.

References

1. Schein, A.I., Popescul, A.H.L., Popescul, R., Ungar, L.H., Pennock, D.M.: Methods and metrics for cold-start recommendations. In: Conference on Research and Development in Information Retrieval, pp .253–260. ACM Press (2002)
2. Fernández-Tobías, I., Cantador, I., Kaminskas, M., Ricci, F.: Cross-domain recommender systems: a survey of the state of the art. In: Spanish Conference on Information Retrieval (2012)
3. Crestani, F.: Application of spreading activation techniques in information retrieval. Artif. Intell. Rev. **11**(6), 453–482 (1997)
4. Berthold, M., Brandes, U., Kötter, T., Mader, M., Nagel, U., Thiel, K.: Pure spreading activation is pointless. In: Conference on Information and Knowledge Management (2009)
5. Fernández, J.D., Martínez-Prieto, M.A., Gutiérrez, C., Polleres, A., Arias, M.: Binary RDF representation for publication and exchange (HDT). Web Semant. **19**(2), 22–41 (2013)

Popular Books and Linked Data: Some Results for the ESWC'14 RecSys Challenge

Michael Schuhmacher[✉] and Christian Meilicke

Research Group Data and Web Science, University of Mannheim,
Mannheim, Germany
{michael,christian}@informatik.uni-mannheim.de

Abstract. Within this paper we present our contribution to Task 2 of the ESWC'14 Recommender Systems Challenge. First we describe an unpersonalized baseline approach that uses no linked-data but applies a naive way to compute the overall popularity of the items observed in the training data. Despite being very simple and unpersonalized, we achieve a competitive F_1 measure of 0.5583. Then we describe an algorithm that makes use of several features acquired from DBpedia, like author and type, and self-generated features like abstract-based keywords, for item representation and comparison. Item recommendations are generated by a mixture-model of individual classifiers that have been learned per feature on a user neighborhood cluster in combination with a global classifier learned on all training data. While our Linked-Data-based approach achieves an F_1 measure of 0.5649, the increase over the popularity baseline remains surprisingly low.

1 Introduction

Within this paper we describe the methods we developed for participating in Task 2 of the ESWC'14 Linked Open Data-enabled Recommender Systems Challenge[1]. For Task 2, the aim was a top-5 item recommendation per user, based on a training dataset with binary ratings. For each user, a relatively small set of books, on average 11.00 (min 0, max 20), to select from was already given. Assigning a score to each item-user pair defines an ordered list from which the top-5 ranked items for each user are interpreted as recommendations.

The training dataset consisting of 72,371 user-book-rating tuples was given, with 6,181 distinct users and 6,733 distinct books. The evaluation/test dataset contains the same 6,181 users, consequently for every user at least one training data recommendation was available. However, out of the 6,903 unique books in the test data, 939 have not been observed before in the training data, thus creating an item-cold-start situation for 1,964 item-user-pairs. While those item-user-pairs might be of special interest for a LOD-enabled system, this subset represents only a small fraction of the 67,989 user-item pairs in the evaluation dataset.

---

[1] http://challenges.2014.eswc-conferences.org/index.php/RecSys

© Springer International Publishing Switzerland 2014
V. Presutti et al. (Eds.): SemWebEval 2014, CCIS 475, pp. 176–181, 2014.
DOI: 10.1007/978-3-319-12024-9_23

2   System Description

For better understanding the dataset and the potential of linked data for improving the recommendation process, we implemented both an unpersonalized baseline using no external knowledge and a machine learning approach exploiting
item features derived from DBpedia. Our baseline does not make use of any
external data, but uses only the information found within the given training
dataset. It is based on the naive idea to recommend top-rated books. Our main
system takes a very different approach as it relies heavily on DBpedia for item
representation and uses supervised learning on the training data for making rating predictions. This system has participated as UNIMANNHEIM in Task 2 of the
challenge.

2.1   Unpersonalized Baseline

To understand the benefit of exploiting Linked Open Data, we implemented
a naive baseline that follows the simple idea to recommend books according to
their overall rating. Our baseline is thus an unpersonalized method that produces
the same recommendations for each user by computing a popularity score for
each book. In particular, we computed for each book b the score

$$pop(b) = \#likes(b)/(\#likes(b) + \#dislikes(b) + 1)$$

where $\#likes(b)$ refers to the number of users that gave a positive rating for b
and $\#dislikes(b)$ refers to the number of users that gave a negative rating to
b. Note that we added +1 to the denominator to avoid that a book with no
negative ratings and a low number of positive ratings achieves a high score. We
refer to this method as the popularity baseline in the following.

For those 939 books that have not been observed in the training data, this
method yields $pop(b) = 0$, i.e. such a book is always less preferred compared to
any of the observed books. According to the results presented in [3] we would
expect that such a method is clearly outperformed by any personalized approach
or any other approach that uses external knowledge. However, we wanted to
implement a naive baseline to better understand in the results of the methods
discussed the next section.

2.2   Linked-Data-Based Recommender

In contrast to the baseline, our Linked-Data-based recommender (LDR) makes
prominent use of external information, namely item features obtained from
DBpedia.[2] The key components are (i) the item representation model employing
features from DBpedia data, (ii) the naive Bayes classifier for rating prediction,

---

[2] As we discovered an implementation bug in the original LDR system as used for the
ESWC Challenge, we present here the fixed system which takes a slightly different
approach to feature representation and classifier learning.

and (iii) the user-neighborhood-based collaborative filtering for reducing data sparsity.

Item Features. In order to overcome the item sparsity and to be able to make predictions for the unobserved items, we opt to represent each item by a set of multi-valued multinomial features. Given the gold standard mappings from book item ids to their corresponding DBpedia entities,[3] we opt to focus on the information available from DBpedia (Version 3.9). We manually chose the following predicates to be queried and added as features:[4]

- Genre: `dbo:literaryGenre`
- Wikipedia categories: `dcterms:subject`
- DBpedia and Yago types: `rdf:type`
- Author(s): `dbo:author`, `dbo:writer`
- Book Series: `dbo:series`
- Publisher: `dbo:publisher`

For reducing sparsity, we furthermore expanded all retrieved Wikipedia categories by their immediate super-category via the `skos:broader` predicate.

Manual categories. The problem in using subjects, genres, and similar properties in the appropriate way is related to the fact that (i) there exist a waste amount of different values, (ii) these values are often scattered over different properties, and (iii) the values can be very specific (e.g., `High_fantasy_novels` instead of `fantasy`). To overcome these problems, we have created a list of 30 categories like `science fiction`, `fantasy`, `horror`, `philosophy`, and so on. To each of these categories we have assigned a simple regular expression (in most cases just the name of the category). Then we have parsed the abstract (`dbo:abstract`), the genre (`dbo:literaryGenre`, `dbp:genre`) and the subject (`dcterms:subject`) of each book and checked whether the pattern defined by the regular expression was identified. This resulted in a new aggregated feature with more coverage and a restricted value set.

Feature expansion. To overcome the problem of sparsely populated features, we computed similarity scores between values of the properties `dcterms:subject`, `dbo:literaryGenre` and `dbp:genre`. For each value pair s_1 and s_2 we computed the Dice similarity between all books labeled with s_1 and all books labeled with s_2. This way we detected a high similarity between, for example, the values `Literary_history` and `History_of_literature`. Given a feature value v, we added all those values v' for which the similarity between v and v' was higher than 0.2. In a similar way, we expanded the author feature by adding to a book all those authors with whom the original author ever wrote a book in co-authorship.

Rating Prediction Classifier. Having multi-valued multinomial variables, we transform all features into a binary features matrix. As we have binary ratings we

---

[3] The challenge data contain some inconsistencies, as e.g. different items have the same DBpedia URI (384 duplicates), or the same title (319 duplicates). We opt explicitly to not fix those errors and work with the dataset as given.

[4] We abbreviate namespaces according to common rules (http://www.prefix.cc).

opt for a classification approach to obtain item recommendations. After initial tests with different established machine learning methods[5] (Naive Bayes, Support Vector Machine, Linear Regression, ADTrees, kNN Linear, kNN CoverTree) we decided to further explore (i) a simple Naive Bayes and (ii) a k-Nearest Neighbors (k-NN) approximation, namely CoverTree [1] (setting k = 7 without further parameter optimization), primarily due to their robustness and good performance in terms of learning/training time. Even though we made several efforts in feature creation and expansion, as described above, it turned out that learning one classifier per user was not a successful approach. The most likely reason for that is the relatively low training instances count of 11.71 items per user as well as the high ratio of unrated to rated items per user of 1.2 (min 0, max 14, median 1). As a consequence, we created a mixture-model which we describe next.

Collaborative Filtering. As a per-user-based classifier was not successful, we followed the idea of user-neighborhood-based collaborative filtering (see e.g. [2]). For that purpose, we first compute user neighborhoods, i.e. clusters of varying size, and not fixed sized neighborhoods, that aggregate together a given user and all other users from the training data that have at least one common book in their ratings list. To account for different and multiple ratings, we compute a simple score

$$UserSim(u_1, u_2) = |\{b \mid r(u_1, b) = r(u_2, b)\}| - |\{b \mid r(u_1, b) \neq r(u_2, b)\}|$$

where $r(u, b)$ refers to the rating of user u for book b. Taking all user pairs with $UserSim(u_1, u_2) > 0$ into account, we obtain a neighborhood per user. However, to mitigate the effect of ratings sparsity, we also learned a global classifier for smoothing, and combined the scores of both classifiers, unweighted and linear.

3   Results and Analysis

Evaluation of our systems was performed with evaluation dataset as provided by the ESWC'14 Challenge. We sorted our item predictions by descending classification confidence to create a ranked results set and computed the F_1-measure@5 (F_1@5). Our results for different variations are shown in Table 1.

Results. The first interesting observation is related to the good performance of the popularity baseline. With an F_1 of 0.5583 the result for the Popularity Baseline are not far away from the best participating system which achieved an F_1 score of 0.5715, thus showing that we provide a rather strong baseline.

With the above described Linked-Data-based Recommender (LDR) configuration, we achieve in the best case an F_1 of 0.5649 when training one model for each feature individually using the CoverTree for classification and combining the output linear and unweighted. However, with a Naive Bayes classifier, we

---

[5] For experiments we used the Weka 3.7.10 Java API with LibSVM 1.0.5, alternatingDecisionTrees 1.0.5, and bestFirstTree 1.0.3.

can achieve at best an F_1 of 0.5567.[6] It turned out, again, that learning one classifier per feature is the superior approach, this time, however, combining the individual classifiers based on the ranking they produce ($F_1 = 0.5567$) instead of the classification confidence values ($F_1 = 0.5430$) was the better approach.

We furthermore analyzed the performance of each feature independently, which revealed that features like the Author ($F_1 = 0.5490$) are by itself more discriminative than e.g. DBpedia/Yago types (0.5225) or the genre (0.5308). When combining the different features, we obtain rather different results.

The different user aggregation methods, global or neighborhood or both, reveal to have also a clear influence on the performance. While the global model, as well as the neighborhood model, each have strengths and weakness depending on the feature used, an equally weighted linear combination of both methods turns out to be always, with the exception of the Book URI, the beneficial strategy.

Table 1. F_1-measure on test dataset for different features and models. Best results per model type in bold.

Features	Naive Bayes			CoverTree	Unsupervised
	Global+Nghb	Global	Neighbour	G+N	
All, one model	0.5405	0.5371	0.5354	0.5572	-
All, linear comb	0.5430	0.5360	0.5359	**0.5649**	-
All, rank comb	**0.5567**	0.5514	0.5439	0.5647	-
Manual categories	0.5270	0.5218	0.5256	0.5382	-
Author(s)	0.5490	0.5441	0.5382	0.5535	-
Genre	0.5308	0.5221	0.5291	0.5364	-
Publisher	0.5317	0.5294	0.5278	0.5407	-
Book Series	0.5247	0.5214	0.5205	0.5253	-
Wikipedia categories	0.5393	0.5356	0.5335	0.5553	-
DBpedia/Yago types	0.5225	0.5219	0.5203	0.5476	-
Book URI	0.5550	0.5561	0.5352	0.5562	-
Popularity baseline	-	-	-	-	**0.5583**

Conclusion. In summary, it was somehow surprising to us, that our unpersonalized baseline system performed comparably well on Task 2 of the Recommender System Challenge. Furthermore, given that our LD-based solution differs significantly from our baseline approach, the marginal difference in F_1-measure seems at first surprising, in particular, as we are only able to beat the baseline with a

---

[6] The original challenge submission (name UNIMANNHEIM) achieved an F_1 of 0.5607 with a Naive Bayes classifier and an one model approach, however, we discovered later that our competition system contained a coding bug in the classifier learning. We thus present here the post-challenge evaluation for the fixed system, which uses a slightly different classifier configuration.

specific combination of features, classifier, and user combination mode. However, one key component of our LD-based recommender is in the end the global classifier learned on all user ratings – which is essentially the same idea that we follow with the unpersonalized popularity score of the baseline. In conclusion, it seems that the usage of a linked data-enabled content-based recommender is not overwhelmingly superior over our naive, unpersonalized baseline approach.

Acknowledgments. We would like to thank our colleagues Arnab Dutta and Johannes Knopp for their valuable contribution to our systems, as well as Orphee De Clercq and Robert Meusel for their support in understanding the data and technology used.

References

1. Beygelzimer, A., Kakade, S., Langford, J.: Cover trees for nearest neighbor. In: ICML'06: Proceedings of the 23rd International Conference on Machine Learning, pp. 97–104. ACM Press, New York (2006)
2. Herlocker, J., Konstan, J., Riedl, J.: An empirical analysis of design choices in neighborhood-based collaborative filtering algorithms. Inf. Retr. **5**(4), 287–310 (2002)
3. Jannach, D., Zanker, M., Felfernig, A., Friedrich, G.: Recommender Systems: An Introduction. Cambridge University Press, Cambridge (2011)

A Semantic Pattern-Based Recommender

Valentina Maccatrozzo$^{(\boxtimes)}$, Davide Ceolin, Lora Aroyo, and Paul Groth

Department of Computer Science, The Network Institute, VU University Amsterdam,
Amsterdam, The Netherlands
{v.maccatrozzo,d.ceolin,lora.aroyo,p.t.groth}@vu.nl

Abstract. This paper presents a novel approach for Linked Data-based recommender systems through the use of semantic patterns - generalized paths in a graph described through the types of the nodes and links involved. We apply this novel approach to the book dataset from the ESWC2014 recommender systems challenge. User profiles are built by aggregating ratings on patterns with respect to each book in provided user training set. Ratings are aggregated by estimating the expected value of a Beta distribution describing the rating given to each individual book. Our approach allows the determination of a rating for a book, even if the book is poorly connected with user profile. It allows for a "prudent" estimation thanks to smoothing. However, if many patterns are available, it considers all the contributions. Additionally, it allows for a lightweight computation of ratings as it exploits the knowledge encoded in the patterns. Our approach achieved a precision of 0.60 and an overall F-measure of about 0.52 on the ESWC2014 challenge.

1 Introduction

Content-based recommender systems ground their approach on the characteristics of the items to be recommended. Items are more similar to each other the more characteristics they have in common. These similarity values are used to recommend items to the users given their profiles. Our approach extends these approaches by using semantic patterns extracted from Linked Data sources. Semantic patters are generalized paths in a graph described through the types of the nodes and links involved. The central hypothesis of this work is that there are patterns in the amount of structured (linked) data on the Web, that could link items otherwise disconnected and, so, discover interesting paths for recommendation [5]. For instance, we could link a book written by Ernest Hemingway with books written by Jack Kerouac, since the latter influenced the first.

We use semantic patterns for both building users profiles and for recommending items. Taking the example of recommending books, we first extract all the semantic patterns which connect all pairs of books that a user has rated, and then, for each pattern, we aggregate the ratings for a particular book. For each book to be recommended, we consider all the patterns in the user profile that point at it, and we compute a smoothed average of the corresponding aggregated ratios (the smoothed average is the expected value of a Beta distribution [9]).

© Springer International Publishing Switzerland 2014
V. Presutti et al. (Eds.): SemWebEval 2014, CCIS 475, pp. 182–187, 2014.
DOI: 10.1007/978-3-319-12024-9_24

Our approach allows easy determination of a rating for an item (i.e. a book), even if the item is poorly connected with the user profile. It allows for a "prudent" rating estimation thanks to the smoothing performed by using the Beta probability distribution. Finally, it allows a lightweight computation of ratings as it exploits the knowledge encoded in the patterns. The lightweight computation is favored by the fact that the semantic patterns are extracted beforehand.

The novelty of our approach resides in the fact that we build user profiles in such a way that they guide the algorithm during the recommendation process. Basically, having patterns associated with ratings in the user profile allows the system to know which patterns to follow to provide relevant recommendations for that specific user.

The paper develops as follows. In Sect. 2, we provide an overview of the related work. In Sects. 3 and 4, we present our method. In Sect. 5 we report the results of our approach. Finally, in Sects. 6 and 7, we discuss and conclude. Throughout the paper, we present our approach with respect to the ESWC 2014 recommender systems challenge[1] which focuses on book recommendation.

2   Related Work

The link between recommender systems and Linked Data has been explored by many researchers. For instance, Di Noia et al. [1], present a content-based recommender system based only on linked datasets. They propose a vector space model approach to compute similarities between RDF resources but do not make use of content patterns for the recommendation task. Fossati et al. [2] propose a news recommender systems based on entity linking techniques in unstructured text and knowledge extraction from structured knowledge bases. Their results show that using the entity relation approach provides the user with unexpected results and more specific explanations which attract the users' attention. Our work shares with these the type of sources used in the recommendation process. However, these works do not explore the use of semantic patterns.

Our pattern-based approach follows up on the work of [11], and is inspired by [4]. It aligns most with the work of Passant who proposes *dbrec* [6], a recommender system built on top of DBpedia, which also introduces the notion of linked data semantic distance. Our approach also shares some similarities with the approach proposed by Sun et al. in [10] which uses a path-based semantic similarity. The work by Peska and Vojtas [7] has interesting commonalities with ours, as they use the Czech DBPedia in order to retrieve non-trivial connections between items, although they do not explore longer paths.

Our definition of semantic patterns is inspired by Gangemi and Presutti [3], who introduced knowledge patterns to deal with semantic heterogeneity in the Semantic Web and to identify units of meaning. Presutti et al. use knowledge patterns to analyze Linked Data as a new level of abstraction that can be used for multiple purposes [8].

---

[1] http://challenges.2014.eswc-conferences.org/index.php/RecSys

3   Semantic Pattern Extraction

Formally, a semantic pattern is a path that connects a source type T_1 to a target type T_{l+1} through pairs *property-type*. This can be defined as a set:

$$\{T_1, P_1, T_2, P_2, \ldots, T_l, P_l, T_{l+1}\},$$

which length is given by l.

In this experiment, we extracted DBpedia[2] patterns of length 1 and 2 between all the books in the challenge training set. The patterns extraction was performed by means of SPARQL queries, like the one in Listing 1.1.

```
PREFIX  db:<http://dbpedia.org/ontology/>.
    rdf:<http://www.w3.org/1999/02/22-rdf-syntax-ns#>.

SELECT DISTINCT ?prop1 ?v1 ?t2 ?prop2 WHERE
    {<Book1> ?prop1 ?v1 .
    ?v1 ?prop2 <Book2> .
    ?v1 rdf:type ?t2 .}
```

Listing 1.1. Query to retrieve patterns of length 2.

When building user profiles, we store both the general pattern, e.g. "http://dbpedia.org/ontology/country, http://dbpedia.org/ontology/Country, http://dbpedia.org/ontology/country", and also the instantiation of the type of the entity involved in the pattern, e.g. "http://dbpedia.org/resource/United_States". In this way, we also collect a list of DBpedia resources which describe the user profile.

4   User Profiling and Rating Estimation

For each user, we consider all the books they rated, and extract all the patterns that link them to each other. Different instances of the same pattern may link elements with different ratings (in our case, ratings are boolean values). We focus on the rating of the end element of the pattern, because that is what we want to predict. In other words, given a known starting point (a book in the user profile), and using one of the patterns in the user profile, we want to be able to predict the rating of the item at the end of the pattern. For instance, in the pattern shown in Fig. 1, we associate the rating of *The Pelican Brief* to the pattern *db_ont:country db_ont:Country db_ont:country*, as we could use it for recommending another book connected through the same pattern, starting from *Dragonfly in Amber*.

We assume that the ratings of the recommendations made using that pattern can be inferred from observations. Thus, we count the positive and the negative pieces of evidence (that is, all the observations, 1 and 0 rating respectively),

---

[2] Version 3.9 available at http://dbpedia.org/Downloads39

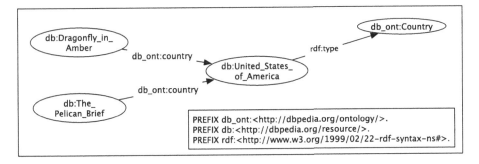

Fig. 1. Example of a pattern of length 2.

and we associate the evidence counts to each pattern, to obtain the following mathematical function f that describes the evidence that is associated to each pair $(user_k, pattern_{i,j})$:

$$f(user_k, pattern_{i,j}) = \{\#p_{k,i,j}, \#n_{k,i,j}\} \qquad (1)$$

To estimate the rating of a newly proposed book, we proceed as follows. First, we identify all the patterns that link any of the user profile to that book. Then, we aggregate all the positive and negative evidence related to those patterns.

$$evidence(user_k, book_i) = \sum_{j \in profile(user_k)} f(user_k, pattern_{j,book_i}) \qquad (2)$$

where $pattern_{j,book_i}$ is the set of patterns which starting item j is in the profile of $user_k$ and which ending element is $book_i$. The function f defined above returns a couple of positive and negative counts ($\{\#p, \#n\}$). The sum $\sum$ is applied pairwise.

$evidence(user_k, book_i)$ returns a pair of aggregated positive and negative evidence counts. Based on these, we obtain a rating for $book_i$ by computing the expected value of a Beta probability distribution. Such a value is computed as follows:

$$rating(user_k, book_i) = \frac{1 + \sum\limits_{j \in profile(user_k)} (\#p_{j,book_i})}{2 + \sum\limits_{j \in profile(user_k)} (\#p_{j,book_i} + \#n_{j,book_i})} \qquad (3)$$

where $\#p$ is the count of positive pieces of evidence, and $\#n$ is the count of negative ones. So, the rating is equal to a smoothed average, and the values 1 and 2 are due to the fact that the prior of the probability distribution is "neutral", that is, when no evidence is available, a pattern has 50 % probability to end in a book rated 1 or 0.

The rating we estimate is a real number between zero and one. Although the initial ratings were boolean ones, and we could still discretize our results by rounding them, the challenge did not require us to do so.

The reasons why we choose this probability distribution are the following: the Beta probability distribution ranges between zero and one, that is, it models the probability for each value in the $[0, 1]$ interval to be the right value for the user rating associated to that pattern; the expected value of the Beta represents a smoothed ratio between positive and negative observations. Smoothing is important, because it allows us to avoid relying too heavily upon small evidence sets.

5   Results

We implemented our approach[3] to address Task 2 in the ESWC-14 Challenge: Linked Open Data-enabled Recommender Systems. We participated as "VUA group". Task 2 requested to calculate top-N recommendations from binary user feedback. We were asked to complete the user-item pairs in the evaluation data by providing the correspondent relevance score. These scores have been used to build a Top-5 recommendation list for each user and have been evaluated with the F-measure@5, i.e. based on the top-5 recommended items. Our system reached Precision@5 equal to 0.6059, Recall@5 equal to 0.4497 and F-measure@5 equal to 0.5162 (values obtained by the evaluation system of the challenge[4]). We ranked only 19th, however the top F-measure@5 was 0.571, which makes our result rather good.

6   Discussion

One novelty of the approach resides in the fact that we build users profiles in such a way that they directly guide the algorithm in the recommendation process. Our algorithm exploits the semantics inherent in the Linked Data source, rather than extracting features from it. We use a Beta probability distribution to aggregate the ratings, which allows to compensate for small samples. The pros of our approach are: easy calculation of a rating for a book, even if the book is poorly connected with the user profile; "prudent" estimation thanks to smoothing of the Beta distribution; consideration of all the contributions, even if few patterns are available; lightweight computation of ratings as it exploits the knowledge encoded in the patterns.

The main drawback of our approach is the computation time for extracting all the patterns between all the books pairs. However this procedure can be performed offline, without affecting the lightweight computation of the recommendation algorithm. Given this, for the challenge we extracted only patterns of length 1 and 2, and we believe this is the main explanation for the rather low recall value (0.4497). In particular, this resulted in some empty user profiles. In these cases, our system is still able to generate a rating for a given book, however this value will be 0.5, resulting in a complete neutral result.

---

[3] Code available online at http://goo.gl/neqbdG
[4] Result plots are available at http://goo.gl/paeXcu

7   Conclusions and Future Work

We have presented an approach for recommending based on Linked Data that allowed us to achieve promising results. The plasticity of the method opens up for further exploration, and the lightness of the recommendation effort leaves us room for further computational extensions. For instance, we intend to add pattern selection based on user preferences. Generally, an important input to our approach is understanding the attributes of the patterns within an underlying dataset. Characterizing datasets thus is an interesting area for future work. Moreover, we aim at extending the length of the patterns adopted in the recommendations, as to both increase the availability of evidence and improve the performance.

Acknowledgments. This research was supported by the EU FP7 STREP "ViSTA-TV" project and by the Dutch COMMIT Data2Semantics project.

References

1. Di Noia, T., Mirizzi, R., Ostuni, V.C., Romito, D., Zanker, M.: Linked open data to support content-based recommender systems. In: I-SEMANTICS '12, pp. 1–8. ACM (2012)
2. Fossati, M., Giuliano, C., Tummarello, G.: Semantic network-driven news recommender systems: a celebrity gossip use case. In: SeRSy, pp. 25–36. CEUR-WS.org (2012)
3. Gangemi, A., Presutti, V.: Towards a pattern science for the Semantic Web. Seman. Web - Interoperability Usability Applicability **1**, 61–68 (2010)
4. Hollink, L., Schreiber, G., Wielinga, B.: Patterns of semantic relations to improve image content search. J. Web Sem. **5**(3), 195–203 (2007)
5. Maccatrozzo, V., Aroyo, L., van Hage, W.R.: Crowdsourced evaluation of semantic patterns for recommendation. In: UMAP Workshops. CEUR-WS.org (2013)
6. Passant, A.: dbrec — music recommendations using DBpedia. In: Patel-Schneider, P.F., Pan, Y., Hitzler, P., Mika, P., Zhang, L., Pan, J.Z., Horrocks, I., Glimm, B. (eds.) ISWC 2010, Part II. LNCS, vol. 6497, pp. 209–224. Springer, Heidelberg (2010)
7. Peska, L., Vojtas, P.: Enhancing recommender system with linked open data. In: Larsen, H.L., Martin-Bautista, M.J., Vila, M.A., Andreasen, T., Christiansen, H. (eds.) FQAS 2013. LNCS, vol. 8132, pp. 483–494. Springer, Heidelberg (2013)
8. Presutti, V., Aroyo, L., Adamou, A., Schopman, B., Gangemi, A., Schreiber, G.: Extracting core knowledge from linked data. In: COLD. CEUR-WS.org (2011)
9. Prokhorov, A.: Beta-distribution. In: Hazewinkel, M. (ed.) Encyclopedia of Mathematics. Springer, New York (2001)
10. Sun, Y., Han, J., Yan, X., Yu, P.S., Pathsim, T.W.: Meta path-based top-k similarity search in heterogeneous information networks. PVLDB **4**(11), 992–1003 (2011)
11. Wang, Y., Stash, N., Aroyo, L., Hollink, L., Schreiber, G.: Semantic relations for content-based recommendations. In: K-Cap 2009, pp. 209–210. ACM (2009)

Increasing Top-20 Diversity Through Recommendation Post-processing

Matevž Kunaver[✉], Tomaž Požrl, Štefan Dobravec,
Uroš Droftina, and Andrej Košir

Faculty of Electrical Engineering, University of Ljubljana, Tržaška 25,
Ljubljana, Slovenia
{matevz.kunaver,tomaz.pozrl,stefan.dobravec,andrej.kosir}@fe.uni-lj.si,
uros.droftina@telekom.si

Abstract. This paper presents two different methods for diversifying recommendations that were developed as part of the ESWC2014 challenge. Both methods focus on post-processing recommendations provided by the baseline recommender system and have increased the ILD at the cost of final precision (measured with F@20). The authors feel that this method has potential yet requires further development and testing.

Keywords: Recommender system · Diversity · ILD · RecSys

1 Introduction

In this paper we present results obtained from participating in ESWC2014 challenge, where we developed and tested two methods for increasing recommendation diversity while preserving user satisfaction.

The focus of recommender systems (RS) is moving from generating recommendations without any additional data about the user to generating recommendations that also consider the user's context [1,3] and personality in order to improve the recommendation results [6]. All these improvements serve to present the user with a selection of items that will be the most appropriate for the situation in which the user desires to consume the selected item.

Recommendation results can be further improved by paying attention to the diversity [4,5,7,9] of recommendations presented to the user. In order to measure diversity one must have additional information available about the recommended items such as their meta-data, descriptions, technical specifications etc. Obtaining this data can be a problem since most of systems either use their own descriptions or do not update their data regularly. This is where Linked Open-Data enabled (LOD) systems offer a significant advantage as they work with data accumulated from various sources over the internet.

1.1 Motivation and Goal

We performed this study as part of the LOD enabled RS challenge of 11th European Semantic Web Conference (ESWC-14) where we focused on task 3 of

© Springer International Publishing Switzerland 2014
V. Presutti et al. (Eds.): SemWebEval 2014, CCIS 475, pp. 188–192, 2014.
DOI: 10.1007/978-3-319-12024-9_25

the challenge - diversity that addressed an interesting aspect of content-based RS - using diversification to avoid over-specialization. As an extra bonus the task also provided evaluation tools that enabled us to immediately measure our results and compare them with those of others.

The purpose of our study was therefore to determine whether we can increase the diversity of items presented to the user by post-processing results provided by a non-diversified RS while maintaining user satisfaction measured by the predicted rating security.

2   Materials and Methods

In this section we describe the dataset, the baseline RS used to generate recommendations, the diversification methods developed as part of the challenge and the evaluation methods used to measure the diversity of recommendations.

2.1   Dataset

We used the DBook dataset provided by the challenge enhanced with meta-data retrieved from DBpedia. Each item from the dataset was described with the DBpedia ontology, featuring 17 fields (author, year of publishing, type etc.) and Dublin Core categories featuring 7067 different values, with each item having on average 5 different categories.

2.2   Recommender System

Since our approach focused on post-processing the results provided by a content-based RS we used a RS developed as part of our previous research [8]. This RS used a rule-based approach that considered all attributes and categories available in the dataset.

We diversified the Top-20 lists using two methods that replaced items in the recommendations list. The idea was to replace some of the Top-20 items with recommendations that would increase the overall diversity of the list without having a strong negative impact on the overall accuracy of the recommender system (measured with F@20 metric).

Figure 1 shows the data flow of our recommendation process.

2.3   Diversification Method

Our diversification methods focused on finding the best items to replace on the top 20 list and the best candidates to replace them with. We used two versions of this algorithm (Fig. 2).

The first version calculated the ILD value of the top 20 list while excluding one item (effectively calculating the ILD@19 instead of ILD@20). This process was repeated until each item on the list was excluded once. This created a list of items and ILD@19 values that was then sorted in ascending order by

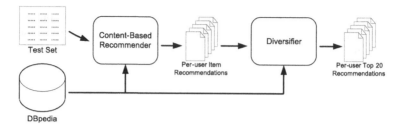

Fig. 1. Recommender system dataflow

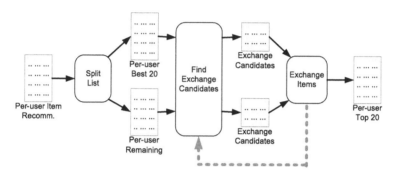

Fig. 2. Diversification method

the ILD@19 value. The idea was that the highest ILD@19 value indicated that excluded item had the smallest impact on the diversity of the list and could therefore be replaced with an item that would add more diversity to the final selection of items. The replacement candidates were selected from the remaining recommendations - in our case we considered items from 21 to 40 (if sorted by predicted ratings), since a larger number of candidates required too much processing time to be completed until the end of the challenge. We removed the item with the highest ILD@19 value and calculated the ILD@20 for each of the replacement candidates. We repeated the process by removing two items from the original list and replacing them with all the possible combinations of replacement candidates and again calculating ILD@20. This resulted with a list of 400 ILD@20 for each user from which we selected the list with the highest value as our top 20 list for each user.

The second version focused on replacing single item at a time, where a joint score in form of $a * avgPR + b * nILD$ was considered instead of pure ILD value. In this formulation $avgPR$ stands for the average prediction rating of the list and nILD for the normalized ILD value of the same list. Parameters a and b allow balancing the top20 list from more accurate/less diverse towards less accurate/more diverse. Similar to the first version the replacement candidates were calculated by excluding the worst item from the top 20 list and replacing it with the best item in the bottom list. The shuffling procedure was repeated until best top 20 list (in term of joint score) was achieved. In test, values 2/3 and 1/3 were chosen for parameters a and b on an empirical basis.

2.4   Evaluation Methods

We evaluated our methods using two different methods. We calculated ILD@20 [9] using attributes based on the equation and Java package provided as part of the challenge documentation. This evaluation was used to calculate the partial ILD (ILD@19 as described above) during the diversification process. We used 14 different attributes in the ILD calculations as these attributes were all used in the recommender system used to generate the preliminary recommendations.

Once we had the Top-20 lists for each user we also used the on-line submission system to receive the official evaluation results and to compare them with those of other research groups.

3   Results

Table 1 shows the results of our baseline recommender system, developed diversification methods and those of a random recommender for comparison.

Table 1. Evaluation results

Method	P@20	R@20	F@20	ILD
Random	0.0008	0.0020	0.0012	0.4853
Non-diversified	0.0203	0.0644	0.0309	0.4549
Diversified - version 1	0.0017	0.0047	0.0025	0.4670
Diversified - version 2	0.0017	0.0050	0.0026	0.4609

4   Discussion

Table 1 shows that both our diversification approaches noticeably increased the diversity of the users Top-20 list, yet did so at the cost of precision and recall. A comparison of our results with those of a random recommender and shows that we get better F@20 in all cases while having a lower ILD value which is logical due to the random RS selection of completely random items. Unfortunately we lacked the time to preform further statistical analysis of our results.

The comparison of results shows that we increased the diversity of our top lists by 3 % (for comparison - the ILD value of the random RS is 6 % larger), while decreasing the F@20 value by as much as 90 %. This would imply that our method focused too much on diversification and might provide better results with further parameter tweaking.

5   Conclusion and Further Work

Since there was a time limit we were unable to perform all the tests that we desired, leaving open quite a few questions. The main issues that we plan to address and present as an article to be published at a later date are:

- Determine whether the number of replaced items from the top list can be fixed or must be calculated iteratively for each user each time the RS generates recommendations.
- The number of replacement candidates to be considered.
- Perform a series of statistical tests in order to determine whether our results are really significantly different from those of a non-diversified (or random) RS.
- Determine the optimal values of parameters a and b for the second method we developed.
- Perform an A/B test to determine how the lower accuracy impacts the actual user satisfaction.

We will also apply these methods to our *Context Movie Dataset* (LDOS-CoMoDa) [2] which also features live users thus making an A/B test a possibility.

Participating in this challenge provided a very good experience since we tackled a completely new dataset and had the appropriate evaluation tools at our disposal.

Acknowledgments. Operation part financed by the European Union, European Social Fund.

References

1. Dey, A., Abowd, G.: Towards a better understanding of context and context-awareness, pp. 304–307 (1999)
2. Košir, A., Odic, A., Kunaver, M., Tkalcic, M., Tasic, J.F.: Database for contextual personalization. Elektrotehniški vestnik **78**(5), 270–274 (2011)
3. Odic, A., Tkalcic, M., Košir, A.: Managing irrelevant contextual categories in a movie recommender system. In: Human Decision Making in Recommender Systems (Decisions@ RecSys 13), p. 29 (2013)
4. Smyth, B., McClave, P.: Similarity vs. diversity. In: Aha, D.W., Watson, I. (eds.) ICCBR 2001. LNCS (LNAI), vol. 2080, pp. 347–361. Springer, Heidelberg (2001)
5. Jannach, D., Lerche, L., Gedikli, F., Bonnin, G.: What recommenders recommend – an analysis of accuracy, popularity, and sales diversity effects. In: Carberry, S., Weibelzahl, S., Micarelli, A., Semeraro, G. (eds.) UMAP 2013. LNCS, vol. 7899, pp. 25–37. Springer, Heidelberg (2013)
6. Adomavicius, G., Tuzhilin, A.: Toward the next generation of recommender systems: a survey of the state-of-the-art and possible extensions. IEEE Trans. Knowl. Data Eng. **17**(6), 734–749 (2005)
7. Adomavicius, G., Kwon, Y.: Improving aggregate recommendation diversity using ranking-based techniques. IEEE Trans. Knowl. Data Eng. **24**(5), 896–911 (2012)
8. Požrl, T., Kunaver, M., Pogačnik, M., Košir, A., Tasič, J.F.: Improving human-computer interaction in personalized tv recommender. Int. J. Sci. Technol. Trans. Electr. Eng. **36**(E1), 19–36 (2012)
9. Ziegler, C.-N., McNee, S.M., Konstan, J.A, Lausen, G.: Improving recommendation lists through topic diversification. In: Proceedings of the 14th International Conference on World Wide Web, pp. 22–32. ACM (2005)

Hybrid Model Rating Prediction with Linked Open Data for Recommender Systems

Andrés Moreno[1,2], Christian Ariza-Porras[1(✉)], Paula Lago[1],
Claudia Lucía Jiménez-Guarín[1], Harold Castro[1],
and Michel Riveill[2]

[1] School of Engineering, Universidad de los Andes, Bogotá, Colombia
{dar-more,cf.ariza975,pa.lago52,cjimenez,hcastro}@uniandes.edu.co
[2] CNRS, I3S, UMR 7271, University of Nice Sophia Antipolis, 06900 Sophia
Antipolis, France
riveill@unice.fr

Abstract. We detail the solution of team uniandes1 to the ESWC 2014
Linked Open Data-enabled Recommender Systems Challenge Task 1
(rating prediction on a cold start situation). In these situations, there
are few ratings per item and user and thus collaborative filtering techniques may not be suitable. In order to be able to use a content-based
solution, linked-open data from DBPedia was used to obtain a set of
descriptive features for each item. We compare the performance (measured as RMSE) of three models on this cold-start situation: content-
based (using min-count sketches), collaborative filtering (SVD++) and
rule-based switched hybrid models. Experimental results show that the
hybrid system outperforms each of the models that compose it. Since
features taken from DBPedia were sparse, we clustered items in order to
reduce the dimensionality of the item and user profiles.

Keywords: Semantic web · Recommender systems

1 Introduction

Recommender systems (RS) are automatic agents that attempt to suggest new or
interesting items to users. A number of different algorithms have been proposed
to improve the performance of recommender systems, which can be classified in
two groups: collaborative-filtering techniques and content-based filtering techniques. Collaborative-filtering techniques (CF) are based on the fact that similar
users like similar items and thus base their predictions in the ratings provided
by similar users. Content-based techniques (CB) build a user profile of interests
based on the features of the items the user has rated. On cold-start situations,
when items have few ratings, neither system can perform well. This is because
they don't have the amount of data needed to find either true similarities among
users (CF) or to construct the user profiles (CB).

In these circumstances, more data is needed, either to describe the items or
the users. Thanks to linked open data initiatives, information about items can be

© Springer International Publishing Switzerland 2014
V. Presutti et al. (Eds.): SemWebEval 2014, CCIS 475, pp. 193–198, 2014.
DOI: 10.1007/978-3-319-12024-9_26

found on the web. Task 1 of the linked open data enabled recommender systems challenge purpose was to predict the rating a user would give to an item in a cold-start situation. In order to be able to use a CB solution, linked-open data is used to obtain features that describe items in machine-readable format.

The paper is organized as follows: we describe the provided dataset, the performance metric used to evaluate the predictions, give an overview of the proposed solution and discuss the obtained results.

Dataset Description. The DBbook dataset contains 75559 ratings of 6166 books by 6181 users. The possible ratings that a user can assign to an item are $\mathcal{O} = \{0, 1, 2, 3, 4, 5\}$. The `ratings` file has 3 fields: a user id, an item id, and the rating. Each item has been rated by at least one user, but the evaluation set includes some books not rated in the training set, representing a cold-start situation. The dataset also provides a mapping of each item id to a DBPedia URI which gives access to a semantic description of items. Given this description, we can define each book with a set of concepts C_i taken from DBPedia. We use the following concepts to describe a book: author, categories, literary genres, and subject. Figure 1 depicts the feature extraction process. The feature space size is 14001 concepts. Each book has an average of 16.49 features with standard deviation (std) of 6.18. Each feature appears in an average of 9.62 books with std of 118, and a max of 4030.

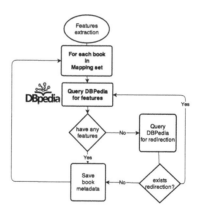

Fig. 1. Semantic features extraction

2   Prediction Model

Burke [1] describes different ways in which recommender system models can be combined. The *switched* strategy maintains different models in parallel and reports to the user the prediction of the model with higher confidence. We use as base model a widely known CF algorithm (SVD++) (Sect. 2.2). However, since traditional CF systems usually make incorrect predictions when no previous ratings about the item are known, the prediction of the switched hybrid model on cold-start situations is delegated to the CB model explained in Sect. 2.1. The measure used to evaluate the predictive performance of the system is the Root Mean Square Error (RMSE). Let T be the rating set of a hold-out set (test set), T_{ui}, the rating that the user u gave to item i and $\hat{r_u}i$ the model prediction, the RMSE is defined as:

$$RMSE := \sqrt{\frac{1}{|T|} \sum_{T_{ui} \in T} (\hat{r}_{ui} - T_{ui})^2} \qquad (1)$$

In the remainder of this section, we will describe the models that take part in our system.

2.1   Content Based Model

On a CB model, a user u has a profile with a list of non duplicate concepts C_u and a set of $|\mathcal{O}|$ vectors $w^o \in \mathbb{R}^{|C_u|}, o \in \mathcal{O}$. For each example of user-item interaction, each of the concepts that are related to the item (C_i) are considered for addition into the user's list C_u. We use an inclusion policy using a sliding window min-count sketch structure [2] based on the work developed in [4]: All concepts seen by the user at least N times during the window duration of the sketch are present in the user's list, and the size of the vectors w^o is updated. After modifying the list and the w^o vectors' length, the weights of the vector are adjusted using a stochastic logistic regression strategy. Let $r_{ui} \in \mathcal{O}$ the rating user u gives to item i and $m_{ui} = meta(C_i \times C_u) \rightarrow \mathbb{R}^{|C_u|}$ a function that takes the concept set of an item and converts it into a binary vector where each coordinate is 1 if the user's concept belong to the items list ($m_{ui}[f] = \mathbb{1}_{C_u[f] \in C_i}$). For each vector w^o, we predict $\sigma(\langle w^o, m_{ui} \rangle)$ and update each of the vectors as:

$$w_u^o \leftarrow w_u^o - \gamma(\sigma(\langle w^o, m_{ui} \rangle) - \mathbb{1}_{r_{ui}=o})m_{ui} \qquad (2)$$

where $\sigma(c)$ is the sigmoid function. The rating prediction under this model is calculated as:

$$\hat{r}_{ui} = \frac{\sum_{o \in \mathcal{O}} \sigma(\langle w^o, m_{ui} \rangle) \times o}{\sum_{o \in \mathcal{O}} \sigma(\langle w^o, m_{ui} \rangle)} \qquad (3)$$

Feature Generation and Evaluation. We use DBPedia to retrieve book features as described in Sect. 1. Using all the retrieved features the predictor performance was lower than expected and, as shown in Fig. 2, if we increase the minimum inclusion rate, the performance declines. A quick evaluation of the features shows that some of them are highly correlated, which led us to consider that clusters of features may provide more information to the predictor. We created clusters of features by co-occurrence, using k-means with cosine distance, convergence delta of 0.01 and 200 iterations. Figure 3 depicts the dataset generation process.

We vary the number of clusters (k) and measure the performance against the test set. In Fig. 4a, we can see that the predictor performance using clusters is

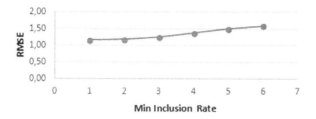

Fig. 2. RMSE vs inclusion rate for book features

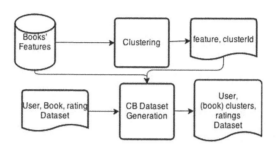

Fig. 3. Content based dataset generation

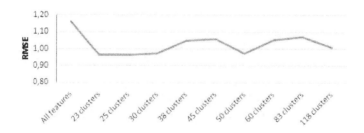

(a) All features vs different cluster's size

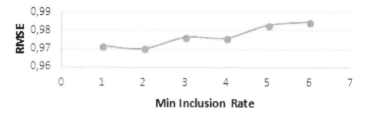

(b) With 50 clusters changing the minimum inclusion rate

Fig. 4. Content based predictor performance using clusters

better than using all the extracted features. Although with 23 clusters we have a slightly better result against the test set, we use the 50 clusters because this had better performance using the evaluation tool.

With these 50 clusters as features, each book has an average of 2.1 features with a std of 0.57. Each feature appears on average in 344 books, with a std of 1332. When trained with these new features, the predictor improves its performance notably with a min inclusion rate of 2, as shown in Fig. 4b. The best RMSE with the content-based predictor on the evaluation tool was 0.969.

2.2 Collaborative Filtering Model

The SVD++ algorithm [3] prediction rule uses the global average of ratings (μ) and the *bias* or deviation from the mean for each user (b_u) and each item (b_i) as model parameters. In order to account for the user-item interaction the SVD++ model represents each user as a vector x_u and each item as an vector $y_i \in \mathbb{R}^k$. Each item is represented by an extra vector $z_i \in \mathbb{R}^k$ that is used by the prediction rule to represent the items the user has rated into her profile. Let $R(u)$ the set of items the user u has rated, the prediction under the SVD++ model is given by:

$$\hat{r}_{ui} = \mu + b_i + b_u + y_i^T \left(x_u + |R(u)|^{-\frac{1}{2}} \sum_{j \in R(u)} z_j \right) \tag{4}$$

When an item has not been seen by the system, the prediction rule only uses the sum of the global mean and the user bias. Parameters of the model are learned using a regularized stochastic gradient descent strategy.

3 Model Validation

To test the performance of the hybrid model, we generated 5 datasets with approximately 80 % for training and the 20 % for testing, each of these datasets had a different percentage of cold-start ratings varying from 5 % to 25 %. The model delegates the prediction to the CB model only when it has not seen the item before. Figure 5 shows the RMSE of the hybrid model as the number of new items in the test set increases. The results show that the hybrid model outperforms CF for a low number of cold-start items.

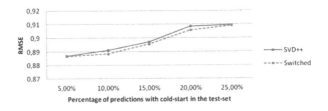

Fig. 5. RMSE of the hybrid model vs SVD++ on cold-start

4   Conclusions

We have described our approach to improve the performance of recommender systems using linked open-data that is freely available on the web. Open data provides descriptions of items that help the recommender system understand better why a user likes an item (a user may like a book because of its author, its literary genre, its main subject, etc.). This approach can help alleviate the new item cold-start problem. However, users may like items based on subjective features such as tone which are not provided in the open-data repositories used. For this reason, we proposed an hybrid model based on rules that uses a pure collaborative approach when enough ratings are present, and uses a content-based approach in the other cases. Our model had a RMSE of 0.8787 against the quiz set provided by the challenge. Open-data such as data from social-networks can also be used to describe users and calculate similarities of new users based on this data. This could further improve the performance of recommender systems under a new-user cold start problem.

References

1. Burke, R.: Hybrid recommender systems: survey and experiments. User Model. User-Adap. Inter. **12**(4), 331–370 (2002). http://dx.doi.org/10.1023/A:1021240730564
2. Dimitropoulos, X., Stoecklin, M., Hurley, P., Kind, A.: The eternal sunshine of the sketch data structure. Comput. Netw. **52**(17), 3248–3257 (2008). http://dx.doi.org/10.1016/j.comnet.2008.08.014
3. Koren, Y.: Factorization meets the neighborhood: a multifaceted collaborative filtering model. In: Proceedings of the 14th ACM SIGKDD International Conference on Knowledge Discovery and Data Mining, KDD '08, pp. 426–434. ACM, New York (2008). http://dx.doi.org/10.1145/1401890.1401944
4. McMahan, H.B., Holt, G., Sculley, D., Young, M., Ebner, D., Grady, J., Nie, L., Phillips, T., Davydov, E., Golovin, D., Chikkerur, S., Liu, D., Wattenberg, M., Hrafnkelsson, A.M., Boulos, T., Kubica, J.: Ad click prediction: A view from the trenches. In: Proceedings of the 19th ACM SIGKDD International Conference on Knowledge Discovery and Data Mining, pp. 1222–1230. ACM, New York (2013)

Deep Learning of Semantic Word Representations to Implement a Content-Based Recommender for the RecSys Challenge'14

Omar U. Florez[✉]

Intel Labs, Santa Clara, CA 95053, USA
Omar.U.Florez@intel.com

Abstract. In this paper, we will discuss a recommender system that exploits the semantics regularities captured by a Recurrent Neural Network (RNN) in text documents. Many information retrieval systems treat words as binary vectors under the classic bag-of-words model; however there is not a notion of semantic similarity between words when describing a document in the resulting feature space. Recent advances in neural networks have shown that continuous word vectors can be learned as a probability distribution over the words of a document [3,4]. Surprisingly, researchers have found that algebraic operations on this new representation captures semantic regularities in language [5]. For example, $Intel + Pentium - Google$ results in word vectors associated to $\{Search, Android, Phones\}$.

We used this deep learning approach to discover the continuous features describing content of documents with vectors of semantic words and fitted a linear regression model to approximate user preferences for documents. Our submission to the RecSys Challenge'14 obtained a RMSE of 0.902 and ranked 6th for Task 1. Interestingly enough, our approach provided better vector representations than LDA, LSA, and PCA for modeling the content of book abstracts, which are well-known techniques currently used to implement content-based recommender systems in the recommendation community.

Keywords: Deep learning · Recommender systems · Neural network language models

1 Introduction

Latent representation of text is an important task in context-based recommender systems. Especially cold-start problems impose a need to trust the content to infer accurate recommendations when few (or non-existing) user ratings are provided. Beyond are the n-grams and bag-of-words models to demonstrate text, continuous representations techniques such as Latent Dirichlet Allocation (LDA), Latent Semantic Analysis (LSA), and Principal Component Analysis

© Springer International Publishing Switzerland 2014
V. Presutti et al. (Eds.): SemWebEval 2014, CCIS 475, pp. 199–204, 2014.
DOI: 10.1007/978-3-319-12024-9_27

(PCA) which have been used to describe the content of a document as a probability distribution of latent variables known as topics.

The idea is that a sparse matrix M that characterizes the user preferences (rows) in items (columns) can be factorized into two matrices U and V of joint latent factor space of dimensionality K. This way the user preference u of item v can be approximated by the dot product $u^T v$. This method is known as *matrix factorization* and has been proved to be effective in the Netflix Prize competition combining better scalability and predictive accuracy than Collaborative Filtering methods [1]. We have followed a similar approach, but have not assume a random initialization for matrix V. Our hypothesis is that the features describing a document can be learned in an unsupervised way considering the method of how words form a document in sentences. This provides a context for each word and thus not every word is independent of each other as in the bag-of-words model.

2   Approach

Our method consists of two steps: (a) feature learning, and (b) user preference learning. While the second step is the traditional matrix, factorization with stochastic gradient descend, the feature learning step uses a neural network to learn a continuous representation of words according to its context in a sentence. Google has shown Word2Vec as a similar deep-learning approach to model semantic word representations, but the task of recommendations on this new representation is still unexplored.

2.1   Feature Learning

We describe a topic representation by learning the word topic proportions with a Recurrent Neural Network (RNN) as in [5]. This architecture is illustrated in Fig. 1 and consists of an input layer $w(t)$, hidden layer $s(t)$, output layer $y(t)$, and the corresponding weigh matrices U, V, and W. The hidden layer $s(t)$ provides recurrent connections to $s(t-1)$ forming a short-term memory that models the context of a word in a document. Thus, the input layer consists of the current word $w(t)$

The network is trained by stochastic gradient descend using back propagation algorithm as in [5]. Hidden and output states are computed as follows:

$$s_j(t) = f\left(\sum_i w_i(t)U_{ji} + \sum_l s_l(t-1)W_{jl}\right)$$

$$y_k(t) = g\left(\sum_j s_j(t)V_{kj}\right)$$

where $f(x)$ and $g(x)$ are sigmoid and softmax activity functions:

$$f(x) = \frac{1}{1 + e^{-x}}$$

$$g(x_m) = \frac{e^{x_m}}{\sum_k e^{x_k}}$$

When the RNN is trained, the output layer $y(t)$ contain $P(w_{t+1}|w_t, s(t-1))$, the probability distribution of a word given a history of words (context) stored in time $t-1$.

To obtain a per document topic distribution, we match the empirical distribution of words in a document d by using a continuous distribution over these words indexed by a random variable θ.

$$P(d) = \int P(d, \theta) = \int P(\theta^*) \prod_{i=1}^{N} P(w_i|\theta) \, d\theta$$

where N is the number of words in document d and w_i is the i-th word in d. As in [2], we use a Gaussian prior on θ. Note that the term $P(w|\theta)$ is approximated by the output of the RNN, so the problem consists of approximating θ_d^*, the MAP of θ^* for a document d can be represented as $max_{\theta_d^*} P(\theta_d^*) \prod_{i=1}^{N} P(w|\theta_d)$. We find θ_d^* with stochastic gradient descend for each document with a fixed number of iterations.

2.2 User Preference Learning

Given a matrix V learned in the previous step with RNN for each document (cf. Feature Learning), the problem of predicting user preferences in a subset of items $v \in V$ consists of finding the regression weights u_i for user i such as the their inner that product approximates the real user preferences y_{u_i} in the training dataset with $y_{u_i} \approx u_i v^T$. After taking the derivative of the squared error and setting it to zero ($\frac{d}{dv}(y_{u_i} - u_i v^T)^2 = 0$), we solve for each user u_i the following equation:

$$u_i = (v^T v)^{-1} v^T y_{u_i}$$

and we are ready to predict preference values for new examples in different subsets of items within V.

3   Why is the System Innovative?

The popular bag-of-words model used in natural language processing and information retrieval has been outperformed by neural networks language models in recent years [3,4]. The novelty of our attempt in the RecSys Challenge strives on the way how features are learned to describe content. The weights of a trained RNN maps provide high quality word vectors that show semantic relationships in large datasets [5]. This way, words are not only similar or belong to the

same topic, but share a similar context. As far as we know, none of the previously proposed architectures has been successfully trained for the problem
of recommendation based on content. Particularly, our experiments show that
this representation provides less RMSE than LSA, PCA, and LDA, as it was
similarly reported for the problem of Language Modelling in [2].

4   Results

Given the 8,170 DBpedia URIs provided in the competition webpage, we extract
the abstract of each book with SPARQL to obtain a vector of size $(8170 \times V)$,
where V is the number of words in the vocabulary. After stop-removal and
removing words with low frequency, we ended up with $V \approx 1,500$. We then
trained 99 RNNs with hidden layers ranging from 2 to 100 nodes to cover a broad
range in the number of latent features to describe content in the DBbook dataset.
Similarly, we have set the same number of topics for LDA, LSA, and PCA in
the experiments. Initially we had considered gradient descend to evaluate the
regression weights during user preference learning, but this approach (with 5, 10,
20, and 100 iterations) didn't provide lower RMSE values than using the normal
equation for linear regression (cf. Feature Learning), so we used the equation
as the best (and fastest) approach. When gradient descend was considered, we
measured 100 values for λ in the range of 10^{-6} and 10^{3}, so in total $9,900$ deep
learning-based recommenders were implemented.

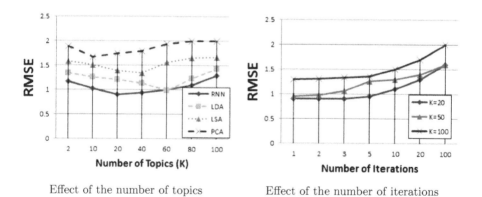

Effect of the number of topics   Effect of the number of iterations

Fig. 1. Experiments to analyze root mean squared errors in recommendations

We compare the quality of different content representations in terms of
RMSE. When a Recurrent Neural Network (RNN) is well trained, the resulting
recommender will be able to linearly combine the latent features learned during
training to better approximate the user preferences of a different items. Our
submission to the RecSys Challenge'14 obtained a RMSE of 0.902 and ranked
number 6 for Task 1. Interestingly enough our approach has always provided

better vector representations than LDA, LSA, and PCA for modeling the content of book abstracts in our experiments, as shown in Fig. 1. Those techniques are well-established methods currently used when implementing content-based recommender systems in the recommendation community.

5   Learned Lessons

During the implementation the recommender system, we come up with the following findings:

- The assumption of having independence between words is plausible, but modeling word contexts provides a semantic relationship between words that improves the latent representation of documents.
- When the matrix V contains enough information to describe the structure in the content of documents, updating U and V with coordinate ascend during a fixed number of iterations provides a minor improvement. In other words, it is possible to train U with a very small number of iterations when enough time has been devoted to train V and thus both steps can be performed independently without loss of recall or RMSE.
- The above approach requires a more aggressive regularization parameter to control overfitting in matrix U. Empirically, large numbers for the regularization parameters λ provide the smallest RMSE with this approach.
- Normalizing the user ratings, commonly in the scale of 1 to 5, has a notably effect than normalizing the vectors U or V during training. The reason is that usually V has a unity variance as it comes from a probability distribution.
- Surprisingly, projecting LDA topics to an orthogonal space with PCA notably improved the prediction results. We believe this is because the linear combination of features and weights provided by the regression algorithms is better suit in a space with low correlation between latent variables.

6   Conclusions

We presented a recommender system that uses the semantic word properties of a type of deep learning algorithm called Recurrent Neural Network. This method provides a lower and less sparse representation of content of text documents. Our results and submission to the RecSys Challenge shows that a RNN provides a lower RMSE values than a latent representation with LDA, PCA, and LSA.

References

1. Bell, R.M., Koren, Y.: Lessons from the netflix prize challenge. SIGKDD Explor. Newsl. **9**(2), 75–79 (2007)
2. Maas, A.L., Ng, A.Y.: A probabilistic model for semantic word vectors. In: Workshop on Deep Learning and Unsupervised Feature Learning, NIPS, vol. 10 (2010)

3. Mikolov, T., Chen, K., Corrado, G., Dean, J.: Efficient estimation of word representations in vector space. CoRR, abs/1301.3781 (2013)
4. Mikolov, T., Sutskever, I., Chen, K., Corrado, G.S., Dean, J.: Distributed representations of words and phrases and their compositionality. In: NIPS, pp. 3111–3119 (2013)
5. Mikolov, T., Yih, W.-T., Zweig, G.: Linguistic regularities in continuous space word representations. In: HLT-NAACL, pp. 746–751. The Association for Computational Linguistics (2013)

Author Index

Ampazis, Nicholas   157
Ariza-Porras, Christian   193
Aroyo, Lora   182
Atanassova, Iana   108, 120

Basile, Pierpaolo   163
Bertin, Marc   108, 120

Cambria, Erik   3
Cantador, Iván   129
Castro, Harold   193
Ceolin, Davide   182
Charlaganov, Marat   95
Chung, Jay Kuan-Chieh   53
Coden, Anni   34
Colpaert, Pieter   114
Corcho, Oscar   77

da Costa Pereira, Célia   21
de Gemmis, Marco   163
De Vocht, Laurens   114
del Bosque, Gerard Casamayor   83
Di Iorio, Angelo   61
Di Noia, Tommaso   129
Dimou, Anastasia   114
Dobravec, Štefan   188
Dragoni, Mauro   21
Droftina, Urocš   188

Emmanouilidis, Theodoros   157

Florez, Omar U.   199

Gelbukh, Alexander   41
Gómez-Pérez, José Manuel   77
Groth, Paul   95, 182
Gruhl, Dan   34

Hayes, Conor   170
Heitmann, Benjamin   170
Hoekstra, Rinke   95
Hołubowicz, Piotr   77
Hussain, Amir   41

Jiménez-Guarín, Claudia Lucía   193

Kolchin, Maxim   89
Košir, Andrej   188
Kozlov, Fedor   89
Ku, Lun-Wei   48
Kunaver, Matevž   188

Lago, Paula   193
Lange, Christoph   61
Lee, Yann-Huei   48
Lewis, Neal   34
Lops, Pasquale   163

Maccatrozzo, Valentina   182
Mannens, Erik   114
Mazurek, Cezary   77
Meilicke, Christian   176
Mencía, Eneldo Loza   150
Mendes, Pablo N.   34
Moreno, Andrés   193
Motta, Enrico   101
Musto, Cataldo   163

Nagarajan, Meena   34
Narducci, Fedelucio   163

Ofek, Nir   28, 41
Osborne, Francesco   101
Ostuni, Vito Claudio   129

Palma, Raúl   77
Paulheim, Heiko   150
Peska, Ladislav   144
Poria, Soujanya   41
Požrl, Tomaž   188

Ramakrishnan, Cartic   34
Reforgiato Recupero, Diego   3
Ristoski, Petar   150
Riveill, Michel   193
Rokach, Lior   28, 41
Ronzano, Francesco   83

Saggion, Horacio   83
Schuhmacher, Michael   176
Semeraro, Giovanni   163

Tettamanzi, Andrea G.B.   21
Tsai, Richard Tzong-Han   53

Van de Walle, Rik   114
Vander Sande, Miel   114
Verborgh, Ruben   114
Virk, Shafqat Mumtaz   48
Vojtas, Peter   144

Welch, Steve   34
Wu, Chi-En   53